In Common No More

In Common No More

The Politics of the
Common Core State Standards

Arnold F. Shober

An Imprint of ABC-CLIO, LLC

Santa Barbara, California • Denver, Colorado

Library of Congress Cataloging-in-Publication Data

Names: Shober, Arnold F., 1976- author.
Title: In common no more : the politics of the common core state standards / Arnold F. Shober.
Description: Santa Barbara, California : Praeger, [2016] | Includes bibliographical references and index.
Identifiers: LCCN 2016005693 | ISBN 9781440837708 (hard copy : alk. paper) | ISBN 9781440837715 (ebook)
Subjects: LCSH: Common Core State Standards (Education) | Education—Standards—United States—States.
Classification: LCC LB3060.83 S47 2016 | DDC 379.1/58—dc23
LC record available at https://lccn.loc.gov/2016005693

ISBN: 978-1-4408-3770-8
EISBN: 978-1-4408-3771-5

20 19 18 17 16   1 2 3 4 5

This book is also available as an eBook.

Praeger
An Imprint of ABC-CLIO, LLC

ABC-CLIO, LLC
130 Cremona Drive, P.O. Box 1911
Santa Barbara, California 93116-1911
www.abc-clio.com

This book is printed on acid-free paper ∞

Manufactured in the United States of America

For Naomi

Contents

Acknowledgments

The Common Core State Standards Initiative (CCSSI) was the first major national education policy initiative launched in the era of social media and mass blogging. For most Americans, when legislators passed No Child Left Behind(NCLB) in 2001, the Internet was a cross between college vanity pages and newspapers' awkward attempts to recycle news online—something like the Drudge Report writ large. By 2009, when the National Governors Association (NGA) and the Council of Chief State School Officers (CCSSO) officially launched the Common Core, the Internet was a dynamic, mass-based phenomenon, filled with netizens of Pinterest, Facebook, and WordPress. The battle over Common Core was waged in chatrooms and on Facebook, on *Education Week*'s blogs, and through pingbacks to and from whatiscommoncore.wordpress.com and edexcellence.net. These self-reinforcing nets of argument seemed interminable, repetitious, sometimes incoherent, yet never quite the same. The librarians of Babel would be veterans.

But unlike those librarians, I found guides to the maze. Many people helped with small parts of the work, but five deserve special mention. Deven Carlson, who is well-versed in the politics of the Common Core, read the entire manuscript with a sharp pencil, both for form and content. Michael Hartney took the manuscript through a political science filter to make sure it stayed on point. Lesley Lavery helped simplify the sometimes baroque intricacies once presented in the text. Michael Petrilli, a veteran of educational politics and evangelist of higher, better, and content-based American standards, provided invaluable help in finding pro-Core teachers and administrators. He also read the entire manuscript and, as always, provided sharp and constructive comments. Anna Bolgrien provided dedicated research assistance on the public's reaction to the Common Core. I also owe thanks to my editor, Jessica Gribble, who was supportive and enthusiastic about the project. All of these ferreted out would-be errors. Any that remain are my responsibility, and any interpretations of the facts are my own.

I also acknowledge here the background interviewees for the project who wished to remain confidential. They shared a love of education, children, and good public policy, even if they could not agree whether the Common Core was savior or scourge. The Office of the Governor of Utah was also exceedingly prompt with an open records request regarding Gov. Gary Herbert's attempt to tamp down anti-Common Core fervor in that state. Some of the more than 7,000 citizen comments that he received in that effort appear through the text. I would also like to thank the staff at the CCSSI who answered some of my direct queries about the critics of their work.

Abbreviations

ADP	American Diploma Project
AFT	American Federation of Teachers
AIR	American Institutes for Research
AYP	Adequate Yearly Progress
BAT	Badass Teachers Association
CAP	Center for American Progress
CCD	Common Core of Data
CCSSI	Common Core State Standards Initiative
CCSSO	Council of Chief State School Officers
CICI	Catholic Identity Curriculum Integration
ESEA	Elementary and Secondary Education Act
ESSA	Every Student Succeeds Act
FERPA	Family Educational Rights and Privacy Act
IASA	Improving America's Schools Act
LULAC	League of United Latin American Citizens
MALDEF	Mexican American Legal Defense and Educational Fund
MOA	Memorandum of Agreement
MTA	Massachusetts Teachers Association
NAEP	National Assessment of Educational Progress
NBPTS	National Board for Professional Teaching Standards
NCEA	National Catholic Educational Association

NCES	National Center for Education Statistics
NCHS	National Center for History in the Schools
NCLB	No Child Left Behind Act
NCTE	National Council of Teachers of English
NCTM	National Council of Teachers of Mathematics
NEA	National Education Association
NEGP	National Education Goals Panel
NESIC	National Education Standards and Improvement Council
NGA	National Governors Association
NORC	National Opinion Research Center
NPR	National Public Radio
NYSAPE	New York State Allies for Public Education
NYSUT	New York State United Teachers
OTL	opportunity-to-learn
PARCC	Partnership for Assessment of Readiness for College and Careers
PISA	Program for International Student Assessment
RTTT	Race to the Top
SBAC	Smarter Balanced Assessment Consortium
SLDS	Statewide Longitudinal Data System
TIMSS	Trends in International Mathematics and Science Study

ONE

The Impossible Dream

When the Common Core State Standards were adopted by 46 states in 2010, supporters of high national standards thought they had gotten it right. After the spectacular flame-out of national standards 15 years earlier, Common Core boosters were determined to foil political opposition. The standards touched only reading and math; they had been drafted by a large and diverse panel of experts; and they were explicitly state-led—all political lessons drawn from earlier attempts. They were dreaming the "impossible dream": a system of rigorous, national standards perhaps with tests to hold states and schools accountable for results.

Still sleepwalking, supporters were gleeful at the rapid, controversy-free adoption by so many states. Massachusetts' secretary of education S. Paul Reville said, "This is a watershed moment, a historical moment for Massachusetts. It's a decision that's good for students, good for equity, good for education."[1] Another observer said the standards were "too strategically smart to be dismissed out of hand."[2] Virtually all American students would, for the first time, be held to the same learning standards for two foundational subjects, a vision shared by some education reformers since the 1960s. And better, the standards had slipped into place, greased by federal money, with virtually no political opposition. Even the No Child Left Behind (NCLB) Act, which had drawn widespread bipartisan support in 2001, was the product of several years of high-wire political bargaining in Congress. Common Core, a product adopted separately by dozens of states, did not even *go* through state legislatures—as educational standards, they were in the domain of state education bureaucracies. Maybe the Core's "fewer, higher, better" standards were politically untouchable. One educational observer wondered why the celebration was so subdued. "The whole notion of national standards has been the third rail of education for two, three decades," he said. "It's a major accomplishment, completely revamping your K-12 math and English standards. I don't understand why [states] are not playing it up more."[3]

Perhaps because it was still just a dream. The standards were *adopted* in 2010, but teachers and parents did not see them for two more years. No school had to change curriculum in 2010, and no teacher was evaluated based on new Common Core-aligned tests. Once the curious music of the dream was gone, so too were the accolades. In five years' time, liberals saw the standards as furtive capitalist aggrandizement, and conservatives thought the Core was an ill-concealed federal plot. By 2015, even staunch supporters admitted that "the term 'Common Core' is toxic."[4] Parents balked at unusual math strategies, and teachers threatened to upend assessments of Common Core materials.

This book explores the Common Core's tortuous political path. The goals of the Common Core—that all students everywhere should have equal, high academic standards—were drawn from a deep well of American education policy sampled by both Republicans and Democrats. Although the specifics of both goals were controversial, the goals themselves were widely accepted and touted as *the* aim of American education. No contemporary politician would or could object. Supporters of the Core were politically cautious, and they banked on widespread frustration with the NCLB Act to bolster acceptance of the standards. But they could not wish away long-standing controversies in American education policy over federal power and the core purposes of education. Would the Common Core lead to a loss of local and state control of standards and curriculum? Did the Common Core thrust a joyless "hidden curriculum" of workforce preparation into the heart of American teachers? Would the standards shackle financially strapped school districts to pre-set curriculum? Did the Common Core strip children and families of privacy? Would the standards undermine teachers' innovation in their classrooms? These questions dogged the Common Core just as they had every other education reform in the twentieth century. The fuse was lit by the starkly polarized politics in the Obama era, weak evidence for the standards' benefits, and festering frustration with American federal education policy. That the Common Core avoided them until *after* its unveiling was indeed a political marvel.

Opponents were successful in voiding participation in the Common Core *process* and even more successful in upending Core-based testing. Both of them were perceived as an assault on state and local control of education, an argument that resonated across party lines. As Congress debated renewing the Elementary and Secondary Education Act, both the House and

Senate explicitly prohibited federal involvement in choosing or designing state standards, including the Common Core. Tests were not abolished, but they were likewise placed in the state domain. Yet, opponents of the standards had scarce success in eliminating the standards themselves. Although "repeal" bills were introduced in dozens of states, legislators enacted them in only three.[5] Two of those, South Carolina and Indiana, replaced the Common Core with standards bearing a twin-like resemblance. Too much political and financial capital was spent building them to be easily lost. And so the standards survived.

What made the debate over the Common Core so novel—or so frustrating—was that the politics surrounding the standards were *not* new. They were merely a reprise of the last battles: the standards wars of the 1990s, the fight over funding in the 1980s, the public's disillusionment with federal programs from the 1970s, the resentment of the role of standardized testing from the 1960s, and even echoes of states' rights from the 1950s. The actors had changed, and indeed the political alliance in favor of the Common Core was strikingly different by some lights—the federal government, bipartisan governors, civil rights groups on one side facing off against bipartisan governors, teachers' unions, and tea party groups on the other. Pro-standards activists came out against the Common Core, while state departments of education that had been shirking meaningful assessments gave them a full-throated defense. The product, too, was new; wags had said that America had a de facto national curriculum because of the market power of the textbook companies, but they were wrong. The Common Core eliminated much diversity. But the controversies surrounding the Common Core had been fixtures in 60 years of American education politics.

WHAT IS THE COMMON CORE?

Although the politics surrounding the Common Core are well-worn, the educational standards themselves are not. As with all academic standards, they specify *when* students should know *what*. The Common Core covers only reading and mathematics, areas that federal education policy had long emphasized, although some states began to work on science standards as well.

The Common Core itself was a product of frustration with the weak, contradictory, and perhaps impossible state standards of the 1990s. David Coleman and Jason Zimba, largely unknown standardized-testing gurus, became start-up entrepreneurs and founded the Grow Network in 2000 to help schools create meaningful reports from the plethora of standardized exams school districts used to characterize student performance. The company was successful enough that McGraw-Hill, the textbook giant, bought the firm in 2004, and both Zimba and Coleman left the firm. But their experience led them to believe that American education was shackled with "vast" and "vague" standards. In 2007, they built on their experience to write the foundational tract for what would become the Common Core, "Math and Science Standards That Are Fewer, Clearer, Higher to Raise Achievement at All Levels."[6]

Theirs was not a novel observation as the Thomas B. Fordham Institute and the American Federation of Teachers (AFT) had been making the same claims since the late 1990s. Existing state standards were vague in part to avoid controversies about how students should be taught—calculators or not? phonics or whole language reading?—in part due to concerns about ethnic, racial, and historical sensitivities, and in part the natural result of the committee-writing process. But what made Coleman's and Zimba's views central to the Core was that their paper attracted the attention of the Council of Chief State School Officers (CCSSO), the equivalent of a state superintendents' trade association. The organization was so impressed with the logic of the paper that they hired Coleman's and Zimba's new start-up, Student Achievement Partners, to help write the Common Core State Standards. At its heart, the standards are two lists of academic standards, one for mathematics and one for English Language Arts (ELA). They were composed by a panel of 30 professors, 30 state education department personnel, 23 business or private foundation members, 11 teachers, 4 school district personnel, and 3 others and sent out to a similarly composed review group.[7]

The bulk of the standards cover common school territory, but the standards work committees drafted them with two distinct differences that reflected Coleman's and Zimba's outlook.

First, the items in the Common Core State Standards are specific. After changes to federal law in 1994, most states had written or revised academic state standards, but most state standards were difficult to translate into concrete lesson plans. Specific standards are those that are descriptive and measurable, but one review of state standards in 1998 found that approximately half of the states' standards were so vague as to be meaningless. For example, at that time, Alaska's standards demanded that students "apply principles, concepts, and strategies from various strands of mathematics to solve problems that originate within the discipline of mathematics or in the real world."[8] Many states still struggled with vague standards in 2010, when a follow-up standards report again found little specific in state standards (although the report found notable improvement in most state standards' content). In that year, Wyoming still required students to "write and share literary texts using appropriate strategies." Iowa implored kindergarten to second-graders to "read to study" and "read for purposes relating to fiction and non-fiction."[9] Jason Zimba offered similar criticism of standards. He told National Public Radio that "previous standards ranged from terrible to not good enough. The best of them were little more than test blueprints. They were not a blueprint for *learning* math."[10]

In contrast to this, the Common Core deliberately specifies *what* students should learn for each grade from kindergarten to eighth grade. (The standards also have lists for high school, but they are not assigned specific grade levels.) In contrast to Wyoming's standard, the ELA standards require third-graders to "introduce the topic or text they are writing about, state an opinion, and create an organizational structure that lists reasons." Eighth-graders should be able to "determine the meaning of words and phrases as they are used in a text, including figurative and connotative meanings."[11] For math, third-grade math students should "interpret products of whole numbers, e.g., interpret 5×7 as the total number of objects in 5 groups of 7 objects each." By eighth grade, students should "understand that solutions to a system of two linear equations in two variables correspond to points of intersection of their graphs, because points of intersection satisfy both equations simultaneously."[12]

Second, the standards are explicit about their college and career focus. Many state standards before the Common Core had mentioned these as goals, but the writers of the Common Core deliberately structured all of the standards to this end. The introduction to the ELA standards, for example, suggests that students should be able to independently "evaluate complex texts," "seek out resources to assist them," and "appreciate that the twenty-first-century classroom and workplace are settings in which people from often divergent cultures . . . must learn and work together."[13] More controversially, the ELA standards suggest that the majority of works used be "informational texts" rather than fiction. David Coleman was emphatic that this was appropriate for work readiness. In a speech to the New York State Education Department, Coleman argued that American schools make "80 percent" of reading time literature in K–6. "Guess what that meant? We destroyed history and science in the elementary school." Further, he ridiculed the non-informational style of high school writing:

> The two most popular forms of writing in the American high school today . . . [are] the exposition of a personal opinion or it is the presentation of a personal matter . . . The only problem with those two forms of writing is as you grow up in this world you realize people really don't [care] about what you feel or what you think. What they instead care about is can you make an argument with evidence, is there something

verifiable behind what you're saying or what you think or feel that you can demonstrate to me. It is rare in a working environment that someone says, "Johnson, I need a market analysis by Friday, but before that I need a compelling account of your childhood."[14]

In his view, the Common Core would make evidence-based, informational writing *de rigueur.* Likewise, the mathematics standards do not include material beyond second-year algebra, notably excluding calculus, because few students require mathematics beyond this to enroll in college.[15] Coleman, in the same speech in New York, compared the math standards to a tree trunk, wide and basic at the base, but later allowing students to branch into many kinds of mathematics:

Arithmetic is the heartbeat of later mathematics, growing in middle school into work with data, with proportional reasoning and geometric measurement, widening but at the same time expanding to a sense of number sense that grows into linear algebra. And then in the high school, what's wonderful with someone with this kind of core trunk, this focus, is they can do a variety of things. They can go into later algebra, towards engineering and calculus, they can do more with statistics.[16]

The product of the two work groups became the Common Core State Standards.

THE MOVE TO COMMON STANDARDS

The Common Core's quick political adoption spoke to the fertile political ground into which it was planted. The groups that launched the Common Core movement placed common academic standards squarely in the American education tradition of educational *equity* and educational *excellence.* These goals had driven state and federal education policy since the 1960s. Former North Carolina Governor James B. Hunt (D) was an early spokesman for the standards, and he hosted policy makers and governors in 2007 to outline what would become the Common Core. But he also provided the political rationale for common standards. In the forward to Robert Rothman's book praising the Core, Hunt explicitly called attention to three political moves the supporters of the Common Core made. First, he argued that Americans had "established an equitable education as a civil right for all Americans." Because the Core had been adopted by more than 40 states, he argued that at least these states could offer an equitable education. Second, he argued that the standards would help American education be economically competitive. They would ensure academic excellence. "Students are competing with their peers across oceans and continents," he wrote. Third, he noted that an "ironclad process" would guarantee the Core's success because it would "emerge" from the states "much as the United States did . . . when the Constitution and Bill of Rights were adopted."[17] The civil rights language was meant to appeal to the left, accountability to the right, and state focus to state and local politicians. It was to be all things to all people.

The two educational reform goals—educational equity and academic excellence—had long track records in American politics, but both sat uncomfortably with Hunt's vision of a latter-day constitutional convention. Both equity and excellence took flight in the states only after the federal government prodded the states to move. It was the federal government that had faulted the states for perpetuating gross inequity in *Brown v. Board of Education* (1954), the 1965 Elementary and Secondary Education Act, and the 1966 Coleman Report. Equal opportunity had been ill-served by the diversity of approaches in the states, and the theory was that it would take the federal government's cash to improve the lot of America's low-income and non-white children. For educational excellence, state governors had been talking about educational excellence for close to 70 years, but it was the federal report *A Nation at Risk* in 1983 and an accompanying "Wall Chart" of shame at the U.S. Department of Education that advertised the "tide of mediocrity" washing over the states that prompted meaningful changes.[18] By all accounts, Hunt was dreaming the impossible dream.[19]

But if the dream was impossible, Hunt was also going where the brave would dare not go. The Common Core was also meant as a rebuke of the federal government's growing presence in American education. Indiana Governor Mitch Daniels was emphatic that the effort would have to be state led if were to be sustained, and the standards initiative was meant to show that the states were finally serious about their educational prerogatives.[20] In 1965, federal policy makers led by Commissioner of Education Francis Keppel convinced Congress that the states could not be trusted to serve the basic needs of low-income and non-white children. The result was the Elementary and Secondary Education Act, which placed the federal government at the financial heart of educational provision. In 1994, a reauthorized version of the act signaled that the federal government no longer thought school spending was enough to rectify inequality and put states on notice that academic standards were necessary. In 2001, the act was reauthorized as the NCLB Act—and it required states not only to adopt academic standards but also to test students annually to show *school* compliance with the standards. If schools or districts failed to meet an appropriate level of progress, the *federal* government specified punitive measures. State policy makers and many in the educator community resented this level of federal involvement, and the states sought to foreclose federally dictated learning standards.

The Common Core was also the historic fulfillment of the goals of governors seeking to embrace uniformity and surrender the crazy-quilt of academic standards. Thirty-six years earlier, in 1973, the Supreme Court had held that "no area of social concern stands to profit more from . . . a diversity of approaches than does public education."[21] The Court was merely affirming the status quo in a country that had, at the time, 16,730 school districts. Funding, curriculum choices, athletic programs, high school lab equipment, library resources, and teacher quality varied dramatically among these districts, and most states did not even require a common set of courses to qualify for a high school diploma. By the 1980s, governors had discovered that "education" was a winning political issue, and many believed that improved academics at home would boost state economic growth.

Yet they were also keenly aware that some states were academic (and economic) laggards. To combat this inequality, the National Governors Association (NGA) called for national academic standards in 1986. The effort blossomed into an historic educational summit in Charlottesville, VA, in 1989, and *both* major-party candidates for president in 1992 supported some version of national standards. But national partisan politics poisoned the effort in 1994. Republicans had gained control of Congress for the first time in 40 years and were in no mood to hand Democratic president Bill Clinton an easy victory. President Clinton tried for at least a national test in 1997, but that effort foundered on Democratic opposition. Democratic interest groups, chiefly non-white groups and teachers' unions, felt threatened by testing. Teachers' unions had been long opposed to external assessment of their members' work—they were trusted professionals, in their view—and non-white groups believed that standardized exams discriminated against their members' children. Thus, politicians of the 1990s could not agree on either equity or excellence. That changed with the unusual politics of 2001. President George W. Bush became president by a disputed margin, and the U.S. Senate was split equally between Republicans and Democrats. The tenuous political control allowed the NCLB Act to pass with elements attractive to both parties. One such provision was the requirement that all states would participate in the National Assessment of Educational Progress (NAEP) by 2003, an exam first administered in 1969 with a nationally representative sample (but not a state-representative sample). Its results, combined with groundbreaking work in the late 1990s, found that schools and states appeared to shortchange non-white students. This finding broke the political coalition of the 1990s as non-white groups swung to strong support of national standards *and* meaningful academic assessments. Public tests *could* force schools to expend effort on those students! Further, NAEP provided concrete evidence that different states did, in fact, have wildly different educational standards. The NAEP provided a common, national benchmark for student success, so policy makers could compare how many students were "proficient" by that standard versus a state's own definition. The differences were stark in some states and only suggestive in others, but it was clear that states were not using a common definition. Neither excellence nor equity prevailed—but it took a national test to prove it. *Both* Republican and Democratic groups found the "diversity of approaches," celebrated by the Supreme Court, wanting. Governors used this political nexus to forge the Common Core.

Ironically, the same NCLB Act that confirmed chasms in educational achievement and broke the political alignment of the 1990s *also* undermined support for federal education reforms. The law's requirements that students be tested annually in third through eighth grade and once in high school and that states identify schools as "in need of improvement" led many states to resent federal dictates about school evaluation. In light of widespread unease, state leaders saw Common Core as one way to regain the upper hand in educational policy. In 2007, working behind the scenes, former governor Hunt's organization, the National Governors Association, and the CCSSO, and several private organizations drafted the key elements of the Common Core. There was scant, if any, federal involvement with the effort; indeed, the effort was entirely conducted outside formal government channels.

But then, in 2009, President Barack Obama and his Secretary of Education Arne Duncan had an ambitious educational reform plan centered on public school choice, teacher evaluation, and early childhood education. Because the Elementary and Secondary Education Act was holed up in Congress, the president and secretary of education sought to use a competition for federal money to induce changes. In this "Race to the Top (RTTT)," states would agree to meet certain reform criteria in return for federal money. (Later, in 2011, the Department sweetened the pot for some reform criteria by offering waivers from elements of NCLB.) One of the criteria was to "participate in a consortium developing high-quality standards"—and the only one in existence was the Common Core State Standards Initiative (CCSSI). Common Core now had a federal inducement. It was effective, and 46 states adopted the Common Core in 2010.

THE CONCEPT OF THE COMMON CORE

In the main, the critics of the Common Core have targeted the process and later adoption of the standards.[22] Yet, despite the later appearance of federal involvement, the Common Core grew out of a confluence of private-sector thinking, education reform philanthropy, and gubernatorial impatience—and private groups played a large role in their formation.

In the year before Gov. Hunt's 2007 meeting invitation, he and former governor Bob Wise (D-WV) held a meeting in Washington, DC, with a panoply of private education reform groups, including the Aspen Institute and the Thomas B. Fordham Institute, to plan an initiative for common national standards. These private groups were central to the argument for national standards because they—and not the public school system—had been calling for changes to American education for a decade or more. Previous political experience seemed to show that working "in the system" would result in little to no change. Indeed, Fordham released a report at the same time as the DC meeting (with insights from some of the same people) presenting four possible paths to national standards; the only path the organization rated as politically feasible was essentially a half-step from the existing NCLB policy model. That model, denoted "Sunshine and Shame," would require states to make test results more transparent and comparable, a move that Fordham ruefully suggested would "do nothing to improve the quality of their academic content standards—which are mostly disreputable."[23]

And so Fordham set out three other alternatives to break up the existing system. First was "The Whole Enchilada," where the federal government would design both the standards and the tests, and states would be required to use lest the federal government yank its educational funding. A federal attempt at this had gone down to an ignominious defeat in 1994. Next, "If You Build It, They Will Come"—Fordham's preferred model—would have the federal government or a private group design the standards. The federal government would offer incentives to adopt the standards. The final alternative was "Let's All Hold Hands," in which the states would join together to develop their own common standards and the federal government would offer incentives to do so.[24]

As it happened, Hunt's and Wise's behind-the-scenes work got the National Governors Association and the CCSSO on board with "Let's All Hold Hands" and a small dose of "If You Build It, They Will Come." In 2007, NGA had begun work on boosting state standards and graduation requirements, and one of its recommendations was for states to adopt a "common core" of standards. CCSSO's gained a new executive director in 2006 who also pushed for better state-led standards, but, according to one insider, "recognized that they lacked resources to develop such standards on their own."[25] In other words, they would outsource the standards to a private group. In January 2009, NGA and CCSSO formed the CCSSI to oversee the effort.

That was Coleman's and Zimba's cue. Although Coleman had been involved in conversations about the Common Core since November 2007—including a trip to the Bill & Melinda Gates Foundation for funding in 2008—the CCSSO and NGA hired them to write the mathematics and ELA standards in 2009. That spring, the CCSSI enlisted the 60-odd professors, state bureaucrats, foundation personnel, and teachers to serve on drafting groups. In April 2009, they formally brought the effort to state leaders. By June, 46 states had pledged support to the as-yet-unreleased standards—a draft would be leaked in July, several months before the standards' official public release in September. This release was a set of skills that the "official" standards, to be released by June 2010, would cover.

That October, Fordham, a key player in pushing national standards for over a decade, offered cautiously enthusiastic support. "Nobody knows how this will turn out, but we think it's worth pitching in to try to help make it turn out well—while reserving final judgment until we see the final product," wrote Chester Finn, the organization's president.[26] The organization's standards reviewers called the Common Core draft "simple and clear" and "praiseworthy," although they did fault the standards for lacking priorities and examples.[27] But that quickly became strong support after the Common Core drafting committee released its final draft in June 2010 with significant changes. By July, the organization found that the Common Core was vastly superior to *most* state standards, and the organization stated that "we would like to see every state with high standards—as good as or better than the Common Core."[28]

There would be something like national standards, after all.

THE ADOPTION OF THE COMMON CORE

The public had very little influence on the drafting of the Common Core, but the standards had public imprimatur from governors and states' chief school officials (typically the state superintendent). To participate in the Common Core, these officials had to sign off on a Memorandum of Agreement (MOA) that committed the state to participation in the Common Core. The bulk of the agreement set out the purposes of the Common Core: They would be "evidence-based," "internationally benchmarked," have "rigorous content," and ensure that students would be prepared for "college, work, and competing in the global economy." The standards would also "accelerate and drive education reform." The MOA also committed states to adopt the Common Core within three years of signing the document and that the Core standards would comprise at least 85 percent of state standards.

State Process

More importantly, the agreement specified the process by which the standards would be created. The memorandum was forthright about the non-public nature of the process.[29] Although it did specify that the standards would be written in an "open, inclusive, and efficient process," the organizations in charge of the standards would be Achieve, Inc., ACT, and the College Board.[30] All were private organizations, and the latter two were intimately involved with academic testing. Those two organizations had long experience with nationalizing college admission standards, and the College Board was the product of the same reform movement that created the NAEP in the mid-twentieth century. Achieve, Inc., had grown out of the frustration with the failure of national standards in the early 1990s, and it was the immediate descendant of a 1996 "National Education Summit" of business leaders and governors led by IBM Chairman Louis "Lou" V. Gerstner. This group was especially interested in a meaningful high school diploma. Further, the MOA noted that the policy forum for discussing the Common Core would be run through major educational interest groups, including the Business Roundtable, the Council of Great City Schools, National Association of State Boards of Education, and the National Education Association (NEA).

Cognizant that national standards in the 1990s failed in part due to vision of federal takeover, the MOA's authors also included a lengthy paragraph detailing the appropriate involvement of the federal government. The MOA was clear that the Common Core was "a state-led effort and not a federal effort," but it did note that the federal government *could* play a role in encouraging both common state standards and common academic assessments. It suggested that the federal government could provide "key financial support" through the RTTT fund, waive requirements about the use of existing federal funds, and support the development of long-term common assessments.[31] When the Thomas B. Fordham Institute scored the possible options for national standards, they wrote that this "Let's All Hold Hands" model was only "maybe" feasible—yet here it was, down to the federal financial incentives.[32]

Easing state adoption was the unique method the MOA specified. States could have entered into a multi-state compact, a binding association defined in the U.S. Constitution, as they have for dairy products, water usage, and nuclear waste, but the states instead opted simply for an agreement. A compact likely would have required Congressional approval first and would have brought the project into the orbit of federal politics.[33] Instead, the governor and state superintendent would have to sign the agreement, although state boards of education (where they exist) would empower the superintendent to do so, just as they had for earlier state standards. This was convenient and sped adoptions if only because the Core was coordinated by the National Governors Association and the CCSSO. Most governors and superintendents had been in the know long before the MOA was issued.

The Federal Process: Race to the Top

Despite the dream of state-led adoption, the federal government's cash proved to be a powerful prod for the states. Congress authorized $4.35 billion to a RTTT fund in the American Recovery and Reinvestment Act of 2009 (usually known as the Stimulus Bill), and the U.S. Department of Education used the fund to boost a range of the Obama Administration's favored educational reforms, including charter schools, teacher assessment, longitudinal student data systems, and "participating in [a] consortium developing high-quality standards."[34] (Although the Obama administration initially planned to require the "Common Core," cooler heads in the U.S. Department of Education sensed that this wording would smack of federal takeover.)[35] This grant competition was meant to contrast with the seemingly punitive nature of the NCLB Act, and states would only have to demonstrate *commitment* to reform rather than showing results. The RTTT criteria were unveiled with great fanfare in June 2009 as President Obama announced that "this competition will not be based on politics or ideology or the preferences of a particular interest group. Instead, it will be based on a simple principle—whether a state is ready to do what works," or at least conform to the president's goals.[36]

RTTT was designed to be separate from regular federal educational funding, and states had a choice to apply for the competitive grant. Forty-six states filed applications with the U.S. Department of Education to demonstrate their commitment to the Administration's educational priorities.[37] Despite obvious partisan differences, state lawmakers were unusually compliant with the Administration's wishes, and many state officials boasted of their lasting commitment to education reform. States that for 20 years had restricted charter schools—public schools freed from some regulations—authorized them or loosened regulations on them. Despite strong pushback from teachers' associations and unions, states stumbled over themselves to outdo themselves in proving their plans to link high-quality data collection with teacher assessment.[38] Illinois was particularly obsequious:

Over the past year, Illinois has exhibited its deep commitment to bold education reforms and to the priorities of RTTT.... The General

Assembly has passed and Governor Quinn has signed four education bills in the last year that (1) establish a comprehensive state longitudinal education data system, (2) allow for alternative certification programs to operate independently from higher education, (3) create new, rigorous teacher and principal evaluation systems that incorporate student growth as a significant factor (the State's default evaluation plan will include 50 percent weighting of student growth); and (4) double the number of charter schools in Illinois and formally explore the concept of an independent charter school authorizer.[39]

Despite President Obama's claim that RTTT was based on a non-partisan "simple principle," a handful of states noted auspicious political circumstances surrounding RTTT. Both Tennessee and Delaware noted how political success and partisan ties favored the reforms—and both went on to be the *only* first-round RTTT winners. Tennessee virtually promised legislative success in the state's RTTT application. "In fact, this application includes a letter of support from all seven Democrat and Republican candidates for governor—a show of bipartisan support that ensures our application will be carried out no matter who holds the governor's office," it read.[40] Delaware was more explicitly personal and partisan. Delaware's reforms would succeed because it was led by a new political star. "Elected just a year ago, Governor [Jack] Markell has the potential to be in office for another seven years," according to the application. "Already, he is a rising leader in education reform, holding the co-chair in the National Governors Association's Common Core Standards Initiative, and the chairmanship of the Democratic Governors' Association."[41]

Gov. Markell's experience was certainly a plus for Common Core in that state, but RTTT was equally motivating around the country. Although the RTTT application guidelines did not specify "Common Core," *every* state application in the first RTTT round mentioned those standards by name, and frequently, even if they had not adopted them—from Virginia and Colorado (eight mentions) to Nebraska (63), Wisconsin (81), and Missouri (86). That the Administration favored Common Core was no secret, but states apparently took the RTTT guidelines at their word. Many states *also* mentioned the American Diploma Project (ADP) led by Achieve, Inc., as a multistate consortium, with 35 states, whose "benchmarks are significantly more rigorous than current high school standards," according to the Commonwealth of Virginia's application.[42] Achieve, Inc., was also a key player in the Common Core, but the ADP standards were less encompassing than the Core. Despite this, only Virginia tried to parry the federal government's preference for the Common Core. Its application reported that while Gov.

Tim Kaine and the state superintendent had signed the Common Core MOA, the authors interpreted that document as only requiring Virginia to participate in the "process of developing the common standards" rather than actually adopting them.[43] Instead, the state noted that its own standards were superior to the Core standards then available (Fall 2009). Not only had the state done its own standards analysis, but also the application listed superior standards ratings from the AFT and the Thomas B. Fordham Institute as well as commendations from the College Board and Achieve, Inc.[44] This was a fatal flaw. One federal application reviewer commented that, "Reviewer guidelines are that the adoption [of standards] in the RTTT notice is specific to the Common Core . . . Virginia, in several locations in its proposal, indicated that they believe the Virginia Standards are superior to the Common Core Initiative and that declaration suggested that they will not adopt the Common Core Initiative Standards."[45] A second reviewer made similar comments.

The grant competition required that states show evidence that they planned to adopt common standards by August 2, 2010. If Common Core was not the obvious choice (as, apparently, to Virginia), the second round of RTTT applications came with instructions: "Applicants for Phase 2 of this competition have the opportunity to submit amendments specifically regarding the adoption of common college- and career-ready standards by August 2, 2010 at 4:30:00 pm ET."[46] Again Common Core was not mentioned but the release of the first-round comments had made the choice clear. Virginia did not submit a second application. RTTT was meant to be a lever for Common Core, and it was an extremely effective one. The standards were officially released on June 2, 2010; and 28 of the 35 states that applied in the second round had adopted the standards by August 2. Figure 1.1 illustrates the rush to adopt the Common Core between the release of the standards' final draft on June 2, 2010, and the RTTT's on August 2, 2010 deadline. Thirty-one states beat the deadline, including three that adopted them on or before the date that the final standards draft was released.

THE POLITICS OF THE CORE

The Supporters

The Common Core had a distinguished cast of supporters, many of whom had long been in the circles of education reformers. Although their reasons for supporting the Common Core differed, all of these individuals and groups had supported clearer content standards and meaningful tests since the 1990s or earlier. Three main groups stand out: governors, foundations and business groups, and civil rights groups.

Figure 1.1   Initial Adoption of the Common Core State Standards

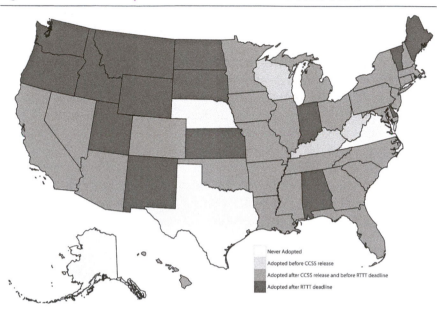

Governors

First were the governors. Former governor and president Bill Clinton, who had supported something like them as president, was supportive, saying, "We cannot be disheartened by the forces of resistance to building a modern economy and good jobs or to rebuilding our education system to give all our children a common core or to give all Americans access to affordable college training programs."[47] In 1996, he had said something similar: "We must start with the elemental principle that there should be national standards of excellence in education."[48] Gov. Jeb Bush (R-FL) was a staunch supporter of the standards, despite the later political risk to himself. Bush had long been a champion of changes to education policy in Florida, and especially assessing educational progress. Calling debate around the standards "troubling," he said that high standards were needed to maintain international competitiveness. "This morning, over 213 million Chinese students went to school, and no one debated whether academic standards should be lowered to protect their students' self-esteem," he said.[49] Other current or former governors supportive of the Core included Mitch Daniels (R-IN), Richard Riley (D-SC), Jay Nixon (D-MO), Mary Fallin (R-OK), Andrew Cuomo (D-NY), and Chris Christie (R-NJ).[50]

Many governors made their common cause higher standards in the 1980s, and by 1990 it was rare to find one that did not at least give lip service to being an "education governor." Fully 60 percent of the governors elected in 1994 or later claimed to have a substantive interest in K–12 education policy.[51] Although governors have often had interests in bolstering education, especially in the South after World War I, education became a central preoccupation in the 1990s. The reasons are not entirely clear. Some had to do with a short but severe financial crunch in the states in the early 1980s that hit school districts particularly hard. Further, many believed that American economic competitiveness was in decline as American industry failed to compete with (especially) Japanese imports. Governors saw an opportunity to leverage these twin crises into a political benefit. "Education is the keystone to economic prosperity," Texas Governor Mark White (D) told a convention hosted by the National Conference of State Legislators in 1983.[52] With traditional local governance in financial distress, the state, through the governors' office, could lead the way. Governors believed that quality education would serve as a way to bolster economic development. A better-educated citizenry was thought to attract better employers and higher wages.[53] Governors also gained additional formal powers with respect to education, especially over the state board (if any) and state superintendents. The number of gubernatorially appointed superintendents doubled to 10 and governors appointed at least some state board members in 36 states in the decade of the 1980s.[54] Informal powers expanded their reach. In Ohio, for example, Gov. George Voinovich (R) made it very clear that he wanted the state superintendent to resign although the governor had no formal power to force the change; the superintendent did. In Wisconsin, Gov. Tommy Thompson (R) successfully gutted the state's education bureaucracy (only to have it restored by the state courts)—but the state's superintendent was no longer an effective voice.[55] Governors saw it to their political advantage to promise bold changes to education, and they had the local tools with which to do it.

But their political vantage point made them little inclined to defer to traditional educational thinking. Governors oversee general government and have a much broader constituency. Because they are blamed for state economic conditions, governors are also very attuned to the voice of business groups—and these groups were unhappy with education. Gov. Voinovich used a group of businessmen to "audit" the hapless state superintendent to convince him to exit. In 1990, *Fortune* magazine ran a special issue detailing ways that businesses could partner with schools to bolster academic achievement; the issue also listed the 10 best "education governors" who incidentally were also given to thinking about education in a business-minded way.

The magazine quotes Lou Gerstner, the future head of Achieve, Inc., saying, "Education is too important to be left to the educators."[56] That thinking prioritized results rather than process, and job skills rather than individual expression.

Business Groups

A second group of Core supporters included a variety of business and education reform foundations. Despite substantial public spending on education, private giving to American education is second only to religion. The sum donated is difficult to calculate, but estimates suggest that private donors contribute about $2 billion a year (in 2005 dollars) to public education, or about 0.4 percent of the total public school expenditures in a given school year.[57] Most of this sum comes from organizations. For the Common Core, the most notable are Achieve, Inc., the Hunt Institute, the Business Roundtable, the Alliance for Excellent Education, the Thomas B. Fordham Institute, and the Bill & Melinda Gates Foundation. These groups have a variety of interest and motives for their work, but each represents a newer, more activist form of philanthropy in education.

Philanthropic giving has been common in American education since colonial days. The West India Company sponsored schools in New Amsterdam in the 1640s, wealthy New England merchants donated large sums to support "free" grammar schools in the 1710s, and the Episcopal Church established schools for slaves in the American South. Until the mid-twentieth century, most gifts were used to complement existing educational programs.[58] The Ford Foundation and others helped support research and advocacy for increased public spending in the 1970s, and about the same time the Carnegie Corporation pushed for middle schools to replace junior high schools.[59] But none of these involved major changes to the "technology" of schooling—the teaching and learning in the classroom on a day-to-day basis. The culmination of this era came in 1993 when Walter Annenberg announced a $500 million gift, the largest ever, to support school efforts to improve education. Like earlier gifts, most of the money flowed to existing schools and existing personnel who could spend the money in the best way they knew how. A decade after the gift, its administrator, Vartan Gregorian, captured the logic of these gifts:

> The Annenberg Challenge did not launch school reform: it empowered and reinvigorated skilled and visionary school reformers who were already active in the field—and did so without ideological or political bias of any kind—reformers who were working on strategies to improve

K-12 education that had been underway since the early 1980s with the support of local and state governments, national agencies, private philanthropies, public institutions, and even federal interventions.[60]

Yet the Challenge was seen as a disappointment by other foundations. Although all admitted the money was beneficial to some, "the school districts and the schools gobbled up those grants like lunch" and leaving minimal lasting effects, according to one Challenge partner organization.[61] The Annenberg Challenge itself noted that its money was spread too thinly and its funds were sometimes captured by local bureaucracy and politics.[62]

In response, newer donors sought to aim at *specific*, high-impact reforms. These included small high schools, charter schools, and school vouchers—but most notably it included Common Core. Here was a well-defined, concrete proposal that could be developed outside local politics and bureaucracy which, if successful, could transform teaching in the schools. Common Core drew the bulk of its private support from newer philanthropies, ones in which wealth was recent and ones which still had substantial links to the business community. The substantial wealth of the Bill & Melinda Gates Foundation, the Broad Foundations, and the Walton Family Foundation all came from the last 50 years. These philanthropies saw an opportunity to leverage a small sum of money to maximum impact. Bill Gates, for example, argued that high schools were "obsolete"—and then directed very targeted funding to make small high schools, either by breaking up existing schools or creating new ones.[63] His foundation later came to Common Core.

Business groups such as the Business Roundtable and Achieve, Inc., had somewhat different motivations. Although they, too, sought leveraged reforms in American education, their goals were more focused on career preparedness. At least since the 1990s, the Business Roundtable has sought to close the "skill-gap" that business leaders say threaten their international competitiveness. In 1995, the Ohio affiliate was instrumental in retooling that state's graduation exams to emphasize employable skills.[64] Achieve, Inc., also got its start in the 1990s under the leadership of businessman Lou Gerstner, then of IBM. Its board members have included CEOs of BellSouth, Procter & Gamble, AT&T, Kodak, Boeing, Intel, State Farm, and Prudential as well as a host of governors. The organization's goals were to boost state standards and improve technology use in the classroom, and it specifically stated that "businesses . . . will require job applicants to demonstrate academic achievement . . . [and] place a high priority on the quality of a state's academic standards and student achievement when determining business location decisions."[65] Although it noted that governors would be responsible for drafting new and better standards, the organization worked in concert with the National Governors Association to do so. By 2005, Achieve, Inc., launched the ADP to prepare students for the workforce and college: "We need states working together and collaborating with many partners like the business community to help graduates leave school fully prepared for the jobs we have to offer," according to the co-chair of the organization (and Prudential CEO).[66] These goals included raising "high school standards to the level of what is actually required to succeed in college or in the workforce" and developing "tests of college and work readiness that all students will take in high school."[67]

The ADP was a clear precursor to the Common Core, down to the "college-and career-ready" language. In 2013, the Business Roundtable issued a press release echoing ADP language—but for Common Core: "Good paying jobs are going unfilled because U.S. workers don't have the skills to fill the positions. We must cultivate a highly educated workforce and we see the Standards as a key component to answering this challenge," according to Robert Corcoran, a General Electric executive on behalf of the Roundtable.[68] Common Core was the culmination of three decades of effort. Although by no means exclusively conservative, these groups have helped hold Republican support for the Common Core.

Civil Rights Groups

The third group includes a wide array of civil rights groups and their legislative supporters.[69] Through the early 1990s, many of these groups were wary of higher standards and especially assessment because they believed that schools had used them to discriminate against group members in the past.

Before the mid-1990s, "quality education" was seen by some in these groups as cover for segregation or discrimination, a view for which public officials provided some support. Research in the 1960s led by James Coleman and others found significant gaps in academic achievement between racial and ethnic groups, but they also found wide disparities in school resources between majority-white and majority-non-white schools. American judges and many civil rights advocates argued that the appropriate remedy was to integrate schools through busing, a view validated in *Swann v. Charlotte-Mecklenburg* (1971). If resources followed white students, the logic went, then school administration must ensure that schools have a proportionate number of white students so that all students would benefit.

This creation of "unitary, nonracial systems" spawned 30 years of controversy about the definition of "quality" education.[70] Did it mean that education would be the same for all students or simply that all students would be in the same classrooms? President Gerald Ford seemed to equate "quality" with non-integrated schools. In 1975, Ford told the Illinois NAACP president that "I don't think that forced busing to achieve racial balance is the proper way to get quality education. The principal objective is to get quality education for all our young people. And I think there must be a better way to do it than the way some advocate."[71] The following year, a reporter asked him explicitly whether "quality" meant "separate": "Mr. President, there are many civil rights groups who believe that the word 'quality education' is a code word that does not, is not in conformity with the Supreme Court's 1954 decision . . . What do you say is your definition of 'quality education'?"[72] Some civil rights activists, however, held a similar view. They suggested that commonality deprecated the contributions of nonwhite groups. Harold Berlak, for example, argued that academic standards "exacerbate inequalities and provoke racial strife" because they seek to create a unified culture. Tests that found significant score gaps between races, such as Coleman's, were not the problem; the content on them was.

> While Presidents Clinton, Bush, and other defenders of the excellence via testing policies are never heard proclaiming that one of the chief purposes of government mandated testing and indexing policies is to employ government power to unify the culture, it is clear that from the beginning that this has been a chief corollary goal of the architects of these policies. The seminal 1992 report, *Raising Standards for American Education* that launched Goals 2000 argued that testing tied to national standards would "bind together a wide variety of groups into one nation."[73]

Others were more concrete. The NAACP and the League of United Latin-American Citizens (LULAC), with others, fought state standards for graduation, admissions to teacher preparation programs, and athletic participation in the 1980s and they staunchly opposed ability grouping students in classrooms. The groups were concerned by obvious racial disparities in test scores and participation rates. One official explicitly said these were "black and white issues."[74]

But civil rights groups' opposition to tests was based on unequal preparation or unequal opportunity. This became the bridge to the Common Core. In part due to the concerted efforts of the interest group Education Trust, civil rights groups came to see standardized testing as a vehicle for change in the 1990s. There was overwhelming evidence that schools were labeling low-performing students as "learning disabled" so they could be taught in different curricula in different classrooms.[75] Others documented an apparent growth in achievement by low-income, non-white students in states with high state standards.[76] Some civil rights groups were in the odd political mix supporting the No Child Left Behind in 2001, perhaps reflecting their constituency. One October 2002 poll found that 77 percent of poor, mostly-non-white urban parents supported the broad elements of No Child Left Behind.[77] By 2015, the core testing element had become solidified. Groups such as the National Council of La Raza, NAACP, Children's Defense Fund, LULAC, and the Mexican American Legal Defense and Educational Fund (MALDEF) called not only for annual, standardized testing—but also for a federal role to ensure "that each state adopts college and career-ready state standards."[78] The Common Core would seem to provide equal standards for *all* children, white or otherwise, and annual tests would ensure that *no* children could be ignored by schools. The president of MALDEF noted, "Because Latinos are an important and growing proportion of the public school population, our community has a particular interest in achieving swift and appropriate implementation of the Common Core State Standards."[79]

Major civil rights groups appreciated the universal focus of Common Core, and they provided an anchor for Democratic Party support of the standards.

The Detractors

Despite the careful framing of the standards—and the rapid adoption of the standards by 46 states—Common Core supporters found themselves in a political firestorm. Low-key opposition had emerged in late 2012 as schools began to explore "Common Core"-aligned textbooks, but opposition exploded in 2014 as state legislators introduced 77 anti-Common Core bills in their home states.[80] That year, three states pulled out entirely and two others created panels to "review and replace" the standards. One governor, a former strong supporter, turned on the standards and sued to prevent their implementation in his state. The Common Core also took hits in the popular media for the first time, too, as comedians Louis CK and Stephen Colbert mocked the Common Core. "Folks, as much as I didn't expect it, I may be coming around to the Common Core because it turns out that Common Core testing prepares our students for what they will face as adults—" Colbert riffed, "pointless stress and confusion."[81] By 2015, hundreds of thousands of parents chose to "opt-out" their students from Common Core-aligned tests largely in New York, New Jersey, and Colorado, threatening both federal funding for their schools and the validity of tracking educational progress.

This took supporters by surprise. The Business Roundtable—three years after the adoption of the Common Core—began running ads in support of the standards. Secretary Arne Duncan initially wrote off opponents as members of "fringe groups" and disgruntled "white, suburban moms," but even he felt compelled to chastise proponents for their poor job of selling the standards. During the political onslaught, Democratic supporters explained that they liked the idea but that the implementation was poor; Republican supporters complained that the effort had been hijacked by the federal government. What *was* clear was that the Common Core was not under attack for educational reasons. They were not the paragon of educational excellence, but even Coleman and Zimba acknowledged that. Instead, the assault was political, and appropriately for bipartisan standards, the attacks likewise came from across the political spectrum.

Opponents on the right, such as Louisiana Governor Bobby Jindal and Glenn Beck, argued that the Common Core was an untoward federal intrusion on the educational prerogatives of the states. Some of these critics supported the Common Core before 2009, but saw Secretary Duncan's and President Obama's credit claiming as evidence that the initiative had been taken over. Others saw the standards through the exceedingly polarized politics of the era—Obama had the highest sustained gap in support between Republicans and Democrats of any president since polling began—and they saw Obama's involvement as *prima facie* evidence that the standards were a Democratic plot. These are discussed in Chapter 3.

Many more centrist critics, including Cristel Swasey, Frederick Hess, and those discussed in Chapter 4, wondered about the validity of the "evidence" that Common Core supporters touted. Frederick Hess, one such critic, imagined proponents merely saying, "Trust us, we're really smart."[82] Some saw the "expert-led" nature of the Common Core problematic and so revived charges against progressive education—the progressivism of John Dewey, not Barack Obama. These critics worried that the Common Core undercut traditional emphases on "classics" and history. Taking the criticism further were those who wondered whether the Common Core sought to undermine parental involvement in education, and perhaps parental control as well. Private schools were faced with a stark challenge, too. If the Common Core was truly common, could these schools maintain their identity? A final challenge to expert-led reform from the center concerned student and family privacy. Although the Common Core itself had nothing to say about data collection, the RTTT had *also* urged comprehensive testing, and the U.S. Department of Education had relaxed rules regarding student data at the same time. Critics saw the emergence of Common Core-aligned tests ominously.

Opposition to the tests, especially those from test-powerhouse Pearson, Inc., bridged the political divide between Republicans, conservatives,

Democrats, and liberals. As discussed in Chapter 5, the Common Core was not conceived to be a set of tests, and the standards themselves have nothing to say about assessment, but no one involved with the standards had any illusions about the inevitability of testing. Supporters had hoped that the tests would be associated with the federal testing regime—the standards would be a salve, and so anything it brought along would be an improvement. Instead, the standards became collateral damage. Most notably, the teachers' unions that had reluctantly supported No Child Left Behind in 2001 turned strongly against the Common Core-aligned tests. The unions had never been comfortable with assessment, but they made the political calculation that they would be politically "lonely" if they did not support the union of standards and assessment.[83] The groundswell of opposition to testing gave unions their opportunity to split high standards from academic assessment. Unions complained that assessments could not be used to measure teacher effectiveness, not even if the same standards were used in every third-grade classroom in the country. Teachers more generally took exception to the classroom disruption the tests created, and associated it with the incoming Common Core. Conservative opponents were only too happy to make common cause with these Democratic groups to help parents "opt out" of exams—and perhaps simultaneously undermine the Common Core.

A final group, clearly on the left, was led by critics like Diane Ravitch, Mercedes Schneider, and Anthony Cody. As shown in Chapter 6, they accepted some of the arguments of conservatives, but the characteristic concerns of these critics were the sponsors, drafting process, and adoption method of the Common Core; a few questioned the explicit college and career targets of the standards. None of the sponsors of the Common Core were formally public, and many were private foundations. Even nongovernmental organizations meant to represent the interests of public officials—the National Governors Association and the CCSSO—were suspect. But private foundations were the target of much of the criticism, especially the Bill & Melinda Gates Foundation. Although private foundations had supported education programs for almost a century, big-time, programmatic reforms came in 1993 with the Annenberg Challenge. This, the largest private gift ever to education, was meant to boost involvement in public education, but a decade later the program was seen as something of a failure.[84] They regrouped and by 2006 had become instrumental in changing school politics in large urban districts such as Los Angeles and New York City. The Common Core effort was a new ground for the organizations' program officers to open doors for political support, shape the outlines of the curriculum, and advance a particular, assessment-based view of American education. Critics on the left found this a dangerous precedent, and some argued that such private support was tantamount to a capitalist takeover of public education. They also noted how unusual the Common Core was in that virtually all of the work was done outside the public sector, away from open records laws, the press, and citizen input. Indeed, the membership of the "work committees" was deliberately not released for months after the work had begun to shield the drafters from public scrutiny.[85] These critics insinuated that the secrecy was sinister and anti-democratic. A final critique of the Common Core, shared with some conservatives, was over the speedy formal adoption of the standards by governors and state superintendents. Conservatives tended to worry about the monetary inducements from a Democratic federal administration, while liberals typically objected to the lack of public discussion about their adoption—indeed, legislatures had virtually no say in the adoption of the standards.[86]

STANDARDS, ACCOUNTABILITY, AND ASSESSMENT

A quick word on the difference between educational standards, accountability, and assessment is in order. In contemporary American education politics, these words frequently appear together, but they suggest different public policies. Standards are those concepts or ideas that teachers are supposed to teach or resources a school is supposed to provide students. Policy makers intend that standards will compel educational *providers* to offer comparable educational quality wherever the standards are met. But standards have a flaw: they are input-focused and often aspirational. Schools or textbook publishers (or hospitals, libraries, or auto mechanics) may "adopt" a set of standards to tell parents and students what they should expect. Standards are a promise. A pre-Common Core example will suffice. In the 1980s, many American states adopted increased high school class standards. These typically took the form of requiring a certain number of courses in a list of subjects. Three mathematics courses, four English, one history, two science, and so on—but the states did not specify *what* would be taught in those classes, only that students would have to take them. Other states required certain topics to be covered, but they never checked systematically whether teachers covered the topics or whether students learned anything.

Those are the domain of accountability policies. Accountability policies compare the *output* of schools or teachers to the standards. These policies attempt to force schools or teachers to meet standards by exposing their performance on those standards to some set of the public, whether to school board members, parents, politicians, or the general public. The NCLB Act required states to issue "school report cards" so parents (and anyone else) could see the demographic composition of schools and how well students met state academic standards for reading and mathematics. Accountability policies draw their power from the ability to shape practice. If something is measured, it is done.

Assessment, the last of the three, is one *method* for accountability. Test-based accountability became the favorite method for federal policy makers in the late 1990s, although it was not the only approach available. (One alternative was known as "authentic assessment.") The advantages of test-based accountability was that all students could be measured against a common standard, allowing a policy maker to compare districts', schools', or even students' performance on the same test. Test-based accountability is also easy to administer—an important characteristic if thousands of schools are to administer an exam. Policy makers can then uncover systematic differences between students and perhaps ameliorate those differences. For example, the NAEP, a federal, representative assessment first given in 1969, showed a distinct and large gap among students from different ethnic and racial groups. This gap reinforced state and federal efforts by politicians on the left and the right for over 40 years. Still, testing critics complain that tests, whether the NAEP or state assessments, do not measure the standards meaningfully *or* that they are academically invalid. These critics are not (necessarily) dismissing standards or accountability, but only the method of accountability.

THE GOAL OF THE BOOK

The Common Core was not supposed to be controversial. There was broad-based agreement on its principles, and American education reformers can easily claim Democratic and Republican support for major contemporary reforms—a focus on teacher quality, academic assessment, charter schools, and high academic standards. But the de facto national standards known as the Common Core have become "toxic" and the associated tests even more so.

Despite the widespread criticism, the critics have been, as yet, notably unsuccessful in rolling back actual state participation in the Common Core. While repeal bills were filed in dozens of states, only three governors signed them. One of these, Indiana, withdrew from the Common Core only to adopt "Indiana Academic Standards" that were a near-verbatim copy of the Common Core. Arkansas promised to rename the standards and explored revising the standards but did so using the Common Core as the starting point.[87] The affiliated tests proved more controversial, and critics did force testing companies to pare down their exams, but still, the exams went on.

This book is about the politics of the Common Core. Why did conservatives continue to recoil from national standards? Why did liberals oppose testing to monitor student progress? And yet, why has Common Core survived—if not in name, in practice?

TWO

A Vision of Equity, Excellence, and Assessment

The Common Core State Standards Initiative (CCSSI) was meant, at the least, to show that the states could remedy a century of educational inequality and boost academic excellence without the help of the federal government. This was a tall order because the federal government had spent 50 years operating under the assumption—with compelling evidence—that the states could not be trusted. Thus, Congress kept states on a short leash with categorical grants and prescriptive policy. But the Common Core shared the federal government's long-term goals of educational excellence and equity. Those goals sprang from very different political sources in the 20th century, but grew together in the 1990s before fully converging *at the federal level* in the No Child Left Behind (NCLB) Act of 2001. As that act stumbled in the early years of the decade, governors and education reformers saw an opening for the states to regain their educational priority; in fact, perhaps they could show that *they* could accomplish the goals that the federal government could not. NCLB was a politically "impossible" act—but it passed, and it effected massive changes in American schools. The Common Core's supporters argued that the standards, built by a likewise "impossible" coalition of states, would lead American education down the path that NCLB only promised.

RACE AND RESOURCES

Common Core booster Gov. James B. Hunt explicitly placed education at the center of the country's longest struggle. His claim that "equitable education [was] a civil right" had motivated federal education policy since the

U.S. Supreme Court held that separate educational facilities were "inherently unequal" in *Brown v. Board of Education* (1954). Treating education as a civil right implied that education was a right or privilege that *must* be enforced by government. And if so, then unequal educational *resources* would violate this civil right whether those resources were educational standards or educational spending. Although the Court's decision famously pointed to the deleterious effects of segregation on the "hearts and minds" of students, the evidence presented to the court—and the theory of action later adopted by the U.S. Congress—suggested that the real outworking of segregation appeared as inequalities in educational resources. Students in African-American schools had teachers held to different standards, sometimes had a different school year, and had access to fewer books and less equipment than their white counterparts. Those disparities were well documented. As shown in Table 2.1, the most extreme case was Mississippi, which spent just 31 cents on African-American schools for every dollar on white schools. Seven other Southern states spent less than 80 cents on the dollar.[1]

But *Brown* did not establish education as a civil right, and subsequent federal court cases confirmed the conflicted place of education in federal policy. In *McInnis v. Shapiro* (1968), plaintiffs argued in federal district court that inequitable school spending violated the Constitution's Equal Protection Clause, the bulwark of American civil rights. And in 1972, plaintiffs

Table 2.1   Ratio of Expenditures in African-American Schools versus White Schools in Selected States, 1950

State	Ratio
Mississippi	0.31
Arkansas	0.62
Louisiana	0.62
South Carolina	0.64
Georgia	0.68
Tennessee	0.69
Alabama	0.76
Florida	0.80
Texas	0.83
Delaware	0.87
Virginia	0.88
North Carolina	0.93
Maryland	0.95

Source: Robert A. Margo, *Race and Schooling in the South, 1880–1950* (Chicago: University of Chicago Press, 1990), Table 2.5, pp. 21–22.

told the U.S. Supreme Court in *Rodriguez v. San Antonio* (1973) that such undisputed civil rights as voting and political participation would be "hollow privilege[s]" without equal, basic education.[2] The courts turned back both challenges. The *McInnis* decision found that there was no way to know what the appropriate level of school resources was, and there was no "discoverable or manageable standard."[3] In *Rodriguez*, the justices held that the Constitution did not "guarantee the most effective speech or the most informed electoral choice" that might come from education, and that a "diversity of approaches" was central to quality education.[4]

Even beyond finances, federal justices were skeptical that education qualified as a civil right. The 1974 federal desegregation case, *Milliken v. Bradley*, found that the Constitution only required educational equity *within* a school district, even if racial (and financial) disparities between districts were great. According to Chief Justice Warren Burger, "No single tradition in public education is more deeply rooted than local control over the operation of schools."[5] *Milliken* placed local control of education ahead of equal educational opportunities. From the federal judicial perspective, the combination of *Milliken*, *McInnis*, and *Rodriguez* meant that school districts were permitted—if not encouraged—to maintain different levels of funding, different qualifications for teachers, and different standards for education.

Even if education did not fit the Constitutional definition of civil rights, education *did* meet a partisan definition of civil rights. Although some Congressional Democrats had been advocating for federal spending on local education since the 1940s, American education was fraught with racial tension—a political tension nowhere more evident than in the Democratic Party, which included both blatant segregationists like Orval Faubus (D-AR) and Robert Byrd (D-WV) but also ardent civil rights proponents like Hubert Humphrey (D-MN) and William Proxmire (D-WI). Many Southern Democrats believed (correctly) that if the federal government provided aid to education, it would only come with desegregation.[6]

Democratic President Lyndon Johnson did just that in the mid-1960s. Although he had a long career opposing civil rights as a Texas politician, as vice president and then president, he moved swiftly to create and consolidate his, and his party's, political advantages. Johnson used his office to cement the Democratic gains among African Americans that had begun in the 1930s and to implement his vision of a completed New Deal, the Great Society. His large congressional majorities easily passed the Civil Rights Act of 1964 and the Elementary and Secondary Education Act of 1965 (ESEA), among other landmark pieces of legislation. The Civil Rights Act placed states on notice that racial issues were *federal* issues; and the ESEA fundamentally changed the governance of local education. Although

ESEA and its later reauthorizations never provided anywhere close to a majority of school financing, the millions of dollars provided to states and schools—especially though the act's Title I—proved extremely enticing even to staunch critics of federal power. Johnson tied the two together by prohibiting any money flowing to segregated schools, and argued that the source of poverty lay "in our failure to give our fellow citizens a fair chance to develop their own capacities, in a lack of education and training, . . . [and] in a lack of decent communities in which to live and bring up their children."[7] In this major foray into education, Title I was targeted explicitly to disadvantaged students and schools. Schools and districts had to take a census of students, classify them by race and income, and report those numbers to the federal government. Districts had done none of this before. As with later federal programs, Title I borrowed the capacity of other levels of government to do its bidding.[8]

Simultaneously, the architects of the Great Society doubted the efficacy of state and local government. Title V of the ESEA was meant to explicitly shore up state educational departments, then little more than backwater governments concerned with statistical reports. Certainly the performance of state and local governments on other civil rights issues had not been stellar in any region of the country. If the ESEA was meant to aid low-income and non-white children, states and local government played to type. "When Title I was implemented, it produced not *a* Title I program, but something more like 30 thousand separate and different Title I programs," according to one observer.[9] A scathing 1969 audit found that school districts used Title I money for swimming coaches and new mainframe computers among other things.[10] The federal government responded by tightening audit controls, and by 1978, ESEA provided 62 percent more money per child than in 1966 despite an almost identical inflation-adjusted appropriation.[11] Even the Title V money was not well used; one policy maker called the states' use of the money the "biggest failure" of ESEA.[12]

Still, Johnson's political gambit provided an enduring basis for federal activity in education. He created a *federal* rationale for funding local education, and he framed that funding as a component of civil rights. Because the federal courts had refused to see education as a Constitutional right, Johnson's work placed federal education activity squarely in the domain of electoral politics.

ECONOMICS AND EXCELLENCE

The states might have been sluggish when pursuing desegregation, but governors in the 1970s were eager to tie educational standards to economic growth. In 1973, only two states required certain classes for graduation from high school; a decade later, 24 did.[13] Improving Georgia education was a centerpiece of Gov. Jimmy Carter's budgets in the 1970s just as it was Georgia Governor Joe Frank Harris in the 1980s.[14] In 1978, the Ohio State Board of Education radically changed its requirements for school districts. In addition to reporting on building expenditures, enrollments, and district programs, school districts would need to emphasize students' academic *outcomes*. In 1981, the board highlighted increases in student competency test scores.[15] Many other states followed suit to require academic competency testing of students in the late 1970s and early 1980s.[16] Some of this was certainly posturing: a former employee of Wisconsin's Department of Public Instruction noted that Gov. Lee C. Dreyfus had an unwritten agreement with the state superintendent: "You're the state superintendent, but make me the best education governor ever, OK?"[17] But there is clear evidence that the states' elected leadership sought to bolster their education credentials— even before the widely cited report *Nation at Risk* was published in 1983.

Nation at Risk was drafted by a little-noticed federal commission that President Ronald Reagan initially wanted to bury. He did not, and it became a rallying point for education reformers. Unlike *Brown* and other civil rights arguments, the authors of *Nation at Risk* made an explicitly economic argument. Only "a high level of shared education" would maintain "the slim competitive edge we still retain in world markets."[18] Although some argued that the "risks" noted in the document were inflated, there is no debate that *Nation at Risk* was a boon to governors.[19] In 1986, Tennessee Governor Lamar Alexander called for a "horse trade" for schools, in which states would create standards and public accountability for schools in return for state dollars and relaxing some internal regulation.[20] With Alexander's leadership and widespread agreement from other governors, the National Governors Association (NGA) published the influential *Time for Results,* a report that generated a flurry of activity leading to an influential 1989 Charlottesville, Virginia, summit. The summit's participants, called by President George H. W. Bush, set out to create national academic standards. The gathering prefigured the Common Core in three important ways: its focus on international competition, its emphasis on the economic consequences of education, and its purported federal–state partnership.

As with the authors of *Nation at Risk*, summit participants at the Charlottesville Education Summit were dismayed at the United States' international academic rankings. The report and later legislation that emerged from the summit, "America 2000," noted poor American performance internationally, and called for title-cased "World Class Standards."[21] How these would be "World Class" was not specified, but Bush and other participants were emphatic that they would help push American students to perform at least as well as the United States' economic peers.

Second, the Charlottesville Education Summit highlighted potential economic benefits of education. Although Bush referenced *Brown* in his remarks, he, and the goals themselves only obliquely referred to inequality of education. Far more pressing to the attendees was the "serious efforts at education improvement . . . by most of our international competitors and trading partners" and that "our employers cannot hire enough qualified workers."[22] America 2000 did promise that "all children in American will start school ready to learn," but placed most of this burden on "parents, families, neighbors, and other caring adults" and community groups rather than federal or state spending, compensatory programs, or curriculum.[23] Economics had displaced civil rights as the primary rationale for equality.

Third, the federal government loomed large. Both Bush and the NGA took pains to note that "America 2000 is . . . not a federal program" and set out clear opportunities for governors. Still, it left a large opportunity for the federal government to be a "catalyst for change."[24] Unlike the Common Core, where states did take the lead, Bush promised that the federal government would write national standards for English, history, geography, math, and science. The federal government would also measure student progress in 4th, 8th, and 12th grade by expanding the National Assessment of Educational Progress (NAEP) to the state- and district-level.[25] Bush had both governors and the public behind him despite the ensuing controversies around the control of education. Eighty-four percent of Americans told the Gallup Poll they supported such standards.[26] Governors at the conference, including Arkansas Governor Bill Clinton (D), were unapologetic: "National goals will allow us to plan effectively, to set priorities, and to establish clear lines of authority."[27]

Despite the appearance of comity in Charlottesville, America 2000 faced significant political headwinds in Congress. Bush's allies introduced America 2000 in Congress in April 1991. "America 2000" proposed four "parallel tracks": publicly accountable schools; "new" high-tech model schools; adult education; and community support programs. Both Republican and Democratic critics seized the opportunity to pillory the four "tracks" of the reform, causing the bill to languish in Congress until October 1992. Congressional Democrats wanted to refocus the bill on disparities in educational spending and protecting teachers' unions from assessment. Ted Kennedy (D) told the *Boston Globe* that America 2000 was "robbing old education programs to pay for new ones"[28] Colorado Governor Roy Romer (D), a key player in the 1989 Summit, said, "When [Republicans] say, 'We don't need more resources, we need results,' that phrase is not helpful. "What they should say is we need results from the resources we've got, and we need some more resources in selective instances."[29] Republicans, for their part, saw strong accountability standards as necessary to make schools and districts change, but were leery that *academic* standards would slip into *fiscal* standards. From the right, conservative Republicans argued that America 2000 would result in intrusive federal mandates.

Of the four tracks, the final America 2000 bill only contained language supporting national academic standards, and, anathema to contemporary Republicans, "opportunity-to-learn" standards that followed the ruling of the recent Kentucky Supreme Court case, *Rose v. Council for Better Education* (1989). The NGA opposed Opportunity-to-Learn (OTL) as "federal interventions," and urged they be stricken from America 2000.[30] Had they been enacted as originally drafted, they would have specified what states and school districts would have to do to ensure that students *could* meet academic standards. Notably, this included teacher quality, school facilities, and financial resources—characteristics that had been explored by James Coleman 30 years earlier, and very much in line with ESEA's original input-based, civil rights focus. Proponents argued that it would be "unfair" to expect students to meet standards if they came from disadvantaged backgrounds or attended sub-par schools. Opponents argued that OTL standards would give the federal government the right to dictate state and local education spending. Further, opponents saw OTL as creating an excuse for low-performing schools.[31] By the fall of 1992, Democrats were using the bill as a political tool. "It's no secret that nobody's really enthusiastic about this bill. Why would we make concessions [to the President] to get it signed?" one aide told *Education Week*.[32] Secretary of Education Lamar Alexander publicly urged the President to veto the bill if it passed, but Senate Republicans saved him the embarrassment by filibustering the bill the month before the 1992 presidential elections. Instead, facing even some Democratic rebellion, the act was amended to read, "no action shall be taken under the provisions of this Act . . . which would reduce, modify, or undercut State and local responsibility for education."[33] In the end, OTL standards remained in the bill in name only.

America 2000 was a stunning failure on the part of America's first "education president." Despite gubernatorial support at Charlottesville, Congress passed *no* major education reform bills in Bush's tenure, and the collapse of America 2000 showed serious fissures in support for *any* of the four tracks. Bush could not count on the support of conservative Republicans (who did support him on school choice), and liberal Democrats were adamant that the federal government's role should be to increase school spending, especially in districts with at-risk or non-white children. It would be left to his successor to move the ball.

Bill Clinton, the "Come-Back Kid," prevailed in 1992, buoyed by unusually strong support from teachers' unions. That year, the National Education Association (NEA) had thrown its political support behind now-presidential candidate Clinton despite his enthusiasm for school choice and testing. The endorsement was a bit awkward, but there was no alternative for the union. *Education Week* noted that the NEA felt compelled to dissemble to justify its support of Clinton: NEA President Keith B. Geiger "deflected" a question about the candidate to tell the newspaper that Clinton "doesn't support a national testing system" despite clear evidence that he did.[34] In 2012, Barack Obama managed only 72 percent support at the NEA Representative meeting; Clinton topped out at 88 percent.[35] Secretary Alexander blasted the endorsement (and Clinton), saying, "The NEA only likes people it can control."[36] Clinton did favor boosting federal funding to schools and opposed some of Bush's more striking proposals for school vouchers, but—regardless of the unions' reservations—Clinton merely turned around and, in early 1994, re-branded America 2000 as "Goals 2000."

The return to America 2000 should not have been a surprise. Bill Clinton had been strongly supportive at the Charlottesville Education Summit, and he had already put his money where his mouth was as governor of Arkansas by strongly supporting (and signing) legislation for school choice and state standards.[37] Goals 2000 had some differences. First, it did not include private-school choice, a continuing Republican proposal (future president George W. Bush unsuccessfully proposed them as part of the NCLB Act in 2001; now-Senator Lamar Alexander did in 2013 as part of ESEA reauthorization).[38] That was a minor dispute in the subsequent deliberations, however. The second major difference was an expansive oversight role by the federal government. One outcome of the Charlottesville Education Summit was the National Education Goals Panel (NEGP), a board to design World Class Standards. It was not really a federal body, however—the controlling members were governors with some federal administration officials. Goals 2000 proposed to strengthen NEGP by including members of Congress, who had pointedly ignored NEGP because they were "incensed" to find out they were ex officio members.[39] More importantly, the president proposed that all states desiring federal funds (i.e., all of them) would be *required* to submit their standards to the Department of Education for approval. While states would retain the authority to design their own standards, the federal National Education Standards and Improvement Council (NESIC) would devise national standards to serve as blueprints, presumably ones that the Department of Education would use when evaluating state standards. Third, Clinton included a proposal for an OTL commission to recommend appropriate spending levels, at least in part to bolster support from the liberal wing of his party.

At this point in 1994, Goals 2000 hit some predictable political roadblocks—the very same ones that hit America 2000, and some of the same ones that confronted Common Core. Congressional Republicans, including Ohio Congressman John Boehner, decried the federal intrusion in the state-level education policy. Congressional Democrats, mindful of teachers' union support, found the emphasis on school accountability troubling because of the potential for non-bargainable teacher evaluation. They also worried that performance-based schools would undercut programs and funding for at-risk students.[40] Further, the bill was seen as an Administration priority—just like America 2000 had been—rather than Congressional priority. "The Administration was very interested in the Goals bill; Congress was very interested in ESEA," a staffer of the House's Education and Labor Committee said.[41]

Goals 2000 passed, and Clinton signed the bill on March 31, 1994. That was more than Bush could claim, but the bill was still far from the expansive, unifying vision of Clinton. There would be national voluntary standards, and there would be NESIC, but neither would have teeth. NESIC could still "approve" state standards, but individual states could *not* be denied money for failing to gain approval. One observer echoed earlier criticism of the "30 thousand separate and different Title I programs" of the original ESEA, saying, "What we have now looks more like 2,000 educational goals."[42] Still, standards-supporters could boast of major victories. When ESEA was reauthorized that year as the Improving America's Schools Act (IASA), NAEP was retooled to allow state-level comparisons (rather than national only), and states were strongly encouraged to participate. Further, the key civil rights funding in Title I was tied to the existence of state *academic* standards and state testing of students in at least three grades. Districts could spend money school-wide even if only 50 percent of the students were low-income, down from 75 percent. This was meant to expand the reach of educational accountability to middle and high schools, which typically have lower percentages of low-income students.[43]

The legislative victories notwithstanding, the curricular components proved toxic. Although all of the standards (technically "voluntary curriculum guidelines") provoked some controversy, none attracted as much as the national history standards. The 600-page document, produced by the National Center for History in the Schools at the University of California, Los Angeles, contained 31 standards for students and about 2,500 suggested classroom activities. The standards—or, more accurately, the teaching examples—touched a deep nerve. Joseph McCarthy made 19 appearances but Daniel Webster none, pioneers were motivated primarily by "greed and rapacity," and the United States was solely responsible for the Cold War.[44] Arthur M. Schlesigner, Jr., and Diane Ravitch, two Democratic critics, said the standards were an "embarrassment" and the examples were "politically biased, moralistic, and judgmental."[45] Lynne Cheney, the chairwoman of the National Endowment for the Humanities, who had enthusiastically signed off on a grant supporting the standards, blasted them as "politicized history" five days before they were to be released in October 1994.[46] If that was not sufficient, the U.S. Senate condemned the standards in a 99–1 vote in January 1995.[47] The standards *were* later issued after trimming out 400 pages of teaching examples and addressing some interpretive issues.

Shortly thereafter, historian Sean Wilentz said the standards' original authors "seem to have been mighty naive" about the political response.[48] The debacle left a lasting scar; the architect of the national history standards was still smarting 10 years later, reiterating that his and his colleagues' original work had been praised as "remarkable in its ambition [and] its clarity."[49] But it also dashed any hopes for any genuine "national" history standards. Common Core's politically aware supporters knew to stay away from history lest they be condemned to repeat it.

The NESIC was not so lucky. Republicans and some conservative Democrats had recoiled at NESIC during the legislative process, but they were outmaneuvered and outvoted. That world changed in November 1994 as younger, more aggressive Republicans took the majority in the House and the Senate for the first time since 1954. Many of the new Republican freshmen were ideologically hostile to this federal activity, and some sought the abolition of the U.S. Department of Education. Few of them hailed from districts where past civil rights issues were politically salient to their constituents—those were the domain of the now overwhelmingly African-American Southern Democratic caucus. The new Republican Congress failed to terminate the Department of Education, but they did succeed in killing NESIC—a result that "crippled the government's ability to impose some measure of quality control" on state and local reform efforts.[50] States would be the final authority on their standards—preserving the hodgepodge of content and expectations that had prevailed before the 1989 Charlottesville Education Summit. A widespread perception among conservatives was that NESIC was an unelected "national school board." Bush's Secretary of Education, Lamar Alexander, had panned the Democrats' version of Bush's America 2000 bill as "the beginnings of a national school board" in 1992, and Alabama Governor Fob James' office echoed this phrase as it rejected Goals 2000.[51] James' office claimed that the federal government would be "controlling what is taught in the classroom. . . . a 'politically correct' agenda mandated by the federal government."[52] The House voted to repeal NESIC in May 1995, just over a year since its creation. The Senate added a rider to an appropriations bill, which the president signed. The controversy over the panel in 1994, however, had forestalled any nominations to the panel, so it never actually operated. NESIC *had* been damaging nonetheless. A strong supporter of educational standards, Gov. Christine Todd Whitman (R-NJ), argued that "perceptions" about NESIC "have . . . begun to undermine the important progress being made by the states in academic standards-based reform efforts."[53] Perceptions, the stuff of politics, had brought down NESIC.

But the standards had also lost much of their political framing. Were they to boost equity? Or the economy? Certainly some continued to make those arguments—Clinton, Ravitch, Finn, Alexander, and others—but the standards sank under the weight of cultural and federalist critiques. Common, national academic standards had bipartisan support at the beginning of the decade, but that goodwill was severely strained by the debacle of the history standards. Indeed, they came at an unusual time in American politics, in the twilight of white Southern Democrats' long hold on that region's politics. Governors Bill Clinton (D-AR), James B. Hunt (D-NC), and Richard Riley (D-SC) were strongly supportive of national standards. They were all pragmatic Democrats who could scarcely advocate local control given their region's experience of local discrimination. They were also keenly aware that their region had long been far behind the more prosperous north, and Southern governors since the 1920s had been amenable to building Southern business interests.[54] Goals 2000 united these desires in a way for Southern Democrats that they did not for Republicans. Southern Democratic governors *had* to be pro-civil rights, but they could also talk business in a way that northern Democrats typically would not. They could thus appeal both to groups who saw the federal government as an equalizer of past (or present) civil rights ills *and* to those who saw academic standards as an economic linchpin.

This world passed away in November 1994 as southern Democratic governors lost easy access to a Democratic Congress. Disputes could no longer be resolved "in the family." Republican majorities in the House and Senate were in no mood for compromise with Democrats or Bill Clinton. That is not to say the goal of Mississippi-to-Massachusetts standards disappeared. Pragmatic, pro-standards governors remained invested—Tommy Thompson (R-WI), John Engler (R-MI), Roy Romer (D-CO), Evan Bayh (D-IN), and others—all of these served on the NEGP over its lifetime, but it would take a new political push at the federal level to restart the "national" option.

Goals 2000 and IASA showed that national standards *were* possible given a careful political approach, and, despite their shortcomings, these pieces of legislation also heralded a revolution in the federal approach to education. One scholar of American education politics noted that "the new federal concern about *every* child was remarkable given the historic focus on only *disadvantaged* children. . . . The key element of the new federal focus on outputs . . . was the national standards" that would be applied to all children.[55] Yet, the debacle over the history standards and strong pushback from conservatives tempered the outlook for broad-based national standards. If supporters could link the benefits of national standards to *all children,* there might be a way through.

NEW POLITICAL WILL: ASSESSMENT

Supporters found that way in the nexus of standards, assessment, and accountability. The Common Core is neither curriculum nor assessment, and standards alone would be unlikely to motivate substantial change in education. In the perfect world, Core supporters argued, the standards would be embraced *with* assessment, because what is measured is what is taught. But—to their great political benefit—Core supporters did not have to spend political capital justifying academic assessment. That battle had already been fought and won. Instead, they were able to *gain* political support for new exams because of widespread loathing for NCLB-inspired exams. Although the Common Core itself did *not* specify exams, they were rolled out at the same time as new, multi-state tests were. Proponents could argue, at least initially, that these new tests were genuinely better than NCLB-inspired state assessments.

Assessment also provided the political glue that held the unique left-right education coalition together. On the right, Main Street Republicans wanted "results" from education and not simply social services. Many Democrats, and especially teachers' unions, claimed that schools needed more money to adequately educate children. Republicans resisted, pointing to 30 years of increased federal and state spending with few concrete academic results. In their view, accountability through assessment showed that schools were lacking. They offered Democrats a compromise—they would agree to more money if Democrats would agree to more assessment of accountability purposes. By the late 1990s, researchers using assessment data uncovered systematic differences in performance and instruction in schools, depending on the race, ethnicity, and income-level of the student. This motivated civil rights groups to pressure Democrats to embrace assessment.

For supporters, the story of assessment is central to the appeal of Common Core, because the combination fulfilled the only at-scale, school-focused element of the 1989 Charlottesville Education Summit: standards that can boost performance. Of the four "tracks" outlined at the summit, only school accountability encompassed *both* standards and assessment, and quite thorough assessment at that. It called for a national testing system; career-ready tests to help potential employers; public reporting of test results by school, districts, and states; and school choice for parents if their local school had poor test results.[56] Although elements of all of these made their way into legislation in the 1990s, the "national" emphasis was only reached through the combination of Common Core and the multi-state testing consortia. (Those assessment consortia quickly lost their appeal for states, undercutting their "national" purposes.)

The road was not very smooth, however. Standards proponents did gain important tools in the 1994 reauthorization of ESEA, Goals 2000 nearly went off the rails in the spring of 1994. The strong bipartisan gubernatorial support of assessment at Charlottesville was driven by the assumption that "World Class Standards" would generate economic growth in the states. Governors' popularity is strongly linked to the local economy, and this certainly was the view of governors around that time.[57] *Governors* thought they had a vested interest in boosting education. Members of Congress, however, have a different set of priorities, and they were wary of Goals 2000.

When Congress enacted Goals 2000 in 1994, they had been written to require standards but prohibit federally funded assessment in an attempt to buy off local-level and teachers' union opposition. This allowed the bill to pass, but tremendously weakened its usefulness. After Republicans took Congress in the fall, the NGA urged Congress to retool the bill. Prominently, the NGA asked that Congress allow Goals 2000 funding to support assessment so that states could "correct the flaws in the existing system and . . . change incentives to improve student academic achievement."[58] Without the assessments, there was no way to hold students or schools accountable for standards.

The political window closed in 1995 as national Republicans saw federal involvement as untoward intrusion and Democrats retreated to defend the race- and need-based categorical grants that aided their constituents. Yet this (temporary) failure in the mid-1990s created an opportunity for a new political alliance by the end of the decade, an alliance based not on standards but on assessment.

In this time period the GOP took a remarkable about-face. In 1995, House Republicans passed bills to terminate the Department of Education and turn much of the federal educational apparatus into block grants for the states. They sought to repeal Goals 2000 outright. Lamar Alexander, William Bennett, and Daniel Coats (R-IN) suggested that IASA had actually "reversed a decade of progress toward a coherent, bipartisan education-reform strategy."[59] Instead, they wrote, "it is time for the federal government virtually to withdraw from elementary and secondary education."[60] This argument held the upper hand in the 104th Congress. But it also played very badly with the electorate. Democrat Bill Clinton ran for re-election in 1996 largely courtesy of the Republican majorities in Congress. Clinton frequently highlighted Republican cuts to federal programs in their attempt to produce a balanced federal budget, and their cuts to education programs in particular. His stance on education commanded voters' affections, too—former New York Governor Mario Cuomo told *ABC News*, "[Clinton] will do for education what John Kennedy did for the space program."[61]

For their part, some ranking Republicans recognized that their caustic approach had been damaging to Dole's election chances, and made their own party's prospects in Congress more difficult even as they continued to hold majorities. "It was a tremendous mistake," recalled Representative Bill Gooding (R-PA).[62] In the next two sessions of Congress, Republicans outbid themselves on education. In 1997, Republicans easily approved a $7 billion hike in education funding, and kept intact virtually all of Clinton's education programs.[63] Although the Republicans' shift from budget cutting to budget boosting was a remarkable shift in itself, of greater import was the marked acceptance of a federal role in local education. No longer did even the Heritage Foundation publicly dispute that *some* federal presence was needed. Two education scholars explain the shift this way: "In a very real sense, this is an example of policies making politics; as elites came to accept established federal funding of education (through the ESEA of 1965) as a reality, the question was not whether, but what sorts of school structures and policies those funds should support."[64]

Although Republicans did embrace additional federal spending on education, they did not embrace liberal Democrats' input-focus education policy wholesale. Instead, they would increase spending, but only on the condition of increased accountability and increased choice. They continued to strongly oppose national standards, or even Department of Education-vetted standards, but they did seek to require annual reporting on state standards.[65] Sweetening the deal for conservatives, Republicans continued to push for public support of private schools as well through voucher and income tax breaks.

In their favor, President Clinton was talking about education in much the same way. In his 2000 State of the Union Address, he called for states to identify their "worst-performing schools" and called them to "shut them down."[66] He was a staunch proponent of public school choice in the form of charter schools and open enrollment, and was, of course, in support of meaningful state standards. That he also sought further increases in federal support for teachers and school-building renovation, identifiably Democratic proposals, was small consolation for liberal Democrats.

This state of affairs led to soul-searching on the left. Many liberal Democrats and interest groups for low-income and non-white Americans had long resisted school accountability because they thought it would turn blame for poor performance back on the schools, teachers, and students and away from bolstering academic and other school resources that had been at the core of ESEA since its original passage in 1965. These groups and their judicial allies believed that if given sufficient resources, students could rise to the challenge and learn just as well as their white peers. Yet, by the late 1990s, accumulating evidence from NAEP and now state exams strained credulity. Massive amounts of school spending did *not* seem to correlate with substantive changes in achievement, and least of all the "test-score gap." This gap, more than any other single piece of political rhetoric, overcame much liberal opposition to standards and academic accountability.[67]

As a political point, the test-score gap had its genesis in the 1960s. By this time, the courts, civil rights groups, and education groups all knew anecdotally that black students performed worse academically than their white peers, but the students' performance was so conflated with racial segregation that it was widely believed that segregation itself caused the gap—this was the logic behind the *Brown* court's remedy for the "hearts and minds" of African-American school children.[68] If this was indeed the case, the solution was to desegregate and to ensure that school resources were equally available for all students. To this end, Congress appropriated funds in 1964 for a national study of American schooling to understand how pervasive the resource gaps identified in *Brown v. Board of Education* were.

The result, the 1966 study *Equality of Educational Opportunity*, strongly confirmed two of these beliefs. First, African-American and Latino children did perform significantly worse than their other peers on academic tests administered by James S. Coleman and his research colleagues—one full standard deviation lower. Second, American schools did have exceedingly wide variation in school resources, and some of that variation aligned with racial segregation. The Coleman Report also found some support that black students did better in classrooms with high-achieving white students, suggesting that racial integration would benefit at least African-American students. These suggested to liberals that an active federal role could repair the educational damage done by segregation and financial inequality—partly. To much consternation, the Coleman Report also found that "variation in the facilities and curriculum of the school account for relatively little variation in pupil achievement."[69] It seemed that neither funding nor curriculum made a difference.

This finding garnered substantial controversy, not least because many of the lowest performing students attended the least-funded schools, making it difficult to separate out the effects of school resources. Further, disparities between school districts were so stark in many states that many found it hard to believe that school resources had little bearing on the work of schools.[70] State courts were not particularly persuaded by the finding, and continued to scrutinize spending as a component of educational equity.

Through the 1970s and 1980s, plaintiffs asked various state courts whether unequal spending was a state-level constitutional issue, in states as diverse as Arizona, California, New Jersey, West Virginia, and Wyoming.[71] California's case, *Serrano v. Priest* (1971), concluded that the *California* constitution effectively required educational spending to be equal and divorced from disparities in district wealth. In 1976, the court found that the legislature still had not fulfilled equity, and ordered more changes.[72] Courts in New Jersey's *Abbott v. Burke* cases have likewise spent 40 years enforcing additional spending in some districts as a way to improve educational provision.

Educational spending is a convenient way to measure education, but, by the late 1980s, even liberal proponents of increasing spending were finding that such an input measure did not always convince courts—and sometimes did not generate material academic results either. Instead of seeking equity, the Kentucky interest group Council for Better Education argued in 1989 that spending should be sufficient for a student to meet the state's educational standards. Under this interpretation, what a student needs is highly variable, and it is highly dependent on *state* standards. In *Rose v. Council for Basic Education* (1989), the Kentucky court held that Kentucky schools needed enough funding so that students' school performance would allow them to "compete favorably with their counterparts in surrounding states, in academics or in the job market" and to "understand the issues that affect his or her community, state, and nation" among other things.[73] A similar series of cases in Ohio likewise turned on the definition of state standards (*DeRolph v. Ohio*, 1997, 2000, 2001, 2002). Other states have had similar suits filed, including Colorado, Illinois, Texas, and New York. Using the adequacy standard, state courts have ordered expanded kindergarten programs, building construction, and job training programs.[74] In many cases, courts have in fact ordered *more* spending even in high-spending districts to compensate for low student achievement there. The irony is that, even as teachers' unions and their allies fought assessment in the name of professionalism, it was only assessment that allowed courts to find that schools (and students) were not meeting state standards.

Further, a widespread perception that urban, heavily non-white schools were crime-ridden and academic failures had led Latinos and African Americans to become increasingly open to school choice and—anathema to teachers' unions—school vouchers. By the late 1980s, there was strong evidence that schools were systematically shortchanging these students by "dumbing down" curriculum or labeling them as "learning disabled" to avoid teaching them with the same academic rigor.[75] Democrats had little political choice, as one policy maker told an interviewer: "the teachers' unions were saying 'everything is fine, just give us more money,' but increasing numbers of African Americans and Latinos were saying 'we want out of these schools.'"[76] Strong, uniform academic standards would force these schools to bolster *all* students' achievement, and especially those "left behind." The use of standards seemed validated as Latino and African-American students' test scores rose meaningfully in the 1990s as states adopted tougher state standards.[77] And those students were part of an increasingly important Democratic constituency.

Now, liberal Democrats had a *partisan* reason to support academic assessment and to make common cause with moderate Republicans who had been supportive of both America 2000 and Goals 2000. Conservatives continued to be suspicious of federal overreach, but the continued test-score gap weakened liberal opposition to a key Republican demand for more accountability.

NCLB

When the ESEA came up for reauthorization in 1999, a coalition of moderates seemed to be poised to finish the work of IASA. Where IASA had made motions toward increased standards and accountability, last-minute dealings took virtually all of the teeth out of it. Goals 2000 likewise had been largely reduced to yet another pot of federal money with few restrictions. But both moderate Republicans and Democrats could agree on limited school choice, state standards, some public accountability measures, and a new focus on "every child" rather than only needy children. The two major plans, the Republicans' "Academic Achievement for All" (or "Straight A's") and the Democrats' "Public Education Reinvestment, Reinvention, and Responsibility Act" (or the "Three R's"), were a stone's throw apart. The

Democrats wanted substantially more funding and direct government oversight of state academic achievement; but, like the Republicans, the Three R's called for school choice and an end to many categorical grants.

Election 2000 did not settle the question. Republican George W. Bush became president, but Republicans had only 50 seats in the U.S. Senate. Thus, when Congress returned to ESEA in January 2001, neither the Republicans nor the Democrats had a strong hand. The Democrats had lost the presidency but gained strength in the Senate; Republicans had gained the presidency but could not push too hard lest Bush's narrow win be used as a political cudgel against them.[78] The narrow balance of power left both conservatives and liberals at the edges of discussion. Conservatives were pressured into accepting federal scrutiny of states and a sizable increase in federal school spending ($22 billion in 2002, $4.6 billion more than in 2001). Liberal Democrat Ted Kennedy (D-MA), the "dean" of ESEA, felt pressure both from moderates in his party and from civil rights groups to accept some elements that would have been anathema in earlier reauthorizations. For Kennedy, that was accountability.

Bush, for his part, was well aware of his tenuous position, and he determined to give Congress a relatively free hand in designing ESEA. Instead of sending a specific reauthorization bill to Congress, he presented a blueprint in January 2001.[79] The notable difference from earlier GOP proposals was a strong emphasis on *federal* accountability, albeit through state standards. Under the 1994 IASA, states were required to have standards and to measure progress, although with the death of NESIC, that was the highest bar they had to meet. Under NCLB, states had to have standards, but they had to show that *all students were making progress* toward meeting them through annual testing in late elementary and middle school in return for Title I funding. The federal government would not be in the business of setting or measuring students' performance, but it would breathe down the neck of states if students did not meet the states' public expectations of them.

Combined with the capitulation of Democrats on public accountability in the late 1990s, this change paved the way for meaningful state standards. Schools *had* to perform up to standard, every year, or very public repercussions would follow. Civil rights groups, too, had come around, as NCLB forbade schools from pulling out low-performing students on test day or shunting them off into remedial classes. The law required *all* students (meaning 95 percent of every demographic subgroup) to meet standards.

Going forward, the standards schools had to meet would carry consequences.

CLEARING THE FIELD FOR COMMON CORE

As NCLB came up for re-authorization in 2007, neither Republicans nor Democrats were eager to extend the law's damaged brand. Bush's political stock had fallen sharply since 2001, buffeted by the federal response to Hurricane Katrina and lingering military troubles in the Middle East, and Democrats had taken control of both houses of Congress. Conservative Republicans who had held their tongue in 2001 regained their voice; and Democrats castigated the president for failing to live up to his promises on spending. "I bought a horse from that man once," Rep. George Miller (D-CA) told Rep. John Boehner (R-OH), when Boehner assured him in January 2007 that Bush would live up to funding promises. "I'm not going to buy another horse from him," he said.[80]

But the collapse of the NCLB coalition belied the substantial reorientation of both Republicans and Democrats toward federal—and national—activity. One scholar of NCLB noted that legislators tasked NCLB with the impossible: It was to build tough, no-excuses accountability *and* provide extensive flexibility to the states.[81] Reformist, pro-standards critics of IASA thought the law had allowed states to circumvent the spirit of the law by setting murky or aspirational standards with little incentive to monitor progress. They further noted that most states were far from compliance even with those soft goals. In 2002, the Government Accounting Office found that 33 states were not in compliance with Title I requirements of IASA, eight years after passage.[82] Twenty-nine of those had made agreements with the Department of Education to lengthen the timeline even further. Four states, Alabama, Idaho, Montana, and West Virginia, were still working with the Department of Education to come to such an agreement.[83] But critics found that even the work of "compliant" states was severely wanting. The Thomas B. Fordham Foundation assessed all existing state standards in 1998. They found that standards were vague, content-light, and focused heavily on the delivery method rather than educational goals. One of its authors wrote, "Deliberately vague standards are in essence a façade behind which public officials can create tests so ideologically mischievous that they lead to problematic local curricula or so academically undemanding that they are as ineffective as the older and discredited competency tests were."[84] The standards appeared meaningless.

There is no question that NCLB forced states to tighten up their standards. Some 37 states did either revise or replace their standards between 2000 and 2006, and the standards had become far more specific. Although reformers on both sides of the political center found this refreshing, Fordham was not convinced that many of the standards were better. They faulted states for valuing committee consensus over coherent vision; a lack of subject-matter experts ("We're not talking about professors of 'math education.' We're talking about real mathematicians."[85]); too little borrowing from other states; and too much attention to process instead of content.[86] For its part, American Federation of Teacher (AFT) noted that elementary and middle-school standards had become much stronger since the 1990s—especially in mathematics—but those that were not were most often clustered (meaning that the same standards applied to a group of grades, like 9–12), simply repeated, or vague.[87] The teachers' union argued that this made it difficult for a teacher to know how to prepare a student in any given school year.

NCLB was meant to remedy this flaw primarily through test-based assessment. It would be strikingly difficult to design a standardized test without concrete standards to assess. The tests would make it crystal clear if states, districts, or school were shortchanging students. Although NCLB only required states to report how many students fell into four categories (below basic, basic, proficient, and advanced), it assumed that state departments of education would have sufficient expertise to set cut scores. This component of the law reflected the concerns of both Republicans who wanted accountability for federal monies, and some Democratic groups who wanted to ensure that Title I maintained a focus on low-income and non-white students.

This provision, key to a school's measure of Adequate Yearly Progress (AYP), proved extremely inviting to many state policy makers. If the cut scores were set low, more students would meet the "proficient" level and thereby enable schools and districts to avoid sanctions. (Recall that the law required 100-percent proficiency by 2014–2015.) In 2009, the Department of Education compared states' cut scores to those in NAEP, the national exam. The results were stunning. Figure 2.1 compares each state's score for "proficiency" in fourth-grade reading and math, expressed in the same units as the NAEP score. The dotted line is the NAEP-proficient level. States above the line required a higher score to meet proficiency than the national exam. Eighth-grade numbers showed a similar pattern: The standard NAEP score for eighth-grade mathematics proficiency was 299. By comparison, Massachusetts' proficiency cut score was 300, Wisconsin's was 262, but Tennessee's was 229—which would give a child a "basic" rating on the NAEP, the lowest category.[88] The wide disparities in test results created recalled the disjointed "Massachusetts-versus-Mississippi" standards of the late 1980s.

Other states used NCLB's flexibility to protect schools and districts from being labeled as "in need of improvement." One study faulted states for deliberately hijacking NCLB's AYP measure to hide districts' academic performance by using large sub-group sizes, wide confidence intervals, and

Figure 2.1 State Score for "Proficiency" Measured as an NAEP Score, Fourth-Grade Tests, 2011 (U.S. Department of Education)

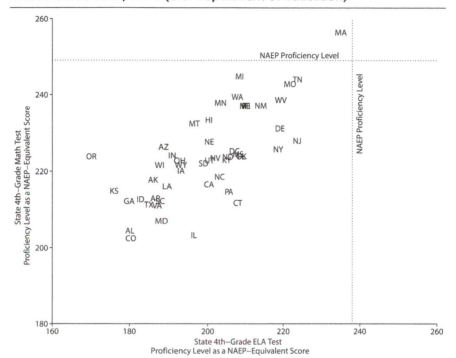

subdividing test results to minimize the number of students' scores used to calculate the measure. (NCLB allowed states to exclude the scores of students from demographic subgroups if their numbers were so small as to compromise confidentiality or introduce substantively meaningless variation to the results—so, if those sizes were large, more student scores could be excluded.) "With the approval of the U.S. Department of Education, many states are reporting educational results under NCLB that defy reality and common sense," according to the study's author.[89] This interpretation gained credence as states continued to implore Bush's Secretary of Education, Margaret Spellings, to allow them to avoid consequences for failing to meet targets. Although Spellings acquiesced to some waiver requests by 2008, critics argued that the granted waivers were "pretty political."[90] Spellings' Department of Education noted that many of the other states seeking waivers seemed to be using "methods of convenience" to "respond to complaints" about performance rather than improving academic performance.[91]

By 2008, this pattern of obfuscation had rendered many of the "soft" accountability measures in NCLB to be meaningless. Not only were standards between states different and sometimes quite low, but districts could continue to ignore "inconvenient" demographic subgroups—leaving children behind. It was clear to both Republicans and Democrats that the key theory of action behind NCLB had failed. Democrats argued, with Sen. Edward Kennedy (D-MA), that NCLB "fail[ed] to reward incremental progress made by schools struggling to catch up" and that it "fail[ed] to supply the essential resources that schools desperately need to improve their performance."[92] But others were not so tempered. Rep. Carol Shea-Porter (D-NH) called the law a right-wing plot to "undermine the confidence in our public schools" and "cripple the teachers."[93] Conservative Republicans, for their part, skewered the accountability measures in the law, not so much for the accountability, but in the apparent federal overreach. Rep. Peter Hoeskstra (R-MI) argued that testing was driving curriculum through its heavy emphasis on mathematics and reading. As a result, schools had become "beggars to Washington."[94] Rep. Bob Schaffer (R-CO) voted against NCLB in 2001 and continued to be a leading critic of the bill—chiefly because it tied states into a uniform accountability scheme:

> You shouldn't get freedom only if you fail. You shouldn't get freedom only if your school's dangerous. You shouldn't get freedom only if your child's not learning. You should have freedom in America by virtue of being an American. . . . If we allow states the freedom to create a competitive education and academic marketplace, we will see teachers rising to the occasion when they are treated like real professionals.[95]

Yet, neither of these critiques was unique to NCLB. Increasing federal school funding is a perennial Democratic hobbyhorse, and torpedoing federal intervention in education was the impetus for the 1995 Republican education agenda. By and large, NCLB's contribution to Common Core was not in resurrecting these criticisms. Instead, NCLB settled the central question motivating the 1989 Charlottesville Education Summit: Shall states have meaningful standards? On the left, even the NEA agreed in principle to state standards. In 2011, the NEA passed a resolution in support of measuring teachers and students against state standards (albeit only if they were "developmentally appropriate, scientifically valid, and reliable").[96] Civil rights groups have become strong supporters of standards despite their initial hesitation in the late 1990s. The Mexican American Legal Defense and Educational Fund (MALDEF) highlighted "high academic standards and expectations for all students" as the primary benefit of NCLB in 2007.[97] Others, including La Raza and the NAACP, also gave this claim in support.[98] Sen. Edward Kennedy (D-MA) praised NCLB in 2008 because "all schools now measure performance based not on the achievement of their average and above-average students but on their progress in helping below-average students reach high standards as well."[99] The left had bought NCLB.

Opponents of federal intervention notwithstanding, many Republicans continued to support the core of NCLB if not the specifics. George W. Bush, perhaps unsurprisingly, continued to herald the law's benefits in 2012, calling it one of "the really positive things our Administration accomplished. . . . We in the federal government ought to demand accountability, which seems to me a very conservative principle."[100] Other Republicans continued to strongly support at least *state* standards. Minnesota Governor Tim Pawlenty (R) supported strong math and science standards as well as linking those standards to performance in 2006; Arkansas Governor Mike Huckabee (R-AR) touted stronger high school curriculum in 2008; and Gov. Mitt Romney (R-MA) while running for president boasted about Massachusetts' testing results: "I don't believe you had the finest record of any governor in America on education," he told Huckabee at a 2008 presidential debate, "The kids in our state scored number one."[101] Even Schaffer, when running for the Colorado State Board of Education in 2006, noted that "fixing NCLB cannot degenerate into a simple flight from accountability."[102]

Although the specific bipartisan coalition that forged NCLB in 2001 had collapsed, the logic behind standards and accountability continued to tie the parties together. This was nowhere more clear than the "test" reauthorization bills both parties introduced in the 113th Congress. Sen. Tom Harkin (D-IA) introduced a bill in 2013 that would have maintained the testing regime from NCLB, although states could use portfolios or performance tasks instead of multiple-choice or other content-based exams. States would have to submit their accountability plans to the federal government for approval, and adopt standards to prepare students for college or career. The Democratic bill would have continued to require robust reporting of results for subgroups, and would require teacher evaluation based, in part, on student achievement.[103] Although Sen. Lamar Alexander (R-TN) introduced a competing bill that scrapped most of the "prescriptive" federal involvement, states would still have to test in third through eighth grade and once before graduation. (Unlike the Democratic versions, states could use any standards they see fit, whatever the Department of Education thought.)[104]

CONCLUSION

In 2015, the ESEA celebrated its 50th anniversary. Although the broad outline of federal involvement in local education remains the same—federal financial support to schools with poor and at-risk children—both the federal government's theory of action and its mode of implementation have changed substantially.

In the spirit of Lyndon Johnson's Great Society, the architects of ESEA tried to rectify widespread disparities in educational resources between school children in the United States. These included classroom materials and teacher quality, and the differences appeared to be linked to poverty and race. The 1966 Coleman Report showed wide achievement gaps, but policy makers chose to remedy resource gaps instead. Between 1965 and 1994, ESEA was essentially a giant categorical grant program that doled out federal dollars to schools that were compliant with federal rules for spending the money. There were few strings attached beyond demonstrating that a school indeed had children that met certain economic, racial, or ethnic criteria. ESEA was a revenue-enhancing program.

By the 1980s, the argument over the role of spending, standards, and accountability reopened. It appeared that the nagging academic performance gaps were not closing, despite 30 years of federal spending. Federal efforts did not seem to be boosting educational equity in outcomes. Many "new" Democrats, and especially Southern Democratic governors, joined cause with moderate Republicans who wanted to see effective education. Governors saw boosting education as a tool to enhance their states' economies (and their re-election efforts) after 15 years of sluggish economic growth. Simply supplementing resources did not seem to be enough. When ESEA came up for reauthorization in 1994, this political coalition fundamentally transformed federal education legislation. Although IASA became a toothless dragon in the legislative process, its emphasis on *academic* standards and *academic* accountability signaled the end of "free" federal money. Schools would have to show results.

That transformation generated angry responses both from liberal and conservative quarters. Liberals, and especially teachers' unions, thought that state or national standards undercut their position as "professional educators." Conservatives were apoplectic over the "national school board"-feel of IASA and its attendant Goals 2000 legislation. State bureaucracies soldiered on, creating widely disparate standards. Though some were honorable attempts, others were clearly meant to obscure poor performance or protect political clients.

But the performance mantra of the 1990s, repeated endlessly by the nation's governors, captured prominent federal politicians by the end of the decade. In 2001, moderate Republicans came to see education as a must-win political issue, and Latino and African-American voters felt that liberal Democrats had consigned them low academic success. Both sides were talking about academic success now; neither side wanted to be held accountable for the "soft bigotry of low expectations."

But the NCLB Act did not satisfy expectations. Its authors—John Boehner, Ted Kennedy, others—tried to combine stiff accountability with great local flexibility. The ensuing decade showed that states would take the flexibility and challenge the federal government to act. Massachusetts *continued* to have vastly higher standards than Mississippi, whatever the state test results said. The federal act, meant to provide the last and the least of American citizens with genuine academic (and therefore economic) opportunity, still failed.

Into this came the Common Core. The states wanted to avoid yet more inflexible federal accountability, but their state superintendents, governors, and many legislators believed that standards were now sine qua non of education policy. Unions endorsed them (if grudgingly), and even conservative legislators were loath to go on record criticizing the idea. The Common Core fit the bill.

THREE

The Conservative Imagination: States, Evidence, and Partisanship

On September 20, 2013, Louisiana State Representative J. Cameron Henry Jr. (R-82) notified Gov. Bobby Jindal that he would file legislation to pull the state out of the Common Core. The standards that were once "voluntary" had "now become a tool of federal coercion."[1] Although Rep. Henry's legislation (introduced in February 2014) was voted down in April, Gov. Jindal borrowed his cause and compared the Common Core to "centralized planning . . . in Russia" on April 23 in *USA Today*. He wrote:

> It's true that Common Core never started out as a curriculum. It's even true that it still is not a curriculum. But just as certainly, if the feds dictate the standards of measure, the local curricula will have no choice but to follow. To succeed on Common Core tests, states will have to adopt curricula that teach to the tests.[2]

In August, Gov. Jindal filled out the argument in a lawsuit against the U.S. Department of Education, in which he claimed that Common Core had become a "federally-commissioned" project used by the Obama administration to "nationalize education policy."[3] The oddity was that Jindal had previously been a vocal supporter of the Common Core Standards. In 2014, *after* Louisiana Governor Jindal's change of heart, the U.S. Chamber of Commerce Foundation ran ads touting his support of the standards by quoting him: "Adopting the Common Core State Standards . . . will raise expectations for every child."[4]

Yet Jindal was not the only Republican governor to have second thoughts; others such as Nikki Haley (R-SC), Mary Fallin (R-OK), Chris Christie (R-NJ), and Mike Pence (R-IN) also wavered.[5]

Like Jindal, Haley railed against federal overreach. She never supported the standards, and argued that she supported local control instead: "Whether [it's] education, healthcare, or any aspect of government, we will fight to keep all standards state based, not federal."[6] To a local Republican women's club, she said, "We don't ever want to educate South Carolina children like they educate California children."[7] She eagerly signed a bill forbidding the implementation of the standards on May 30, 2014. The bill also included protections against lapsing back into the Common Core: new South Carolina standards could not be enacted without a joint resolution of the state legislature—lest the State Board of Education simply re-title the standards.

Mary Fallin was more circumspect and recognized that the Common Core "brand" had been damaged by partisanship, whatever the standards' benefits were. She was the chairwoman of the National Governors Association (NGA) in 2014—the same organization that spearheaded the Common Core—and continued to praise high, rigorous standards. Still, she signed a bill in June 2014 revoking Oklahoma's participation in the Common Core because she said she was "listening" to parents and teachers in Oklahoma. She couched her decision in a conflict between the federal government and the state, but gave a local political reason: "The words 'Common Core' in Oklahoma are now so divisive that they have become a distraction that interferes with our mission of providing the best education possible for our children. . . . I am committed, now more than ever, to ensuring these standards are rigorous."[8] Oklahoma replaced the Core with its pre-Common Core Standards.

Despite her local reasoning, her case provided "proof" for conservatives like Jindal and Haley that the standards were "forced" on the states. After Oklahoma dropped the standards, the U.S. Department of Education revoked the state's waiver from the requirements of No Child Left Behind (NCLB)— a move widely interpreted as punishment from the federal government.[9] The U.S. Department of Education relented in November 2014, but only after the Oklahoma State Regents for Higher Education certified that the state's standards, the ones that the state had before Common Core, were "college- and career-ready."[10]

Other Republicans who had been committed to the Common Core backtracked after legislators and constituents rebelled against the standards. Anti-Core groups offered lines of attack to legislators, but "lack of evidence" for the standards was offered at dozens of hearings. The resulting political pressure prompted at least two governors to reconsider their support.

New Jersey's Christie ordered a commission to "study" the standards in July 2014, but he did little else to challenge their adoption or implementation. Indeed, he appointed a strong Common Core supporter to the state's Education Department in December 2014. Christie's appointee told a state senate panel, "The support for Common Core is very broad in New Jersey."[11] Christie was a likely Republican presidential contender for 2016 at this point, and his motions likely had more to do with holding some political support from further-right elements of the Republican Party than with his own opposition to the standards.

Mike Pence was less committed to the Common Core, but he was aware that Indiana had played an important role in designing the standards. When the state legislature began to hold hearings on the standards, he publicly proclaimed he was opposed and, in March 2014, he signed the first bill in the country to pull the plug on the Common Core, an act that he trumpeted frequently.[12] New Indiana standards would be "uncommonly high. They will be written by Hoosiers, for Hoosiers and will be among the best in the nation," he said.[13] He spoke the language of local control, but suggested that his priority was evidence-based standards whatever the source. "Where we get those standards, where we derive them from, to me is of less significance than are we actually serving the best interests of our kids," he told reporters.[14] The Democratic state superintendent, Gina Ritz, promised the standards would be different: "There will be a change . . . we're not looking at carte blanche adoption of every single Common Core standard."[15] To the great disappointment of opponents, the new Indiana standards *were* different by omission. In many places, the new standards were verbatim copies of the Common Core.[16]

As the experience of these governors shows, the conservative fight over the Common Core is much the same as a rift between more business-minded, fiscal conservatives and small-government, social conservatives—"tea party" conservatives. This is exactly the same rift that challenged the national standards in 1994, and state standards throughout the 1990s. Many of the original proponents of the "World Class Standards" at the 1989 Charlottesville Education Summit were "Main Street" conservatives whose primary interest in government was to hold the line on taxes and build a positive political environment for state businesses. Republican governors who continued to support the Common Core through its turbulence, especially Gov. John Kasich (R-OH), were cut from the same cloth. Tea party conservatives, by contrast, had deep suspicion about the motivations of government— and especially if that government was run by a starkly polarizing president.

The conservative opposition to the Common Core—ranging from elected officials like Bobby Jindal to media personalities like Glenn Beck—sprang from three sources, although all of them shared a distrust of government expertise. Conservatives critiqued the Common Core because of their ties with the federal government, their association with a highly partisan Democratic presidential administration, and supporters' claims of expertise and evidence. None of these were unique to conservatives (particularly the last), but they were the most prominent critics.

FEDERAL POWER OR LOCAL CONTROL?

The first conservative critique is a simple, long-running distrust of federal intervention in state or local matters, education or otherwise. Federal animosity toward the states in education has been a 50-year driver of the Elementary and Secondary Education Act (ESEA). Here, conservatives are merely returning the favor. This is Jindal's official reason for opposing the Common Core.

The most obvious expression of this critique comes from tea party groups that came to prominence in the late winter of 2009. Although the "tea party" is a nebulous network with no organizational leadership, affiliated groups typically share a veneration of the Constitution, animosity toward the contemporary federal government, and pronounced fiscal conservatism.[17] Early on, the movement's protests centered on the bank bailouts and the 2009 "stimulus bill," but the plethora of local groups grew to oppose other causes as well, typically when the federal government played a role. They took a leading role against the Affordable Care Act in 2010, and they helped propel Republicans to their House congressional majority in the fall of that year. But protracted struggles over that bill and the subsequent 2012 Supreme Court decision that left the Act standing sapped tea party groups of their fervor.

The Common Core reinvigorated them. Tea party organizers told *The Washington Post* that, unlike their efforts on ObamaCare, defeating the standards was "winnable."[18] The right-leaning *National Review* said the Core has "lent the movement new purpose and substance."[19] These groups have gained in prominence both by their support of Common Core "repeal" bills and testing opt-out bills.

They had notable success in pressuring state lawmakers to introduce bills to delay or repeal Common Core participation, although bills passed only in Indiana, Oklahoma, North Carolina, and South Carolina. Governors proved more amenable to pressure, and most governors made public statements of concern about the Common Core, whether Republican or Democratic. Six issued executive orders reiterating that the state had full control of standards and curriculum. In Arizona, for example, Gov. Jan Brewer (R) issued an order on September 20, 2013, stating that "no standards or curriculum [shall] be imposed on Arizona by the federal government," and that "the power to make important education decisions . . . must occur at the local level." In an indication of the now-freighted name, the state's standards were no longer to be called "Common Core" in Arizona.[20] Governors in Iowa, Georgia, Iowa, Maine, Mississippi, and Oklahoma (all Republicans) issued similar orders in 2013 and 2014.

Outside the halls of government, tea party groups have successfully kept the Common Core in the public eye, and they continue to create significant headaches for Core supporters and the federal government. Core supporters have been quick to belittle opponents as "fringe groups" or bearers of "conservative extremism" speaking "nonsense." At one point, Arne Duncan argued that opponents of the Core were conspiracy theorists, saying, "It's not a black helicopter ploy."[21] Yet Duncan has become the number one public defender of the Core, and, in an event for newspaper editors, he compared questions about the Core to questions about Pres. John Kennedy's Bay of Pigs Invasion—perhaps unintentionally drawing a comparison with an uncomfortable event in need of greater transparency.[22] The potential threat to the Common Core also motivated national and state chambers of commerce to redouble lobbying efforts and field television advertisements in support of the Common Core—in 2014, four years after the standards were adopted.[23] Tea party groups have hit a political nerve, and hard. They have forced a top *Democratic* official to defend the standards against charges of federal overreach despite evidence to the contrary even as *Republican*-leaning business groups try to paper over differences between themselves and Republican governors and legislators. They should have seen it coming. One of Arne Duncan's senior advisors told a Washington, DC audience in March 2009 that if common standards were funded by the federal government, "you can't keep ideology or politics out of the ball game."[24]

The power of the federal critique is that it is valid on its face. Tea party groups' criticism was neither "fringe" nor "black helicopter." The design and rollout of the Common Core all but invited their anger, and their distrust of the process is widely shared by groups on the left. In keeping with their anti-federal focus, Tea party groups' central complaint was that the Common Core State Standards were, at best, an exercise in federal hypocrisy and, at worst, an unconstitutional, "socialistic" government power grab.[25]

The charge of federal hypocrisy typically meant that, despite Secretary Duncan's and others' frequent protestations that the standards were "state led," the federal government either bribed or coerced the states into adopting the standards using Race to the Top (RTTT) or waivers from select parts of NCLB. As one North Carolina Tea Party writer puts it: "It is offensive,

in light of the Tenth Amendment, to accept federal bribe money to implement its instrumentalities of indoctrination."[26] Dozens of persons complained to Utah Governor Herbert about federal control, including this
one: "Utah should not accept federal dollars to hold our children ransom
to this curricula that was written and implemented without parental approval
and was pushed on the states through the back door." Others objected to
the distance of the Common Core from teachers and local control. One constituent wrote:

> We all talk about local control. To a state political figure it's taking back
> control from the Feds; to a local politician the state is using the exact
> tactics of the Feds. To a teacher like myself, all of the self-investment
> and opportunity to prove myself as a teacher . . . is stifled by regula-
> tions sent down from those who are continually on the cutting edge
> and never able to come to a knowledge of the truth.

And it was not just that the federal government was lurking behind the
"state-" led effort: for them, even the standards were a product of swamp-
land. One tea party writer argued that

> Common Core standards were actually initiated by private interests in
> Washington DC and not by state lawmakers. Both the NGA and the
> CCSSO are both DC-based trade associations (organizations founded
> and funded by businesses that operate in a specific industry). In fact,
> most of the creative work was done by ACHIEVE, Inc, a progressive
> non-profit group based out of DC.[27]

As the "Common Core" tests went online, others noted the connection of
one of the test writers, the American Institutes for Research (AIR), to Washington, DC, as well. One Utah constituent wrote, "AIR is one of the world's
largest behavioral and psychological research centers. How has it gotten so
large? Primarily with grants and contracts from the federal government."
    These were the mild-mannered comments. Others saw more nefarious
forces at work through the federal government. Glenn Beck argued that the
"federal overlords" refused to see that a "top-down, heavy-handed approach
to improving America's K–12 system doesn't work."[28] One Alabama critic
argued that "civilization as we know it during our lives is coming to an end
if we allow the federal government to tell us everything we're going to do
with our education system."[29] And another, in a book subtitled *Obama's
Final Solution for your Child's Mind*, linked the Common Core to a century
of fights over American education—that between Progressive reformers like

John Dewey's child-centered movement and those defending "individual-ity and liberty":

> Progressives have already infiltrated our school systems with revision-ist history and pseudoscience. The Common Core is just the final phase of their control. Wouldn't it be nice to just have one national/world mindset and stop having to deal with all these pesky states and localities? Wouldn't it also be better to shape citizens who are func-tioning little worker bees. . . . This worked so well in Eastern Europe and the Soviet Union.[30]

Although Coleman, Duncan, Petrilli, and Zimba were unlikely to be the four horsemen of the Apocalypse, tea party groups' critique and their criticism hit a nerve for many politically active Americans, including centrist subur-ban parents and groups on the left. The staunchly pro-Democrat, pro-teachers' union, and anti-school choice Network for Public Education found common cause with the tea party on the standards, according to its co-founder, Anthony Cody. He wrote, "The substance of the Tea Party [sic] criticism of Common Core standards is solid. And it aligns pretty well with what many of us a bit more to the left have been saying for years." Among other points of agreement, he noted that "there is little question that this is federal bribery bordering on coercion." He also recalled his opposition to the secretive process in 2009, also in common with tea party groups: "We are apparently about to be handed a set of standards that will dictate what is taught in millions of classrooms across this nation."[31]

Was It a Federal Project?

The Common Core State Standards Initiative (CCSSI) devotes almost a quarter of its "myths & facts" Web page to debunking the "myth" that the federal government was important to the design or implementation of the standards. The federal charge stung; Michael Petrilli, the president of the pro-Core Fordham Institute, took pains to emphasize that "Republicans in Con-gress are working to ensure that not another cent of federal funding, and not a whiff of federal coercion, is allowed going forward when it comes to the Common Core."[32] He repeated similar charges in an in-print debate with Joy Pullman, the managing editor of a conservative publication *The Feder-alist.* He wrote that despite Obama's credit claiming and Duncan's cheer-leading, "Common Core is a conservative triumph, as the vast majority of states have moved from vague, low-level, and often leftish academic stan-dards to challenging, straightforward, no-nonsense ones."[33]

The Common Core certainly suffered by appearances: even though the effort was certainly managed by the states, its most visible cheerleaders were President Barack Obama and his Secretary of Education, Arne Duncan. The president and Duncan may not have written the standards, but they pulled the strings, chiefly through RTTT, which was designed to entice states to adopt the Core. Although this use of federal money was novel, the federal government frequently uses cash inducements to motivate state action. But political suspicion ran high, and Common Core supporters had to take great pains to show that the federal government was *not* responsible for the adoption of standards despite the appearance of federal incentives.

The NGA and the Council of Chief State School Officers (CCSSO) made some public attempts to keep the federal government at bay, although the national character of the standards invited early and persuasive federal support. Former North Carolina Governor James B. Hunt wrote that "the initiative has always been a state-led effort . . . they have *emerged* from the state, much as the United States did almost 225 years ago when the Constitution and Bill of Rights were adopted."[34] Yet in December 2008, the NGA and CCSSO had explicitly called for federal involvement. In *Benchmarking for Success*, the organizations noted:

> Federal policymakers should offer funds to help underwrite the cost for states to take the five action steps described above [adoption of a common core of standards]. At the same time, policymakers should boost federal research and development (R&D) investments to provide state leaders with more and better information about international best practices, and should help states develop streamlined assessment strategies that facilitate cost-effective international comparisons of student performance.[35]

The Obama administration was happy to comply. It was well known that the incoming Obama administration was keenly interested in pushing the standards. Alice Cain, an education advisor to Rep. George Miller (D-CA), noted that common national standards and assessments were a high priority for Barack Obama in 2009. At the time, "the Administration was really stressing the standards component . . . Common Core, basically. It wasn't too long before they started talking about common assessments," she told a researcher.[36] A federal official was reported to be attending the Common Core's foundational meeting at the Chicago Airport Hilton on April 17, 2009, and the original drafts of the RTTT regulations included a requirement that states adopt the "Common Core."[37] These inconveniences were overlooked as the Obama administration took quite public credit for Common Core. In the countdown to the 2012 elections, *The Washington Post* noted that the Obama administration had been unusually successful at pushing education reform. Those changes included expanding charter schools, implementing teacher assessment, issuing waivers to NCLB, and "a common set of standards aimed at raising achievement . . . to prepare for life after graduation" (though not denoted as "Common Core"). As of September 2012, the U.S. Department of Education claimed that 28 states changed laws to compete for the money. Gene Wilhoit, CCSSO's executive director, credited the U.S. Department of Education with action when he told *The Washington Post* that "they've taken their concept of reform, like it or not, laid it out very directly, put the resources around it and moved to drive state practices."[38]

How effective was federal money? It was as it turns out exceedingly so. Table 3.1 shows the dates states adopted the Common Core. It was no secret to the states that the federal government wanted Common Core. Although the Department of Education had taken out the phrase "Common Core," the RTTT score sheet gave points for "participating in a consortium developing high-quality standards."[39] States took "high-quality standards" (correctly) to mean Common Core, and they were eager to receive federal funds. New York's application was enthusiastic. "We envision that the enthusiasm resulting from the work of the Common Core Standards will spark a revolution in the design of formative, interim, and summative assessments . . . and bridge the knowledge gap that currently impedes instructional strategies that promote effective differentiated instruction."[40] And out West, Utah was supportive. "The adoption of nationally recognized, relevant Common Core Standards will provide a more stable set of expectations for teachers, students, parents, higher education, and other interested stakeholders."[41]

There was no doubt that the federal government pushed the standards.

The RTTT made Core supporters' claims of "state-led" difficult to maintain. The CCSSI appeared to believe simply repeating "state-led" would convince critics. On its "myths" page, the organization argues that "the federal government played no role in the development of the Common Core."[42] The organization highlights that the Common Core was developed before the 2009 stimulus bill passed, which funded RTTT. This is true—the work that became the Common Core was drafted by a small cadre of individuals who did not work for the U.S. Department of Education. It is also true that many governors—Republicans and Democrats—were on board with common standards for much of the 1990s and early 2000s. The Common Core was itself was *not* a federal project. Yet, given the standards were coming

Table 3.1 Initial Adoption of Common Core State Standards, by Date

Never Adopted	Adopted by or before Final CCSS Draft		Adopted before RTTT Deadline		Adopted after RTTT Deadline	Adopted after RTTT
Alaska	Kentucky	February 10, 2010	North Carolina	June 3, 2010	Indiana	Idaho
Nebraska	West Virginia	May 12, 2010	Minnesota	June 11, 2010	Utah	Maine
Texas	Wisconsin	June 2, 2010	Arkansas	June 12, 2010	Vermont	North Dakota
Virginia			Michigan	June 15, 2010	Delaware	Washington
			Missouri	June 15, 2010	Kansas	Montana
			Hawaii	June 18, 2010	Oregon	Wyoming
			Ohio	June 18, 2010	Alabama	
			Maryland	June 22, 2010	New Mexico	
			Nevada	June 22, 2010	South Dakota	
			New Jersey	June 23, 2010		
			Illinois	June 24, 2010		
			Oklahoma	June 24, 2010		
			Arizona	June 28, 2010		
			Mississippi	June 28, 2010		
			Louisiana	July 1, 2010		

Rhode Island	July 1, 2010
Pennsylvania	July 2, 2010
Connecticut	July 7, 2010
Georgia	July 8, 2010
New Hampshire	July 13, 2010
South Carolina	July 14, 2010
New York	July 19, 2010
Massachusetts	July 21, 2010
Florida	July 27, 2010
Iowa	July 29, 2010
Tennessee	July 30, 2010
California	August 2, 2010
Colorado	August 2, 2010

Note: The U.S. Department of Education awarded "low" points toward the RTTT competition for common standards adopted after August 2 but before December 31, 2010. Indiana, Oklahoma, and South Carolina subsequently withdrew from official participation in the Common Core. Alabama later withdrew from the "process" but retained the standards.

together at the very time that Barack Obama and Arne Duncan were preparing the RTTT carrot, it is a stretch to say the federal government had "no role."

More troublesome to the Core was the organization's claim that "The Common Core is a state-led effort that is not part of No Child Left Behind or any other federal initiative. . . . [Race-to-the-Top] did not specify the Common Core or prevent states from creating their own, separate college- and career-ready standards. States and territories voluntarily chose to adopt the Common Core to prepare their students for college, career, and life."[43] It was true that no state was *required* to adopt the Common Core, and the federal government did not prevent any state from using its own standards. Yet, the U.S. Department of Education nearly breached this defense when it revoked an ESEA waiver for Oklahoma when it backed out of Common Core, and Gov. Jindal's (R-LA) lawsuit against the Department of Education suggested that the circumstantial evidence against the claim was at least legally suggestive. But it was misleading to say that the "Common Core . . . is not part of . . . any other federal initiative." States adopted the standards to meet a *federal* deadline for *federal* money; Kentucky did so even before the standards were final—because of federal inducement. Common Core was very much a state-led idea, but the federal RTTT was indisputably responsible for its adoption.

Does It Matter?

Still, supporters of the Core were politically savvy. The Common Core was already in the works before the federal effort, and supporters *had* spent considerable time with state education chiefs and governors to ensure that they were supportive of the project. There was no secret agenda, although the federal government help was fortuitous in that it dramatically sped up adoption. But supporters did not rely on the federal government; instead, they convinced textbook publishers and later the College Board (now led by the Common Core's own David Coleman) to adopt the standards. States— even if they had *not* adopted the Common Core to increase their chance of winning RTTT money—would find it more difficult to escape them. As it was, the states adopted the standards, federal influence or no, and as districts purchased curricula to match the standards, it would be hard to turn back the clock. When Republican legislators in Wisconsin introduced a bill to revoke the state's participation in Common Core in 2014, top Democrats asked the state's Legislative Council whether the bill would be constitutional.[44] The council noted some Wisconsin-specific difficulties, but then noted that the federal government could revoke its waiver from the ESEA (as it did temporarily with Oklahoma) and that many school districts *had already* spent significant time and resources preparing the Common Core.[45] The Democrats repeated the last claim. Minority leader Peter Barca (D) critiqued the repeal movement in a press release at that time: "I have never before seen such an outpouring of support from educators, who stood up in unison to back Common Core standards when they were last threatened by Wisconsin Republicans. At the time, it was made very clear that making dramatic changes would be very costly and challenging."[46] Using the same argument, State Superintendent Tony Evers pled with "colleagues" to oppose dropping the Common Core. He argued that tossing the Common Core "would throw out not only the expertise, but the time, energy, and expense our educators, parents, and students have invested in learning our new college and career ready standards and preparing for our new state tests."[47] Supporters in other states made similar arguments about the costs. These were not federal incentives.

It is telling that, despite the pushback in states like Utah, Indiana, Arizona, and others, changes to the Common Core Standards themselves have been minimal. In Indiana, anti-Core activists were appalled when the "new" Indiana academic standards were little more that the Common Core Standards warmed over.[48] Arizona simply renamed the standards. Although Utah's attorney general did find that the Common Core process "infringed upon local and state control of education" through "federal coercion," he argued that the Common Core did not materially affect the curriculum or future local control.[49] The "Utah Core" was essentially the Common Core.

Thus, tea arty critics were right. The federal government did make the Common Core exceedingly attractive. And federal support was essential to propping the door open to roll the standards out in a timely, unified fashion. And the door was open just long enough for states and districts to spend significant resources to make changes to an undefined "something else" difficult practically and politically. There were federal fingerprints all over the *process,* despite the CCSSI's protestations otherwise.

But the Common Core was not a federal project. Despite the federal government's financial aid and later offers of waivers from NCLB, there was not a strong federal influence on their actual implementation. The federal government backed down when pressed on Oklahoma's rejection of the Core and—a subject of Chapter 5—it did not take action against the many states that dropped out of the RTTT-required and federally funded *testing* consortia, where the Common Core–aligned tests faced much more grassroots and professional trouble.

OBAMACORE

A second major group of conservative opponents of Common Core were motivated by simple partisanship—Common Core was seen as a Democratic plot to take over American education. In many cases, their resort to partisanship served as a way to gin up the base against the Common Core when other legitimate critiques were too pedestrian to energize parents and other voters. Few elected politicians made the appeal in so stark of terms, but one of Utah Governor Herbert's constituents did:

> Common core is used to indoctrinate our children!!! Wake up Gary! Do your own homework on this subject yourself! . . . We already have an uphill battle teaching them faith, family, country, love, respect, humility, and honor in this socialist, narcissistic society we live in. Please let's do away with common crap in this state before this next generation of OUR Utah children become entitled government leeches like the rest of the country is. You want Utah to become a blue state? Then keep common core and we'll see how short a time it takes to get there.

Sen. Rand Paul (R-KY) likewise suggested that Common Core had lost its bipartisan appeal. It was instead a Democratic project. "If there's a Republican candidate out there," he said, "let's just say there's a hypothetical one that's for Common Core. I'm saying that that hypothetical candidate that's for Common Core probably doesn't have much chance of winning in a Republican primary."[50] Others, including Joy Pullman from the conservative *Federalist,* skewered potential GOP 2016 candidates who were insufficiently opposed to Common Core, including Scott Walker, Mike Pence, Bobby Jindal, Mike Huckabee, and (especially) Jeb Bush.[51]

Many partisan, conservative critics took to calling the act "ObamaCore" after the president's divisive health insurance legislation. Stanley Kurtz, a conservative commentator, suggested that "ObamaCore" was "one of the most important and disturbing of [the president's] many transformative plans." In his view, the Common Core was a power grab by *a president* intent on "circumventing Congress." In line with Obama's ideology, the Common Core's "new non-fiction requirements create a huge opening for leftist indoctrination." Although Kurtz admitted that the states were involved, he states that "Obama is most at fault."[52] Conservative gadfly Phyllis Schlafly used the same language in an October 2012 post to galvanize anti-Obama voters. "ObamaCore . . . fits right in with Obama's attitude that there is no higher power than the federal government. If Obama is reelected, he will be able to accomplish this task with help from Secretary of Education Arne Duncan, a graduate of Chicago politics." Like Kurtz, Schlafly argued that the standards would "indoctrinate [children] to accept the leftwing view of America."[53] The "ObamaCore" trope became so widespread that Glenn Beck's anti-Core seminars in 2014 included instructions *not* to use the term. Beck himself claimed that he "never called it Obama Core or alleged that it came solely from the president," but Beck frequently connected the president with the educational "controllists" to motivate opposition.[54]

Beyond ideological talking heads, however, the Republican Party itself took aim at the standards. Despite the many supportive Republicans, the Republican National Committee endorsed a resolution rejecting the Common Core because it was "an inappropriate overreach to standardize and control the education of our children so they will conform to a preconceived 'normal.'"[55] The center-right Thomas B. Fordham Institute sympathized with the GOP's worry about the Obama administration's role in pushing the Common Core—before calling the resolution "inane" because it seemed to be an attack on standards themselves.[56] In 2013, Sen. Charles Grassley (R-IA) attempted to add budget language to prevent federal money being spent on the Common Core assessments.[57] And Republican presidential candidates and would-be candidates in the 2016 campaign took considerable heat from Republican primary voters and caucus-goers over Common Core. Jeb Bush, in particular, felt pressure to modify or at least re-package his support of the Common Core as he ran for the Republican nomination in 2016.[58] Bush did not back down from his statement, but he emphasized what he called the conservative parts of the proposal.

Other prominent Republicans were less stalwart. None changed his tune as abruptly as Bobby Jindal, who was discussed elsewhere. Former presidential candidate and erstwhile Common Core supporter Mike Huckabee told Iowa Republicans that "Common Core may have originally been . . . a governor-controlled states' initiative to keep the fickle federal fingers of fate off of education," but now "it has morphed into a frankenstandard that nobody, including me, can support."[59] Huckabee did support the original Common Core groundwork, conducted by the American Diploma Project (ADP) and Achieve, Inc. ("in the mid-1990s"). But that was where his support ended. "Common Core is a disaster. It should be killed off, but states should not abandon high education standards, certainly conservatives should never abandon high education standards."[60] Other Republicans followed suit to express support for the central idea of the Common Core, high standards, but all of them noted that the Obama's administration's involvement was "wrong."[61] Clearly, the Common Core had become a Democratic project, at least to likely GOP voters. Other Republican governors, including Chris Christie (R-NJ), Scott Walker (R-WI), and even Rick Snyder (R-MI) all supporters of the Common Core to some degree, felt backed into a political corner by the partisan nature of the Common Core. In 2013, Snyder signed a state budget denying funding to any Common Core activities. He was frustrated, he said, but he could not override the Republican legislature.[62] (The legislature approved funding several months later.)[63]

That Common Core came in for such direct partisan treatment was unexpected. Former governor Jeb Bush (R-FL) had a staunchly conservative record as an unabashed proponent of public *or* private school vouchers and high state standards. By most measures, he was a center-right conservative, and he said that his support of the Common Core was in line with those values.[64] Other Republican governors were instrumental in putting together the Common Core coalition, including Bobby Jindal (LA), Tommy Thompson (WI), and Sonny Perdue (GA). Indeed, the state-centered focus of the Common Core was one of the defining differences between it and earlier national curricular reforms. Unlike America 2000 or Goals 2000, the Common Core was controlled (and copyright) not by a federal agency, but by two state-based associations, the NGA and the CCSSO.

That Common Core itself was controversial in partisan terms was also a surprise because the broad outlines of American education policy had largely lost their partisan hue that had tinged them as recently as the mid-1980s. Although Democrats continued to push for more funding and Republicans for increased school choice, elite members of both major parties often put aside those differences to agree on core policy values. One shared value was that education was a driver of economic development; another was that seemingly slipshod standards were a cause of American ills. This bipartisan agreement underlay America 2000 (1989), versions of Goals 2000 (1994), IASA (1994), the Higher Education Act (1998), NCLB (2001), and Common Core (2010).

But if George H. W. Bush, Bill Clinton, Lamar Alexander, George W. Bush, Ted Kennedy, and John Boehner could reach past genuine ideological differences, their constituents frequently could not. Less prominent, re-election-seeking politicians rejected these elite bargains. Although disputes over core *policy* waned, specific *legislation* became partisan flashpoints. Both America 2000—the Charlottesville initiative—and Common Core had the misfortune to be attached to waning political brands. When governors unveiled "America 2000" at Charlottesville in 1989, the standards were encumbered by a president in search of a campaign issue. When governors unveiled the Common Core State Standards in 2010, they were encumbered by the most polarizing president since polling began.

The Common Core became sucked into national politics by the voluble support of President Obama and Arne Duncan. Things might have worked out well. By the end of 2008, President George W. Bush was despised by Democrats and disliked even by fellow Republicans as was his widely panned NCLB. Despite initial bipartisan support for NCLB, few education reformers thought the law had worked out well, and many were calling for radical changes in the reauthorization bill. In 2008, Sen. Barack Obama had run an upbeat campaign, and the bipartisan distaste for NCLB offered an unusual policy opening at the federal level—"something" had to be done. The background political support for Common Core was well underway by early 2009. Obama did not have to convince elite stakeholders of its merits; most states were already on board. With a small federal push, Common Core might have circumvented the partisan rancor of Goals 2000.

But then, President Obama's opening bid, the American Recovery and Reinvestment Act, precipitated a permanent collapse in self-identified Republican support, a situation unprecedented since the Gallup Poll began tracking presidential approval.[65] At the same time, *CNBC* editor Rick Santelli helped mobilize the creation of the "tea party" in reaction to the stimulus bill.[66] By the summer of 2009, fewer than 20 percent of Republicans approved the job Obama was doing—a level he never reached again. (By contrast, Bush had support from 20 percent of Democratic adults as late as 2004.)[67] In late 2009, as the Democratic Party pursued the Affordable Care Act (ObamaCare), the president's ratings suffered further; by the end of 2010, Republicans returned to a House majority and took more state legislative seats than at any time since 1928, a feat they repeated in 2014. The president's persistent failure to acknowledge differences with congressional Republicans only solidified their opposition. Obama offered no olive branches to Republican legislators, and they had no truck with him.

Of itself, the national partisan polarization under Obama should have done little to education reform. Common Core was unknown to most voters and legislators in 2009, and for those in the know, it *was* a bipartisan, state-created project. But by 2012, the president had taken credit for the initiative, Arne Duncan had become its chief public defender, and the following year architect David Coleman was hiring Obama campaign staffers at the College Board. The reading public could be forgiven for thinking the standards were an Obama project. If the president made the connection, suspicious Republicans were eager to believe him.

It was well known that the president and Duncan were supportive of the standards; early drafts of RTTT gave points for adopting the Common Core. But leaving aside RTTT, the president boasted about improving "college- and career-ready" standards in the states as he ran for re-election in 2012. That year, the Democratic platform claimed that "the President challenged and encouraged states to raise their standards so students graduate ready for college or career and can succeed in a dynamic global economy. Forty-six states responded, leading groundbreaking reforms that will deliver better education to millions of American students."[68] *The Washington Post* took them at their word, and the newspaper ran a story claiming that Obama had "overhauled" education "largely bypassing Congress and inducing states to adopt landmark changes"—especially Common Core.[69] In 2013, the president highlighted Common Core in his state-of-the-union speech, saying, that "we . . . convinced almost every state to develop smarter curricula and higher standards."[70] There was no talk about state-led here; the president was taking full credit for the work.

Arne Duncan was similarly sanguine about the Administration's role in the Common Core. After the Republican National Committee voted to oppose the Common Core in April 2013, Duncan told the U.S. Chamber of Commerce in April that they should become politically active. Duncan said, "I don't understand why the business community is so passive when these kinds of things happen."[71] As the standards took more political hits, Duncan gave an "impassioned defense" of the Common Core in a speech to newspaper editors in June 2013, telling them to challenge critics for evidence. "Challenge them to produce evidence—because they won't find it. It doesn't exist," he said. While Duncan said that the federal government did not write the Common Core, *The Washington Post* noted that, "There is some irony in the fact that Arne Duncan keeps saying that the Core is not the work of the federal government while he, the federal secretary of education, goes around attacking its critics."[72] Instead, Duncan was solidifying the impression that the Common Core was "a major policy success for the Obama administration," as the *Post* termed it.[73] He was so visible a defender that *Education Week* lampooned him—twice—with a "top ten" headline that would not appear: "Secretary Duncan Declines to Back Common Core, Acknowleges [*sic*] His Support 'Created Appearance' of Federal Overreach."[74]

And then there was David Coleman. In May 2013, he argued that Republican governors had to be convinced of the Common Core on evidence because a partisan appeal would be—as it became—a liability. "When I was involved in convincing governors and others around this country to adopt these standards, it was not, 'Obama likes them,'" Coleman said. "Do you think that would have gone well with the Republican crowd?"[75] That was political realism, but Coleman also praised Dan Wagner, the data analytics chief for Obama for America, the president's campaign organization. "Let's remember who won the [2012] election. . . . Perhaps more exciting than the person who stood to the side and handicap the election [Nate Silver] is the person who led the Obama campaign's use of data to galvanize a generation of low-income people to vote like they had never had before . . .

there is no force greater."[76] He also announced that the College Board was hiring Jeremy Bird, a national field director for the president's re-election effort. Together, Coleman's remarks insinuated that, whatever the evidence, this education reform was a Democratic operation.

With Obama, Duncan, and Coleman directly tying the Common Core to Democratic Party politics (or policies), the Common Core became tied to the president. But more than this, prominent Republican Jeb Bush *also* made the connection in statements that he may well regret. Bush met privately with Arne Duncan some five times after 2010, and Duncan was a keynote speaker at Bush's 2010 education summit. Bush has repeatedly praised Duncan in public, and called Barack Obama a "champion of education reform." Obama has returned the favor, and Duncan frequently used Gov. Bush's name in support of the Common Core.[77] When South Carolina sought to end its commitment to Common Core, Duncan said, "GOP leaders like Jeb Bush . . . . have supported Common Core standards because they realize that states must stop dummying down academic standards and lying about the performance of children."[78] In September 2011, Bush even praised the federal incentives RTTT offered. He told *NBC* that the president's pressure on recalcitrant states through RTTT was useful: "I think Secretary Duncan and President Obama deserve credit for pushing—for putting pressure on states to change, particularly the states that haven't changed at all. They're providing carrots and sticks and I think that's appropriate."[79] If an established Republican scion praises the president's involvement with the Common Core, it is very hard to believe that the Core is *still* a state project. Bush recognized the political problem belatedly, only in 2014 telling the pro-reform journal *Education Next* that "the opposition to the Common Core has been mostly fueled by President Obama and his administration attempting to take credit for and co-opt a state-led initiative."[80]

President Obama's approval ratings among Republicans, and his eager endorsement of the standards, suggested that the Common Core would remain a partisan wedge so long as Obama remained president. Although core Democratic constituencies had major reservations about the standards, the identification with Obama (obviously) did not fuel the same suspicion and outrage on the left. But the partisan connection made a groundswell of anti-Obama opposition on the right viable, durable, and perhaps terminal to the Common Core project in some states.

EVIDENCE

The Common Core was the dream of many Main Street Republicans. They wanted national standards and national tests for accountability so that employers could have confidence in the quality of graduates. They supported national standards in the 1990s. When that failed, they tried to use the state-led approach to gain support from tea party conservatives. This would do little violence to the overall effort, and being state-led would also protect the effort from federal politics. By 2007, NCLB was associated with unpopular Republican George W. Bush; by 2010, conservatives sought to avoid an association with a presidential administration that was deeply unpopular with Republicans in general. When the Obama administration and the U.S. Department of Education began to push the Common Core overtly, Main Street Republicans (and Core supporters more generally) had to fall back on other "legal fictions" to continue to defend the proposals. Supporters retreated to the tireless mantra of "internationally-benchmarked" and "evidence-based" standards. David Coleman noted that without evidence, the standards would be "vast, vague, and useless."[81] Who could be against those?

The breadth of these defenses was readily apparent. "International benchmarking" was a centerpiece of one founding documents for the Common Core, *Benchmarking for Success: Ensuring U.S. Students Receive a World-Class Education.* The authors of the report argued that "many states are working hard to improve standards, teacher quality, and accountability, but policymakers lack a critical tool—international benchmarking."[82] The document listed five "actions" that state leader should take, four of which include the words "international" and one "nations and states around the world."[83] Others, after the widespread adoption of the Common Core, have echoed the same arguments repeatedly, and the following three quotations are only representative of the hundreds of similar comments that appear in *Education Week* and on school district Web sites. Commenting on a study of the similarity of the Common Core with several other standards, a senior staff member at the CCSSO said, "The study continues a line of evidence that the Core Standards . . . have a solid research base and will help teachers and students."[84] Maine's Commissioner of Education, Stephen Bowen, argued that not only did teaching professionals want the Common Core, but they were independently strong: "I have heard it over and over from teachers—they want us to adopt the Common Core. They are rigorous, and there is a sense there will be staying power to these standards so they can work with them for some time to come."[85] And U.S. Secretary of Education Arne Duncan, writing in the *New York Times,* emphasized the standards' self-evident benefits:

A second transformational reform is the voluntary adoption by at least 36 states of the state-crafted Common Core Standards, which measure students' readiness for college or careers. For the first time, most states will apply rigorous, internationally benchmarked standards in math and English, bringing tougher standards to more than three-fourths of all U.S. public-school students. It is time to end the insidious practice of dumbing down academic standards—and lying to students about their readiness for college and careers.[86]

Unfortunately for Core supporters, conservative critics—who were not always opponents—did not accept these self-referential assertions. They argued that the "evidence" for the Common Core was thin and overextended. Frederick Hess, of the American Enterprise Institute, argued that "given how avidly Common Core boosters celebrate 'evidence,' they really ought to be able to muster more than 'Trust us, we're really smart.'"[87] This was a serious charge, as the political appeal of the Common Core was that they were *better* than existing standards by some impartial measure. The evidence was politically important because it gave conservative politicians and think tanks space between themselves and the U.S. Department of Education and the Democratic Obama administration—even critics of the Department of Education, such as U.S. Senator Lamar Alexander, have suggested some state standards were poor. "Most of us realized that [students] weren't learning enough in school to get a job at the [local] Nissan plant . . . . The bottom line with the Common Core dispute . . . is, if we could eliminate the trend toward a national school board, you'd eliminate 95 percent of the concern about the higher standards," he told Tennessee reporters.[88] With this critique, conservatives called for a measure of humility in implementing education reforms; perhaps reformers, or Common Core boosters, did not have the "best" standards at hand. Perhaps they should not be rolled out all at once. Perhaps some diversity in implementation should be encouraged rather than tolerated, in a federal fashion, as in federal*ism*. "If the feds had stayed out, if advocates hadn't tried to sign everybody up, you could have imagined something that was much more coherent, people could see what it meant in practice, and if it delivered what was promised, and it's easy to imagine other states would have been wanting to sign up," Hess said.[89]

Conservatives took on four phrases that Common Core supporters used to justify evidence: "international benchmarking," "evidence-based," "rigorous," and "college- and career-ready." These phrases appeared together with great regularity; they formed a central pillar of Core supporters' argument, and all of them concerned evidence. David Coleman even suggested that evidence "was the secret power behind the Common Core."[90] (Supporters typically invoke "evidence-based" to suggest that student learning is affected by the standards.) Although conservatives were making a political argument (*should* governments require uniform standards?), their arguments would be hypocritical rhetoric unless *they* had credible evidence.

In each case, proponents of the Core made two assertions: first, that these phrases *characterized* the Common Core State Standards; and second, that these characteristics *caused* changes in student academic achievement. Both assertions turned on the availability and interpretation of evidence. Initially, supporters of the Common Core were caught off guard on both counts, according to members of the standards' validation committee and scholarly observers, but the umbrella organization regrouped to provide promotional material addressing some of the criticism.[91]

Part of the difficulty was that "evidence" meant different things to critics and supporters. Supporters said that they had looked at other countries' materials, surveys, and a handful of studies, but critics wanted evidence that standards brought real academic improvement. Hess' definition provides an example: "Benchmarking usually means comparing one's performance with another's—not just borrowing some attractive ideas," he wrote.[92] In other words, Hess argued that benchmarking compares *outputs* of public policy rather than the *inputs*. This was a fundamental disagreement.

The most notable example of this disconnect was found in supporters' bullet-point "myths and facts" sheet. The first two "myths" were direct responses to charges like Hess' regarding evidence and international benchmarking ("common standards means bringing all states' standards down to the lowest common denominator"; "the Common Core State Standards are not internationally benchmarked"). The organization claims "the standards were informed by . . . the highest international standards" to prove that the Common Core State Standards are at least equal to the "best in the country."[93] A critic was then directed to "an appendix listing the evidence that was consulted in drafting the standards, including the international standards that were consulted in the development process."[94]

The appendix (which appears in the mathematics standards) had the following entry:[95]

Mathematics documents from: Alberta, Canada; Belgium; China; Chinese Taipei [Taiwan]; Denmark; England; Finland; Hong Kong; India; Ireland; Japan; [South] Korea; New Zealand; Singapore; Victoria (British Columbia).

The bibliography also listed two international mathematics assessments, the Program for International Student Assessment (PISA) and the Trends in International Mathematics and Science Study (TIMSS), and several think tank and academic papers. The most important of these were a set of think tank papers by Alan Ginsburg and various co-authors and another set by William Schmidt and others. Both scholars had conducted extensive research on standards and are well regarded. Ginsburg was a researcher and later policy director at the U.S. Department of Education for four decades, and Schmidt was a professor of education at Michigan State in the Center for the Study of Curriculum. Their scholarship, some of which was prepared specifically for the Common Core project, took a particular view of "benchmarking," which emphasized curricular sequence and coherence. In this research, the scholars identified high-performing countries and then compared their content standards for similarities.

Despite the list in the math appendix, the bulk of research on (math) standards was concentrated on a very small list of countries whose students routinely performed well on international assessments. Schmidt's work focused on the "A+" countries, which he and a co-author identified as the six countries with the highest TIMSS mean middle-school student scores, which are Singapore, (South) Korea, Japan, Hong Kong, Flemish Belgium, and the Czech Republic.[96] Ginsburg's cited research identified Singapore, Hong Kong, and South Korea as high-performing countries because they "represent" high-performing countries on TIMSS and PISA.[97] Having identified the high flyers, Schmidt and Ginsburg presented the sequence of mathematical topics (sometimes called "competencies") used in common by these countries, and both found a high degree of overlap. For example, Schmidt and others discovered that all of the "A+" countries introduced whole numbers in grade 1, decimal fractions in grade 4, and three-dimensional geometry in grade 8.[98] Ginsburg's work took a slightly different approach and instead compared the activities students needed to perform at each grade level for a given competency. For whole numbers, Ginsburg's work suggested that first-graders learn to count objects in a set, third-graders understand even and odd numbers, and fifth-graders learn to approximate and estimate large numbers.[99] This "benchmark" informed the placement and order of the math standards. It was a benchmark of inputs, not outputs, but it was a benchmark.

Common Core Standards supporters also appealed to "rigor." The CCSSI defined "rigor" to mean "high-level cognitive demands by asking students to demonstrate deep conceptual understanding through the application of content knowledge and skills to new situations."[100] The Fordham Institute's definition emphasized content, a "sensible order," and increasing difficulty.[101] By these lights, the Fordham Institute found that the Common Core State Standards were reasonably rigorous. In 2010, Fordham judged the standards, and their work suggests that the Core met the CCSSI's goals for rigor but not quite Fordham's. Still, the group praised the Common Core for being clearly more rigorous than state standards in 76 cases out of 102. (Fordham compared reading and math standards for 50 states and the District of Columbia: $51 \times 2 = 102$.)[102]

Others also defined rigor by comparison. Even scholars who had become critical of the Common Core suggested that they could be judged comparatively: In the Common Core's English Language Arts portions, three education scholars "saw a decrease in emphasis on comprehension and an increase in emphasis on language study. . . . These shifts may represent important increases in quality, but we are not prepared to make that judgment."[103] As here, supporters of the Common Core typically used the pre-existing state standards as a comparison.

In and of itself, this was valuable work—high-performing countries did appear to follow a particular sequence when introducing mathematics concepts, and comparison of inputs is the first step to evaluate public policy. With this, supporters of the Common Core were able to show at least some proof that the standards were *characterized* by the terms they set out. But critics like Stotsky and Hess did not allege that the standards committee did their work in a dark room. It was that the standards were not "benchmarked" by their definition. What Hess and others wanted to see is a link between standards and *performance,* or "a higher standards or end goal." The Fordham Institute anticipated this criticism in 2009:

> Merely finding and naming a country that has similar content in its standards or locating similar content in another test or framework . . . is not compelling evidence. In fact, most of these determinations were originally derived from expert opinion, preference, or survey results. They were not an attempt to "validate" the standard per se, inasmuch as that means that the standard is necessary to accomplish a higher standard or end goal. In other words, much of the cited evidence in the common standards is suggestive, not dispositive. Frankly, we're not that optimistic that all academic standards can or must be "validated," partly because we don't define a good education strictly in terms of college-and-career readiness, and partly because true validation studies are hard to do well.[104]

The Common Core coalition itself admitted as much early in the process. Gene Wilhoit, the executive direct of CCSSO, told the House Committee on Education and the Workforce in 2009 that even though "there are gaps in the evidence . . . this is the first time that we have gone from just an opinion sort of thing about what should be taught to [a] more [*sic*] strong evidence-based kind of process."[105]

Conservatives doubted that supporters could marshal evidence for those gaps to show that standards *cause* improvements in academic achievement. A standard of evidence requiring an effect from the Common Core or any educational reform proved exceedingly difficult, just as other researchers found for the effects of low-income vouchers, class-size reduction, teacher merit pay, charter schools, and direct instruction.[106] Fordham's reticence was well placed.[107]

Conservatives sought indications that standards would move academic achievement. Was there "evidence" that the Common Core would increase achievement? In short, they argued no. Work by the U.S. Department of Education and scholars at the Brookings Institution could not find a relationship between state standards and the NAEP despite multiple attempts.[108] The director of the U.S. Department of Education's Institute for Education Sciences, Grover "Russ" Whitehurst, found no relationship between the difficulty of state standards and the performance of students on the NAEP. He and a research colleague tested both the absolute level of NAEP performance versus difficulty of state standards *and* the relative level of change in students' performance versus standard difficulty. For example, despite the substantial difference between California's high standards and Arkansas' low standards (as rated by the AFT and the Fordham Institute), students in the states made almost identical gains on the NAEP test between 2000 and 2007.[109] They concluded, "The lack of evidence that better content standards enhance student achievement is remarkable given the level of investment in this policy and high hopes attached to it."[110] Another scholar, in reaching the same conclusions, noted that while "the word 'benchmarks' is used promiscuously as a synonym for standards, . . . the term is misleading by inferring that there is a real, known standard of measurement. Standards in education are best understood as aspirational, and like a strict diet or prudent plan to save money for the future, they represent good intentions that are not often realized."[111]

Why would there *not* be a relationship? The evidentiary rationale for the Common Core State Standards was that higher and uniform state standards would force improved learning in the classroom. Higher standards would prompt districts to select better-quality material; and uniform national standards would eliminate the possibility of cheating on results because low performance by students could not be hidden by setting a low bar for meeting "proficiency" on state standards.[112] But most of the actual variation in student achievement occurs within states and within schools and not between states. Presumably, all schools in California were held to the same state standards; the same was true for Arkansas. Figure 3.1 shows the mean and one standard deviation spread in NAEP scale scores for eighth-grade

Figure 3.1   Mean and Standard Deviation of NAEP Eighth-Grade Math Scale Scores, by State, 2011

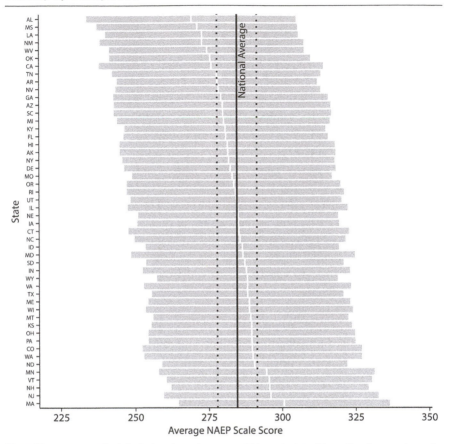

Note: Shows one standard deviation about the mean within each state. The national mean shows the standard deviation between mean state scores. *Source:* U.S. Department of Education.

mathematics for each state compared with the national mean and one standard deviation between state scores. In every state, the spread *within* the state was three to four times greater than the spread *between* states. As such, the evidence would strongly suggest that reformers concerned with boosting student achievement look elsewhere—at teacher quality, school choice, funding, or opportunities to learn. The evidence suggested that using the Common Core State *Standards* to improve academic achievement was a flawed policy proposal.[113]

Others suggested that the lack of a relationship existed because the Common Core was not *actually* that similar to the standards in high-performing countries. The Common Core might have asked fourth-graders to *under-stand* fractions just like an A+ country, but the Common Core did not expect fourth-graders to *practice* fractions like an A+ country. One detailed study of national standards in high-performing countries found that approximately 75 percent of math standards revolve around "performing procedures" like adding fractions or finding the area of circles. By comparison, only 38 percent of the Common Core math standards do. Instead, the Common Core placed a much greater emphasis on memorizing at lower grade levels (for example, about 67 percent for the Common Core math standards emphasize memorizing or recall versus 25 percent for Finland in grades 1 and 2).[114] It may be, then, that the practices—the curricula—in the classroom were vastly more important than the topics taught.[115]

The "evidence" that the Common Core would produce better-educated, globally competitive students did not appear to exist in any consistent way. This failure was not a fault of the standards themselves—they were standards, not curriculum and not teachers. It would be truly stunning if simply introducing fractions in fourth grade, and not in third or fifth, and without specifying how to introduce them produced dramatic effects. All of curricula, teachers, demographics, and family life play outsized roles. But that was not the message NGA and CCSSO trumpeted. Instead, they repeated the claims of evidence, benchmarking, and rigor again and again in the Core's drafting stages and then especially in its defense. Why did Common Core supporters give such a central place to "research" and "evidence" when *even they* knew the research support was thin?

CONCLUSION

As for so many things Common Core, the answers were meant to build political support. Governors at the 1989 Charlottesville Education Summit bought the argument that economic competitiveness was inextricably linked to academic performance and academic standards, and "World Class Standards" no less. But it was not academic performance or even "World Class" that destroyed the 1990s attempts at high national standards. Instead, the national standards were brought down by the workmanship of Gary Nash and his colleagues on the history standards and by charged disputes over the "new math" pushed by the National Council of Teachers of Mathematics. Although the NGA and CCSSO had to keep the federal government at bay as the Core moved forward, it was almost more important to show that *these* standards were not the product of ideologically driven academics with axes to grind or teachers swept up by some squishy constructivist fad. Relentlessly beating the drum of "evidence," "evidence," "evidence" would, they thought, provide their conservative governors with political cover. Although Gov. Gary Herbert (R-UT) maintained his support for the Common Core in Utah, the uproar over the Core was such that he was forced to ask the attorney general whether the standards were adopted legally, open a public comment forum, and create a "Standards Review Commission" that was charged with taking public comment and re-reviewing the standards. The commission's second charge (of six) was to evaluate whether "the standards [are] based on best practices and/or sound research."[116] Similarly, the otherwise skeptical conservative Representative John Kline (R-MN) praised the Common Core for being "research and evidence-based" and its "potential to support those states whose standards are falling short."[117]

The use of "evidence" was meant to placate a distinct political constituency. Two scholars of the process write: "One particular set of inferences, among the differing ones that could be drawn from research, . . . were selected and framed in such a way as to persuade key policy audiences that common standards held the potential to rectify pressing educational and economic problems."[118] They found that emotional appeals were largely absent (save allusions to *Nation at Risk* and World War II) because Common Core supporters were soliciting the support of elites—and *political* elites at that. This focus was central to understanding the ensuing evidentiary controversy. These elites, chiefly governors and business groups, had long ago bought the argument that high standards would lead to economic development. They needed "research" to "prove" these standards were better, but they were not necessarily interested in the theory of action implied by the standards. They were not in the trenches of education research, and they had little experience with (or need to) weed through the thicket of over-drawn conclusions, biased samples, and spurious relationships that characterize much education research, including some of that in the mathematics appendix. Instead, "trust in how the standards were developed . . . meant that the research base was rarely a topic of discussion at the state level."[119] Echoing Sandra Stotsky's more vociferous critique of the standards' use of evidence, another (unnamed) validation committee member commented that "it was pretty clear from the start that nobody thought there was sufficient evidence for any of the standards . . . it [was] thoughtful professional judgment."[120] In other words, the process was exactly what Gene Wilhoit told Congress would *not* happen with the Common Core.

The evidence that was rock solid was that many existing state standards were of low quality, variable, and often useless as educational tools. The Fordham Institute and the American Federation of Teachers (AFT) had produced several years of reports showing well-documented evidence of these disparities, and education sector easily showed that state departments of education played statistical games assessing even those standards.[121] Common Core was indisputably an improvement. But when conservative critics spoke of "evidence," they meant evidence that *these* standards, as designed, would actually produce real academic results. And to date, no one was able to show that a student learning from a Common Core–aligned textbook did substantially better than a student, in the same conditions, learning from a non-Common Core–aligned textbook. Common Core supporters and conservative critics talked past each other.

In different political times, conservative critics might have been convinced to let the evidence slide. But the appearance of federal meddling (whether true or not) destroyed any leniency these critics might have had. After all, one of the central tenets of the Common Core effort *was* that it would be state-led. Conservatives suspicious about national curriculum in the 1990s were not mollified that President Obama and his secretary of education frequently claiming credit for the effort further emboldened critics. This confluence undercut the standards' natural constituency.

FOUR

A Semblance of Ideology: Parents, Private Schools, and Privacy

Many conservatives doubting the evidence behind the Common Core *could* be convinced that the project itself was valuable. Governors Chris Christie (R-NJ) and Gary Herbert (R-UT) were among those conservatives, although virtually every other Republican governor in 2009 was supportive of the Common Core. Their objections were less to the Common Core standards themselves than to a time-honored aversion to federal activity. A change in federal leadership combined with genuine opportunities for local control could overcome their opposition. A second group, however, was adamantly opposed to the *design and content* of the standards themselves. The most visible of these critics were Glenn Beck and Phyllis Schlafly, who suggested that the Common Core was a "big progressive poison pill for the entire education system."[1] Yet, as with the first more pragmatic group of conservatives, many of their arguments were not new. Instead, they were reminiscent of the fight over the national history standards in the 1990s. They suggested that the government was imposing a politically correct uniformity on American children; that the Common Core was a progressive guise to take over private schools; and that Common Core–aligned tests were being used to invade the privacy of students and families.

THE COMMON CORE AS IDEOLOGY

The charge that new academic standards are an ideological tool was a common conservative complaint throughout the 20th century, with some justification. Ellwood P. Cubberley, an influential Progressive, a century ago promoted the use of schools to promote "self-reliance and initiative," cleanliness, obedience, and "the Anglo-Saxon conception of . . . popular government."[2] Cubberley had no reservations about proclaiming who should make decisions about standards: "Each year the child is coming to belong more and more to the state and less and less to the parent."[3] He and other reformers were concerned that education pre-1920s was rote, dull, and divorced from the industrial needs of the United States; students needed education to suit them for "real-life" tasks. Parents may have been suited to prepare their children for life in an agrarian age, but parents were ill-suited for an industrial society they had not experienced. Using a softer touch, reformer John Dewey advocated much the same thing. Schools, according to John Dewey, were to serve the "welfare of the entire community" and tailor education to students' expected future careers.[4] Later, Dewey praised the nascent Soviet system: "It is hard not to feel a certain envy for the intellectual and educational workers in Russia. . . . An educator from a bourgeois country may well envy the added dignity that comes to the function of the teacher when he is taken into partnership in plans for the social development of his country."[5]

Conservatives fought against the technocratic groundswell that Dewey and especially Cubberley represented. One, William C. Bagley, asked in 1934, "What do you think of a theory which holds that, in the absence of an immediate 'real-life' problem or purpose, . . . ignorance becomes a virtue?"[6] By the 1940s, however, they lost; the humanistic, moralistic, and demanding McGuffey readers were out, along with Latin and geometric proofs.[7] Although the favored school standards varied through the 20th century, the pursuit of real-world problems remained. The 1958 National Defense Education Act, a first step in federal encouragement of local curriculum, was meant to "promote the development of technical skills essential to the national defense" in elementary, secondary, and collegiate education.[8]

When Common Core became a project of David Coleman and Jason Zimba in 2007, they might have thought they took the high road—the one advocated by Bagley. The 1930s critic had been an advocate for a common national curriculum if only because Americans were a mobile people.[9] But Coleman and Zimba also took the Cubberley-like charge of writing work-ready standards. In a critique of Florida's math standards, Coleman and Zimba asked "Is [a standard] truly necessary for college and work and thus should be provided for all, or an element of advanced math for only some students to pursue?"[10] This was the very same proposal advanced by early-20th-century Progressives: Education should be, above all, tailored for future work, and appropriate for *all* students. This belief infused the Common Core.

Thus, radio and television personality Glenn Beck did not have to connect too many dots to characterize the Common Core as a product of central state planning. Using statements like Coleman's and Zimba's, Beck concluded that "the Common Core experiment is really about creating *workers*, not *thinkers*."[11] Coleman did not help his cause when he said that, "as you grow up in this world you realize people really don't give a [expletive] about what you feel or what you think."[12] This attitude—and the Progressive vision of education—allowed Beck to slam the Common Core as a project of "government planners" seeking to reshape "students' views on fundamental questions about their nation."[13] Certainly, the Common Core itself did not include the 600 pages of politically charged teaching examples that accompanied the 1994 national history standards, but the Core did suggest a different way of teaching mathematics and a strong emphasis on "information texts" at the practical expense of literature.

What made the Common Core such an affront? For the math standards, it was the unusual math approaches that, while not required by the standards, were strongly suggested. One often-cited example was the "counting-up" method of subtraction, which was included in standard 1.0A.6: "Use strategies such as counting on; making ten (e.g., $8+6=8+2+4=10+4=14$) [or] decomposing a number leading to a ten (e.g., $13-4=13-3-1=10-1=9$)."[14] The standards also listed more traditional strategies (such as knowing that subtraction is the inverse of addition), but major math curricula such as McGraw-Hill's *Math Expressions* adopted the first recommendation wholeheartedly.[15] These strategies had been a lightning rod of controversy—comedian Louis CK's widely seen Common Core lampoon centered on "nonsense" math problems. "My kids used to love math. Now it makes them cry!" he said.[16] In Utah, this mathematics method was among the most scorned elements of the Common Core. Gov. Herbert's constituents called then "absurd," "asinine," "confusing," "disorganized," "insane," "bizarre," and "ridiculous." Whatever the merits of the math algorithms, these did not seem the stuff of mind control.

On the other hand, the English Language Arts (ELA) standards became the proxy for the 1990s national history standards. Phillis Schlafly's Eagle Forum (also a foe of the history standards) suggested that the Common Core textbooks required students to identify themselves ideologically and adopt "pro-big government statements," such as "The commands of government officials must be obeyed by all."[17] As such, Schlafly wrote that "Obama Core is a comprehensive plan to dumb down schoolchildren so they will be obedient servant of the government."[18] Michelle Malkin criticized textbooks but she aimed at the standards themselves:

Under Common Core, classics such as *To Kill a Mockingbird* and *The Adventures of Huckleberry Finn* are of no more academic value than the pages of the Federal Register or the Federal Reserve archives—or a pro-Obamacare opinion essay in *The New Yorker*. . . . Literature and history are all about competing ideological narratives, in other words. One story or "text" is no better than another. Common Core's literature-lite literacy standards are aimed not at increasing "college readiness" or raising academic expectations. Just the opposite. They help pave the way for more creeping political indoctrination under the guise of increasing access to 'information.'[19]

Malkin also compared the Core to outcomes-based education, the early-1990s reform that ignited a similar conservative backlash because state standards then included prescriptions about what students were "to be like."[20] In this vein, Beck quoted one English professor approvingly: "The Common Core . . . is the attempt to take away the great stories of the American people and replace them with the stories that fit the progressive, liberal narrative of the world."[21]

Parents, too, picked up this theme. Prompted by their children's experiences, or by Beck, Malkin, or Schlafly, parents lamented to Gov. Herbert about the "loss of classics" when Utah adopted the Common Core. "Return to the classics! Return to biography, return to historical fiction or nonfiction! I am appalled by the content in the literature! There is a reason the classics are classic! The refinement of language; setting a standard; the advanced vocabulary; the reasoning and complexity of plots; etc.," one wrote. Another complained of the Common Core's focus on informational texts and wrote, "Students need to read the classics. Technical manuals and books that don't capture student's interest will not help them learn to love reading."

Although Beck, Erickson, Malkin, and Schlafly had expressly political goals in mind, Sandra Stotsky, a Common Core validation committee member, used more temperate language to express a similar point. Stotsky was less worried about political indoctrination per se than the declining ability of students to comprehend difficult or complex arguments. Stotsky argued that the Common Core implied a 50-percent rule: half informational texts, half literature (which included all fiction, including poetry and plays).[22] That percentage was far too high for her. She argued that requiring such a preponderance of informational text would undercut the "college- or career-ready" goals of the Common Core. She wrote, "From about the 1900s—the beginning of uniform college entrance requirements via the college boards—until the 1960s, a challenging, literature-heavy English curriculum was understood to be precisely what pre-college students needed." Reducing literature would make students less able to comprehend complex arguments or parse ambiguity.

Common Core decreases students' opportunity to develop the analytical thinking once developed in just an elite group by the vocabulary, structure, style, ambiguity, point of view, figurative language, and irony in classic literary texts. . . . [The National Council of Teachers of English] offers as examples of informational or nonfiction texts selections on computer geeks, fast food, teenage marketing, and the working poor. This is hardly the kind of material to exhibit ambiguity, subtlety, and irony.[23]

Stotsky, who had been a standards writer for the Commonwealth of Massachusetts and a standards evaluator for the Thomas B. Fordham Institute, did more than complain; and she released a 2009 revision to the Massachusetts standards in 2013. Unlike the Common Core Standards, her revised version included four categories for fiction literature: contemporary prose fiction; poetry; drama; and myth, legend, traditional narrative, and classical literature. These standards also included an extensive list of sources and authors as examples, inviting a deliberate comparison to the paucity of such sources in the Common Core.[24] The core of her argument was not that standards were a bad thing but rather the observation that standards become a ceiling for education rather than a floor. If the standards were weak on literature, schools would be unlikely to strengthen that curricular area.

Supporters of Common Core responded that these critics had confused the *implementation* of Common Core with the standards themselves. The Common Core ELA standards, for example, included an explicit note: "Given space limitations, the illustrative texts listed above are meant only to show individual titles that are representative of a wide range of topics and genres."[25] States and teachers would *have* to supplement them because the standards highlight only the concepts students should learn, not the content. This was part of the political insight of the Core's designers, who knew that *any* list of books would attract criticism. Further, they responded that the division between literature and informational texts was for the child's *whole* school experience. Some courses, like those in history, social studies, mathematics, or the sciences, could have a preponderance of informational texts, leaving ELA classes to assign literature—just like they always had. Indeed, the split might encourage additional reading in non-ELA classes.

PARENTS AND PRIVATE SCHOOLS

Because private schools cannot compete with "free" public schools on price, they differentiate themselves through their academic credentials, mission, or values. This was especially true for the religious private schools that enroll 80.6 percent of all private school students.[26] Despite their differences, these schools purchase curriculum from the same market as public schools, and their students take the same college placement exams as their public school peers. The politics in this private sector took up many of the same arguments as the public sector: the standards were lower, the documents were drafted without public input, or they were a federal imposition. But the standards also faced two challenges more germane to religious, private schools. First, opponents argued that the standards threatened parental influence in education. Second, opponents alleged that the Core's "fewer, higher, better" mantra pushed spiritual or religious content to the margins of the curriculum as the "better" standards dominate.

These charges were more serious because they lay at the heart of long-running conflicts in American public education. Who should be in control of children's education? If the state had ultimate control, then how much should it defer to the wishes, beliefs, and desires of parents? Critics like Beck and Malkin suggested that the Common Core preemptively settled the question at the expense of parents. But the Common Core brought the same questions, with far more bite, to the 15 percent of American students who do *not* attend public schools. Parents of these students had made an explicit educational choice to leave the public system, and the Common Core appeared to undercut their liberty.

Parental Influence

The first complaint regarded the erosion of parental control. Because parents have to *choose* to send their children to private schools, they have an outsized influence on the goals and content in these schools; they are schools "of choice" in the sense that unhappy parents can easily pull their children out. Private schools often emphasize (and sometimes require) parental participation in education either at home or at school. To the extent that the Common Core weakened parental participation or control, it was a threat to private education. It should be noted that the "parental responsibility" argument also appeared in the public school space. One Utah commenter wrote the governor, "[Common Core] has made me heartsick for months. I feel powerless, and the children in Utah are victims." And another: "The role of public education in this state is to support parents, nor replace them. When parents are involved in the education of children, everybody thrives." Nevertheless, because parents have to make an active choice to use private education, this critique is especially salient in that sector.

The primacy of parents in education is a widespread Christian conviction. The U.S. Conference of Catholic Bishops, which took a neutral view on the Common Core, emphasized this as a right of parents: "Parents possess the fundamental right to choose the formative tools that support their convictions and fulfill their duty as the first educators."[27] Others might look to Catholic bête noire Martin Luther: "All who are called masters . . . must derive from [parents] their power and authority to govern,"[28] or to the Apostle Paul: "Do not provoke your children to wrath, but bring them up in the discipline and instruction of the Lord."[29] This understanding of education put the overwhelmingly Christian, religious private schools—and their parents—fundamentally at odds with the standardizing rationale undergirding the Common Core.

Pro-Common Core groups in the private school space acknowledged this friction and sought to highlight how parents can be involved. The National Catholic Educational Association's (NCEA) Catholic Identity Curriculum Integration (CICI) program gave boilerplate advice about the role of the home in education and highlighted that parents should communicate with their children's school. "Our [Catholic] church clearly states that parents are the primary educator of their children . . . if a parent reads the [Common Core] standards and does not think a particular standard is a good goal for their [sic] child at this time, they [sic] should address this concern with the school. . . . Parents should provide students with love and support, recognizing that all students make mistakes."[30]

Unfortunately, actions by local and national figures have only confirmed what many Catholics, other private school supporters, and conservatives feared.

Some of the most explicit claims of expert-led authority came from Massachusetts' former Commissioner of Education Paul Reville. At a January 31, 2014 panel at the Center for American Progress, he argued that opposition to the Common Core was small minded because "the children belong to all of us" and not to the parents.[31] The Heritage Foundation's publication, *The Daily Signal*, quickly compared his statement to one made by *MSNBC* host Melissa Harris-Perry the previous year when she said in an ad for the network, "We have to break through that private idea that kids belong to their parents."[32] That statement garnered two weeks of coverage in the right-leaning blogsphere and on *Fox News*, including a comparison of Harris-Perry to Vladimir Lenin by Rush Limbaugh and a cheeky tweet from Sarah Palin: "Dear MSNBC, if our kids belong to you, do your kids belong to us, too? If so, can we take them hunting after church in our big pickup truck?"[33] Reville's statement likewise bounced around the blogsphere. He made out better than Harris-Perry, though—he was only linked to Hillary Clinton's 1996 children's book *It Takes a Village* by archconservative Breitbart.com.[34] Yet the nerve that this high-profile Common Core supporter hit was not isolated to left-leaning "collectivist" statements such as this. Others saw the Common Core Standards as an attempt to implement this view.

In the religious sector, the same argument was made by Milwaukee Archbishop Jerome E. Listecki. When parents' group Milwaukee Catholic Parents Against Common Core delivered a 1,000-signature petition to the archbishop in June 2014, he replied, "Parents already are welcome to review any and all aspects of our schools curriculum, but to think that parents are more qualified than our academic experts to select said curriculum is ridiculous."[35] The group answered with a letter indicating that the diocese had not "consulted" parents nor asked for their support. They also asked that he consider the position of David L. Ricken, Archbishop of Green Bay: "Schools of this diocese [should use] the diocesan standards previous in place and not substitute for them the 'common core standards' . . . There is no track record of existing data to help us determine if these standards will actually improve our students' performance."[36] Listecki refused to reconsider, and he suggested that parents were not sufficiently trusting of the Church's authority or safeguards. He told Wisconsin Eye, the state's equivalent of C-SPAN, that "What I hear when I hear people talk about their distrust for Common Core is their distrust for authority . . . . I think what happens is that distrust of authority lends itself to think that education can be used a way of shaping a social adjustment, a social reconstruction without the parents, without the community being involved in those social reconstructions . . . [but] in the Catholic environment, we have individuals who are very vigilant about what we use in class."[37]

Parents' and school groups were not convinced by the vigilance of their administration. The parents' group, Toledo (Ohio) Catholics Against Common Core, highlighted a statement by Pope Francis linking "educational experiments" and the "dictatorship of one form of thinking" to the "horrors of the manipulation of education that we experiences in the great genocidal dictatorships of the 20th century. They have retained a current relevance under various guises and proposals."[38] The Family Research Council, a conservative policy organization more influential with non-Catholic Christian schools, listed parental control as the number one problem with the Common Core, writing that "the children of this nation belong first to their parents and families, not to their communities or governments."[39] An 11-page letter distributed by the Milwaukee parents' group charged the diocese with violating that tenet—and compared its school system with Judas Iscariot. "The Archdiocese violated parents' TRUST. Parents trust school personnel to be truthful to the parents when in fact they 'took the 30 pieces of silver' and compromised their professional integrity to 'transform' our children to [sic] the elitist designers of conformity."[40] Amplifying the parental critique, the Listecki controversy was picked up by conservative media outlets, including Glenn Beck's *The Blaze*, the MacIver Institute, and *Fox News*.

Many religious private schools took a measured approach. Approximately 100 of the 195 Catholic dioceses in the United States used at least part of the Common Core Standards in their curriculum in 2014, and some Catholic school personnel defended the standards in terms similar to those used in the public space. Former Grand Rapids, MI, Catholic superintendent Jim O'Donnell argued that Catholic schools *could* empower parents to educate their children and that Catholic school personnel had the prerogative to select assignments and books that integrate faith into the Common Core Standards. "Catholic schools have always had high standards for the education of students with alignment to our Catholic underpinnings. Common Core Standards are simply the next iteration," he wrote.[41] The U.S. Conference of Catholic Bishops, perhaps sensing division in their ranks, took a neutral position on Common Core in the Catholic schools, but did offer that the standards, as standards, were not inimical to a Catholic education. Their statement showed concern that the standards were too narrowly tailored to "college and career" rather than "the formation of the human person in the pursuit of his ultimate end [i.e. purpose]."[42] And they stressed that Catholic schools should be at least as academic as their public peers, a comparison that suggested Common Core might be necessary.

How could the Common Core attack parental control? Putting aside arguments about the process of adoption, critics suggested that the materials were deliberately obscure. Glenn Beck, for example, argued that it introduced methods or books about which parents are unfamiliar so as to make them more dependent on outsiders, an interpretation shared by RedState .com's influential Erick Erickson.

Glenn Beck's 2014 book, *Conform,* was a paean to local control at the expense of the Common Core, but his critique is broader than 50-state federalism. Beck argued that the Common Core was "a systematic approach to dumb down our kids and further remove parents from the process so that students will be easier to indoctrinate and control."[43] He later cited an official from the Michigan Elementary and Middle School Principals Association as an example of the "controllist" agenda: "Educators go through education for a reason. They are the people who know best about how to serve children. That's not necessarily true for an individual resident . . . they may not know what is best from an education standpoint."[44] The book, which was released to coordinate with a national anti-Common Core event on July 22, 2014, was Amazon.com's best-selling Common Core book through the fall, and a year out was still in the top 20.

Beck did not attack the standards *as* standards directly, but Erick Erickson, editor of the influential conservative blog *Red State*, did. After recounting problems his wife and daughter had with homework, he argued that Common Core supporters sold out parents. "This issue, once under the radar, is going to keep growing into a major political issue as more and more mothers are less and less able to help their children with homework." At the January 2015 Iowa Freedom Summit (an event for potential 2016 GOP presidential candidates), former governor Mike Huckabee (AR) repeated that "The Common Core . . . has truly morphed into something dangerous to students—and to their parents—because when the federal government gets control, they really have no idea what works in each locality."[45]

"Parental control" is the private sector's analogue to "local control" in the public sector, and it taps many of the same emotions and arguments. Ironically, parents opposed to the Common Core in the private sector had to fight it in every school or diocese because there was no higher political level. That made the Common Core all the more resilient.

Character of Schools

The second major private school critique of standards turned on the concern for the "character" of schools raised by the U.S. Conference of Catholic Bishops. What *is* the character of private schools? Private schools did not have to adopt the Common Core, and so the voluntary nature of the Core has put arguments about the *implications* of the Common Core in stark relief.[46] While public schools must worry about issues of local control and federal monies, "these same concerns are really nonissues for private schools, Christian or otherwise, who are not bound by the same mandates or regulations as public systems," wrote Sheri McDonald, principal of Mariners Christian School in Costa Mesa, CA. "Private schools have the luxury of weighing the value of the standards on the basis of their own merits. . . . Are there truths within the standards that should in fact be a part of that nonnegotiable body of knowledge that makes up the core of what should be taught in Christian education to best serve students?"[47]

Many, perhaps a majority, of private schools have adopted the Common Core, and some quite willingly. These schools typically defend their choice by acknowledging their small place in the larger educational universe. McDonald wrote, "The majority of our students matriculate into public high schools, so we must be aware of and aligned to the expectations for our students."[48] The U.S. Conference of Catholic Bishops used the same logic as they defended the choice of some schools' selection of the Core. They noted that "such realities" as the alignment of the ACT and SAT to the Common Core suggested that "Catholic schools must take into consideration the horizon of the local, state and national education landscape and the influence and application of the CCSS. To ignore this would place our students at a significant disadvantage for their post-secondary education, which is not an acceptable option for our families."[49] The controversial Milwaukee Archbishop Listecki noted that the Common Core presented an "opportunity" for students.[50] Others were less positive; the Diocese of Manchester (NH) informed its congregants that it would *not* be adopting the Common Core State Standards, but that schools were to be "cognizant of all such standards and their impact," in part to prepare students for a transition into public high schools.[51] For other private schools, the question has been one of marketing and curriculum. Despite warnings about creeping government control, some schools have used it as a way to encourage parents to sign up because "your child will get the same education in a distinctive environment." A principal of a small Christian school in Florida was quoted in favor of the standards, saying, "Our teachers know what to teach, and the parents know what their children should be doing in school. Sure, it is a change, but it is real change that is needed if we are going to prepare our students for college and a successful future."[52]

The NCEA was a strong supporter (with funding from the Bill & Melinda Gates Foundation, to the anger of opponents).[53] The organization pressed many dioceses to adopt the standards contemporaneously with the states in 2010. NCEA offered workshops on integrating Catholicism with the Common Core and provides other resources, including curriculum guides and training. To shelter itself from criticism, the organization also supported the CICI organization to emphasize the "whole child" elements of the Common Core.[54] As dioceses ran into parental opposition, supporters pointed to the necessity of matching state standards—but they also emphasized their "adaption" rather than "adoption" of the Core.[55]

Yet a persistent criticism of the standards from the private sector was that they undercut schools' identity. Given the cost of attending many private schools, they instead emphasize differences, whether religious, programmatic, or pedagogical. The U.S. Conference of Catholic Bishops provided a mild rebuke of the standards because they were "were adopted too hastily . . . with inadequate consideration of how they could change the character of our nation's Catholic schools."[56] For other Catholics, the standardizing elements of the Common Core posed steep roadblocks for religious or philosophical reasons. A widely cited open letter signed by 132 Catholic academics from major institutions including Georgetown, Texas

State, Notre Dame, Princeton, and Marquette urged American archbishops to "seek an orderly withdrawal" from the Common Core. Gerard Bradley, a law professor at Notre Dame, wrote the letter:

> We write to you . . . because of what the particular deficiencies of Common Core reveal about the philosophy and the basic aims of the reform. . . . these aims will undermine Catholic education, and dramatically diminish our children's horizons . . . Common Core shortchanges the central goals of Catholic education: to grow in the virtues necessary to know, love, and serve the Lord, to mature into a responsible, flourishing adult, and to contribute as a citizen to the process of responsible democratic self-government.[57]

The Cardinal Newman Society, a Catholic opponent of the Core, also took exception to the narrow college-and-career focus. In its Summer 2014 newsletter, the Society argued that "Catholic education is much greater than college and career preparation. . . . The Common Core may diminish a school's Catholic identity by 'crowding out' important elements of authentic Catholic formation, emphasizing skills and practicality over vocation, and failing to teach reason from a foundation of truth."[58]

Private school Core critics also disputed the need for the standards in the first place, a charge also heard in the public school sector. The Cardinal Newman Society, citing the pro-Common Core NCEA, argued that "Catholic high schools already have a 99 percent graduation rate, . . . [and] most Catholic school graduates attend four-year colleges (85 percent), as opposed to fewer than half (44 percent) of government school graduates."[59] Non-Catholic Christian school publishers drew the same comparison. A Beka Book, a large publisher of textbooks for Christian schools and home school students, said it had carefully studied the standards, and that its textbooks "were found to already meet almost all Common Core content standards." It would be open to changes in the future, unless the standards had "philosophical implications" or would require changes in teaching methodology.[60] Bob Jones University Press, a competing publisher, was blunt: "We oppose any federal intervention in education." And even if it were not, the publisher would do nothing because BJU's materials exceeded the standards. "BJU Press is not changing any of its materials in order to be compliant with Common Core State Standards nor intentionally doing anything to align with them. . . . Moreover, some Common Core State Standards actually align with *our* standards," the publisher noted.[61]

Were parents and other critics successful? As the Milwaukee case shows, 1,000 angry parents was not sufficient to move hierarchy. Others, though, met with success. An anti-Common Core parents' group in Pittsburgh succeeded in convincing Bishop David A. Zubik to announce that the diocese would *not* adopt the Common Core—and the groups' Web site was widely copied by other anti-Core groups. Zubik was careful to note that even though the diocese was a member of the NCEA, it was not a governing board and it would not influence his decision about the Common Core. Throughout his announcement, he noted how "parents raised questions" and thanked them "for the loving concern that you have shown about the education of your children."[62] Yet, just as in the public sector, critics of the Common Core were forced to fight to "repeal" the standards in their schools. In this, the designers of the Common Core had been politically savvy—it is harder to dislodge programs than to prevent their adoption, even without the pull of federal money.

PRIVACY

Common Core critics on the right—but also on the left—expressed concern about the privacy of individual students and family members. As with other Common Core complaints—the tests, the curriculum, the pedagogical methods—concerns over student privacy were incidental to the standards themselves. But, despite Core proponents' wishes, politics drew this side issue into the policy vortex. Arne Duncan acknowledged the connection in his defense of the Common Core when he dismissed the claim that the standards were a scheme to gather student data: "They say that the Common Core calls for federal collection of student data. For the record, it doesn't, we're not allowed to, and we won't. And let's not even get into the really wacky stuff: mind control, robots, and biometric brain mapping."[63] Critics, though, did not think it was so "wacky." The standards themselves did not require data collection at all—as supporters were fond of saying, they were standards not curriculum, and they were useful only as implemented through curriculum. The tests were not even part of the standards. That was too clever by half. Because most states adopted Common Core as part of the federal Race to the Top (RTTT), the standards became intimately associated with that initiative's other priorities, including extensive student testing. Critics point to the assessment priorities of the RTTT program, to the existing data collection by the U.S. Department of Education for research purposes, and to the pro-assessment policies advocated by affiliated interest groups and think tanks as evidence that students' privacy is at risk with the standards.

RTTT was the Obama administration's signature initiative, and it was one meant to remedy the political defects of the No Child Left Behind (NCLB) act. NCLB had become a monument to bureaucratic obfuscation and deception as states, districts, and schools found ways to game the system to avoid the sanctions for failing to meet student performance goals.[64] Although the act only specified schools or districts as being "in need of improvement," practitioners and the press quickly translated that to "failing schools." In early 2009, Secretary Duncan took that line to argue that NCLB had "50 ways to fail." RTTT, on the other hand, would offer rewards to schools and districts for making the right choices.[65]

Despite the change in language, the Obama administration's RTTT program was entirely consistent with prior federal education policy. RTTT still emphasized student performance, elements of school choice, and low-income, non-white children's educational needs, but it clearly linked those goals with assessment. The U.S. Department of Education evaluated states' applications for RTTT money with a 500-point rubric of which 280 were given for meeting-specific requirements related to data systems, district assessment, measuring teachers, and promoting student achievement. Although some of these goals could conceivably be met without using some form of standardized tests, tests *were* the preferred policy instrument. Since the first Elementary and Secondary Education Act (ESEA) in 1965, the federal government has sought to boost students' *academic* achievement. The 1966 Coleman Report, which found wide performance gaps between groups of students, served as the justification for this focus. With the 1994 reauthorization of ESEA, states were required to measure *students'* performance, measured to state standards; NCLB in 2001 only toughened these requirements. Indeed, the core policy benefit to annual testing was to identify which *students* were consistently underperforming their peers. There was no way for this to work without identifying students.

That is, federal education policy *only* worked by collecting student data. Politically, neither Duncan nor Obama was going to back away from identifying learning gaps, either. Non-white interest groups are among the strongest supporters of student assessment because they argue (with strong evidence) that low-performing non-white students are more likely to be ignored by schools and states. Individual student identification keeps pressure on *particular* schools for *particular* students.

As documented elsewhere, the problem for federal policy was the potpourri of standards and testing regimen across the states. Federal education policy had long struggled with preserving federalism while advancing national goals. Education reformers noted wide variability in standards and assessment among the states, and in some cases even among years in the same state. Not only did each state have vastly different standards—both in content and in quality—but each district would very likely have a different curriculum.[66] Many critics perceived that the implementation of NCLB was long on punitive measures but short on results. Common Core seemed to be part of an answer. Now, policy makers concerned about differential achievement between states and students would no longer—*could* no longer—be fobbed off as simply a difference between states or curricula. The standards would be at least 85 percent identical, and textbook publishers would be pressured for their material to conform. Any differences among students could be attributed to teachers, schools, or *students* as those most responsible for teaching and learning. Thus, the Obama administration saw Common Core as a convenient way station to measuring student achievement.

Second, critics pointed to data collection practices by the Department of Education. In concert with standards adopted "by a significant number of states," as the RTTT document put it, RTTT also sought to "break down data barriers" that had hamstrung research on student performance and school accountability in the past. The director of the Data Quality Campaign, an interest group pushing for regularizing state data, wrote "No Child Left Behind mandated that data be reported for particular populations, which began to bring transparency to a system that had survived on the safety of aggregated data. . . . [But] to maximize the power of data, not only for accountability purposes but to inform continuous improvement, we need to be able to follow individual students over time."[67] The Data Quality Campaign saw success as many states adopted tracking numbers to follow students from K–12 to college, maintain records of student course taking, and annual student test scores.

Data quality was not a truly private sector (or state-level) undertaking. Since 2005, the U.S. Department of Education had awarded grants to states to improve their data systems, and the 2009 stimulus bill extended the competitive grant for states to build databases.[68] That optional grant was supplemented by RTTT. The Department of Education instructed reviewers to award points for implementing the systems if they created unique student and teacher identifiers and linked those identifiers to students' transcripts and test scores from elementary through college. States were also to track student demographic information. It is this database that privacy advocates found troubling.

The State Longitudinal Data System (SLDS) was not part of Common Core, but many school districts used the new standards and the new data collection hand in hand.[69] Critics saw it as part of an assault on student privacy by the federal government. One critic worried about the scope of access: "The sinister side of these longitudinal systems is that the U.S. Department of Education broadened its interpretation of educational privacy laws (FERPA) in 2011 . . . [to allow access to] any organization or group tangentially involved in your child's education. This can include testing, technology, textbook, and research companies."[70] The change to the Family Educational Rights and Privacy Act (FERPA) was significant largely because it allowed schools to contract out data collection and processing *without* parental consent. The Department of Education's chief of staff, Joanne Weiss, boasted of the benefits of "mashing" data together to create " 'data backpacks,' where students can carry their own transcripts and port-folios, personalized college-choice tools, financial aid shopping sheets, and yes, more school and college scorecards."[71] For the Department of Educa-tion, this was a good thing; for critics, it looked Orwellian.

Arne Duncan told reporters that the Department of Education was not involved in student data collection. He said, "They say that the Common Core calls for federal collection of student data. For the record, it doesn't, we're not allowed to, and we won't."[72] It was true that the *Common Core* does not call for federal data collection, but Duncan's claim that "we"— the Department of Education—did not collect data was difficult to square for an agency that collected and aggregated data for, at the very least, the national Common Core of Data (CCD) (unrelated to the Common Core State Standards) and federal student aid programs.

Critics, such as Cristel Swasey, a widely cited anti-Core blogger, were more blunt: Duncan "directly lied to the American Society of News Edi-tors."[73] In her estimation, he might have been technically correct but was still engaged in the "witchery of wordplay." She highlighted the role of RTTT for building "interoperable" state databases and the Department of Education's partnerships with private organizations to actually collect the data (especially the Council of Chief State School Officers [CCSSO]). The Department of Education also provided vendors with the National Educa-tion Data Model as a template for database builders when designing their own systems. Some of the data the Department of Education suggested they collect were routine, like name, ethnicity, and address. Other suggestions were more suspect; the department recommends collecting student religious affiliation, diet, and medical lab results.[74] The department claimed that 18 states and "vendors" use the model in their own databases. Badged federal agents may not be scraping data from students' tests, but badged federal agents are coordinating with others to do so.

Third, privacy advocates point to the politics of association. Many of the groups that had been instrumental in the design and motivation of the Common Core were *also* pushing for better data collection, and they sup-ported collection for the same reason that Arne Duncan supported it. These pro-Core, pro-data groups worried that teachers, principals, and school administrators would try to hide unflattering data to protect current practices and personnel. Cheating scandals in Atlanta, GA, and Washington, DC, provided fodder to feed this suspicion. In Atlanta, many low-income schools that showed "miracle" gains in scores drew legal attention and resulted in charges that dozens of teachers had engaged in racketeering to "defraud the government, cheat students, and protect their own careers."[75] A state investigation found that 178 principals and teachers were involved; the trial itself began with 21 teachers pleading guilty to a variety of crimes.[76] In Washington, DC, similar charges emerged after Chancellor Michelle Rhee's controversial tenure. Some 191 teachers were "implicated in possible testing infractions," including some at an award-winning school.[77] In both cases, teachers and principals were accused of changing data to protect themselves or their school. Although testing opponents drew a different conclusion, pro-testing groups suggested that leaving tests to schools merely invites self-preserving behavior.

Under NCLB, states seemed to engage in similar behavior. NCLB requires schools to meet "proficiency" criteria based on student test results. Researchers at the National Center for Education Statistics (NCES) and at the think tank education sector documented dramatic variation in what constituted "proficiency." "With the approval of the U.S. Department of Education, many states are reporting educational results under NCLB that defy reality and common sense," according to Kevin Carey at education sector. "Some states claimed that 80 percent to 90 percent of their students were proficient in reading and math, even though external measures such as the federally funded National Assessment of Educational Progress (NAEP) put the number at 30 percent or below. One state alleged that over 95 percent of their students graduated from high school even as independent studies put the figure closer to 65 percent."[78] NCES likewise found disparities in a study released in 2009. The Department of Education compared state proficiency scores on state tests to those on the NAEP, a national exam. To be proficient on the NAEP math test, an eighth-grader would need a score of 299 that year. To be proficient on a Massachusetts state exam, a student would need to score an equivalent of 300 (harder than the federal standard), but a Tennessee student just 229.[79] Even if most states were not protecting low-performing schools with an easy cut score, there was *no way* to compare among states.

The pro-data groups typically approached data collection with this problem solving in mind. In a report calling for more and better education data collection, the Thomas B. Fordham Institute lamented that "we have witnessed hundreds of policymakers struggling to make decisions in the face of incomplete information" especially because "what gets measured and reported in education is what gets taken seriously."[80] Education Sector argued that multiple measures of students' lives would improve government service. "Educators and community leaders lack data to help them understand how [social services and educational] systems interact and to help them make decisions and coordinate their work. It means they can't take advantage of powerful tools to detect patterns or risk factors across interventions—patterns that might be impossible to discern from school data alone. This cross-agency information is particularly important to serving at-risk youth, such as children in foster care, who are most likely to use multiple public services," the organization noted in a report on New York City.[81] Achieve, Inc., was quite upfront about data, too: States "must follow students through K–12 into postsecondary and the workforce."[82]

These were Common Core supporters. But what about David Coleman himself? Coleman's own background was in collecting and analyzing student data at his company, Student Achievement Partners. In the foundational Common Core tract of 2008, he and Jason Zimba implored policy makers to "[modify] the accountability system so that it measures more than mere proficiency."[83] And in May 2013, as College Board president, Coleman lauded the deep, detailed data of the Obama campaign: "What made the difference in 2012? . . . The incredible precision and insight gained from data. Not only knowing where people are, but testing different various interventions, seeing what works, keeping focus on delivering them." He promised to do the same with student data. He said he would leverage the "largest set of data by some counts" held by the College Board to enlist an "army" to propel students into college.[84]

It was hard not to draw a connection between Common Core and expansive data collection. The chief architect of Common Core cut his teeth on intensive data analysis. He promised more such analysis in public. Pro-Core policy shops—the same groups that were instrumental in the run-up to the Common Core—wanted better, more comparable data. When anti-Core activists complain that the Common Core "requires" states to collect all manner of personally identifiable information, they are not "correct." The Common Core itself does not require any—but it is just that the Common Core's strongest supporters want that data.

PUSHBACK: PARENTS OPT OUT

As top-line political challenges to the Common Core proved difficult to surmount, parents increasingly took matters into their own hands by opting out of Common Core-aligned tests. Individually, these protests would have been negligible to the implementation of Common Core, but collectively, their opt-outs garnered widespread political attention—and in some districts, considerable financial attention as well. From a testing perspective, the Common Core exams had an unenviable position because the tests had *no consequences* for students but they had *federal* consequences for schools and districts. When students opted out of a test, teachers might miss an additional opportunity to check students' progress. For schools, though, federal law required a 95-percent participation rate from each subgroup in the school. If the school missed this requirement of NCLB, the U.S. Department of Education could dock federal monies for which the school or district would otherwise be eligible. Thus, even if opt-outs could do little to dislodge tests or the Common Core, some schools and districts were acutely aware of the consequences of unhappy parents. Still, the political importance of opt-outs was complicated by the affiliation of opt-out groups with teachers' unions, a distinct socioeconomic bias, and the small actual number of students opting out.

Objections from parents' groups were altered and amplified by an alliance (or co-optation, per critics) with teachers' unions. The anti-testing New York State Allies for Public Education (NYSAPE) presented 10 "demands" to state officials in 2015, four of which related to testing directly, but the remaining six were of this flavor: "[We demand] teacher-created state tests," and "decouple test scores from teacher evaluations." The group had begun with parents, but it quickly became closely aligned with teachers' unions, and in 2015 prominently co-signed a resolution with local teachers' unions, the Badass Teachers Association (BAT), and the Long Island Opt-Out parent association among others to oppose testing.[85] New Jersey opt-out groups also began with parents, only to see the New Jersey Education Association take the issue statewide with organizing assistance and television advertising.[86] Although "parents' groups" can command greater political legitimacy than what would seem to be self-interested union politics, this close alliance suggested that the organized opt-out movement was partly an extension of local Democratic disaffection with teacher accountability.[87] Some teachers' unions recognized the difficulty. The president of the Rochester, NY, teachers' union said, "[If] unions remain silent on this issue, people would say they don't care enough about kids to speak out, to protect them from these tests. And then when you speak out to protect students from these invalid and oppressive tests that are impeding teaching and learning, the unions are accused of using kids."[88]

These politics could have been expected. But more troubling to supporters of the Common Core was an apparent distinct socioeconomic pattern in opting out.[89] Although most districts had a noticeable share of refusals, districts with the *most* refusals tended to have fewer non-white and non-Asian

Figure 4.1   PARCC Test Refusals by Percentage White, 2015

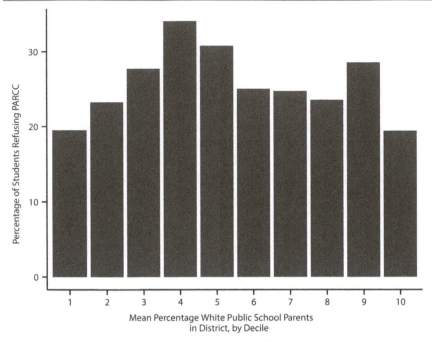

Source: New York State Education Department; U.S. Bureau of the Census.

students as shown in Figure 4.1. The income pattern was also striking in that the districts with most refusals were middle-income districts, as shown in Figure 4.2.[90] This pattern helps confirm Secretary Duncan's inartful assessment of Common Core opposition—urban, non-white residents were far less likely to object. Indeed, they were far more likely to support the Common Core as well, as shown in Chapter 1. This disparity provided excellent cover for especially Democratic politicians to continue to support the exams in the name of closing student achievement gaps. New York Governor Andrew Cuomo (D), for example, pushed for half of a teacher's tenure evaluation to be based on student scores after noting a yawning gap between officially "highly qualified" teachers and low student test passage rates. The teacher evaluation system without test score was "just baloney," in the governor's view.[91] Some parents also noted that the test scores are used for admission to selective public schools—options that are often meant to benefit non-white students.[92]

A final limitation on the opt-out movements was the small absolute numbers. Although some schools and classrooms did see dramatic vacancies—

Figure 4.2   PARCC Test Refusals by Median Household Income, 2015

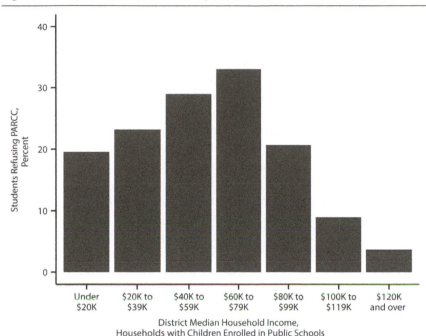

Source: New York State Education Department; U.S. Bureau of the Census.

in Colorado, some schools had fewer than 10 percent of students *take* Common Core-linked tests—the vast majority of students took the tests.[93] In New York State, for example, about 49,000 of 1.1 million eligible students opted out of the state ELA tests in 2013–2014; in 2014–2015, the anti-testing group United to Counter the Core estimated that 193,000 student opted out of the 2014–2015 ELA exams. New Jersey, which had active, organized opposition to the state's tests, had a 3.8 percent refusal rate for third to sixth grade and higher in high school in 2014–2015, according to the state department of education.[94] Colorado's 12th-grade exam had a 17 percent opt-out rate for fall 2014 but much lower rates in elementary and middle school.[95]

Still, elected officials were worried about this opposition. In Colorado, the state board of education passed a resolution to hold high-refusal districts harmless for violating the federal requirement that 95 percent of students be tested. "Districts still need to engage in good faith efforts to test all students in accordance with state and federal law and maintain documentation of parent refusals," the state superintendent said.[96] Colorado Governor

John Hickenlooper (D) said that parents "are not doing their kids any favors by opting out" and defended the state's participation in PARCC. U.S. Secretary of Education Arne Duncan, too, was ominous. If states did not raise their participation rates, he hinted that individual districts could lose their federal aid, a significant share of most districts' budgets. "We have an obligation to step in," he told a conference of education news writers. His department suggested that it was considering imposing penalties on "egregious" districts, and it specifically denied a request from Colorado to waive the 95-percent participation rule. "High-quality, annual, statewide assessments provide information on *all* students so that educators can improve educational outcomes, close achievement gaps between subgroups of historically underserved students and their more advantaged peers, increase equity, and improve instruction," an assistant secretary of education wrote in her denial.[97]

The scattered opposition to Common Core-linked testing became widespread enough that 39 states began efforts to reduce the number or kind of tests in 2015.[98] The broad-based opposition to the number of tests suggested that opponents of the Common Core had found a strategy for neutralizing the *effect* of the standards.

CONCLUSION

The motivation behind the Common Core State Standards was to improve standards for schools across the country. Some states would have had high standards and some schools even higher, but Core supporters were motivated by the desire to have a very high floor. That districts or states could not abandon common parts of the standards (but *could* add 15 percent) meant that districts would be equal and could be evaluated against every other district in the country. Further, the common aspects of the Core would allow data to be collected to compare teaching practices and learning environments in a way never before possible. There would be no excuses.

For opponents, this looked like an assault on local control and even individual liberty. Private schools, which were largely outside state regulations on curriculum, found themselves confronted with Common Core-aligned curriculum and sometime active support from private school trade organizations. Others worried that the "common" part of the Common Core would erode the individuality and character of private education that made their schools distinct. Despite the turbulence these debates caused, neither was as effective as assaults on a seemingly peripheral part of the Common Core universe, the associated tests. Parents who were concerned about privacy or "overtesting" simply had their students refuse to take the tests—and prompted lawmakers and the federal government to respond to the threat of grassroots disruption of the student assessment framework of NCLB.

Although the *vocal* opponents of the Common Core and testing were a small minority of parents, they tapped into widespread unease. Both testing and the Common Core faced strong opposition, and the opposition had not abated two years after the Core's introduction into schools. In late 2015, *Education Next* found results that gave the Common Core the odds of a swing-state politician. Some 46 percent of parents opposed the Common Core as such with some 37 percent of parents in favor. Proponents could take some solace in parents' support for accountability measures paired with the Common Core, though: When asked about using the standards "to hold schools accountable," parents' support for the Common Core rose to 47 percent and opposition fell to 41 percent.[99] A better result, perhaps, but the public's unease gave supporters little on which to build for the future. The large fraction of parents opposed to the Core gave vocal opponents fertile political ground. The Common Core was in peril.

FIVE

The Ghost of Education Future: Teachers, Tests, and Time

Under attack from some conservatives, proponents of the Common Core eagerly pointed to support from the teachers' unions that represent many of the teachers who would, after all, have to implement the standards in their classrooms. In 2013, Randi Weingarten, the president of the American Federation of Teachers (AFT), proclaimed that the Common Core would "transform the DNA of teaching and learning to ensure that all children, regardless of where they live, have . . . [what] they need to succeed."[1] She praised the AFT's involvement in funding the implementation of the standards, even as she later called for a "mid-course correction" in how they were actually being implemented.[2] Even the National Education Association (NEA), which had historically been more suspicious of standards, supported the effort because of "broad support from many groups of stakeholders" and because it "wanted to be sure that the concerns and voices of teachers were considered."[3] Supporters knew that many educational reforms had died in the classroom, as teachers failed to understand or see the value of new methods.[4] For Common Core, union support was crucial because even critics credited teachers' unions with the ability to break education reforms.[5] Having the unions on board was a political coup, *especially* because Race to the Top (RTTT) encouraged states to measure teacher performance partly with student test scores.

Yet this support was perched on an unusual political precipice. Both unions were strong critics of No Child Left Behind's (NCLB) emphasis on testing and its apparent attack on teacher professionalism through teacher quality standards. Although no one doubted that tests would be part of the Common Core package when Common Core became a known entity among educational elites, the political winds seemed to favor the unions. Indeed, if the NCLB of 2001 had been the Republicans' best hope at changing federal education policy, the Democrats seemed to have a near lock on it by 2009. In 2007, Democrats took control of both houses of Congress just as NCLB came up for reauthorization. Public support for adamantly pro-NCLB president George W. Bush was nearing record lows for an American president. Although the AFT was initially supportive of Democrat Hillary Clinton for the Democratic nomination (as were some NEA affiliates), both dutifully stumped for Barack Obama in 2008.[6] It seemed that unions would have a friendly Democratic Congress, a working relationship with a Democratic president, and the leverage that general NCLB fatigue would provide.

To unions, it seemed a good time to be on board; they could shape it all: the standards, the tests, and the implementation if they were in early—as the NEA's statement suggests. Common Core would be introduced in a Democratic environment. The NEA boasted in 2011 that even though the Common Core committees had few classroom teachers as members, "the standards project staff listened carefully to our teachers and made substantive changes in the standards based on the recommendations of our teachers."[7] At this point in 2011, most states were only beginning to tinker with the implementation of the standards locally; the promised exams were still four years down the road.

But as the haze around the as-yet-unfinished standards lifted, *members* of teachers' unions became restive. The tests that accompanied the standards *were* going to be used to evaluate teachers—that was also all but required by RTTT—and the results from students were likely to be bad. In New York, tests were to be used to determine up to 40 percent of teachers' and principals' ratings. Observers got an early read on what the new tests might look like when Kentucky, Georgia, Florida, and New York gave new standardized, Common Core–aligned exams in 2012 and 2013. State education chiefs warned of drops in the number of students meeting proficient targets, and that was, in fact, what happened. In Kentucky, math proficiency rates fell by a third; in New York, rates fell by 30 percentage points; just 41 percent of Georgia students were proficient in algebra; and half of Florida's students did not meet the reading standards.[8] The stress the tests would create on teachers was appropriate, New York Commissioner of Education John King said, because, "It's the fault of all the adults that we have a system that leaves 65 percent of students who start ninth grade unprepared."[9] In December 2015, King took the helm of the Department of Education when Arne Duncan stepped down.

Those adults—teachers and principals—took exception to the tests (and Commissioner King) for their link to teacher performance. The Common

Core Standards may have been fewer, higher, and better—but the tests were also much harder. For years, virtually all teachers had been rated as "highly qualified" as required under NCLB; the new tests challenged that legal designation. (Most states defined "highly qualified" based on a teacher's credentials and subject-matter degrees.) The New York State United Teachers (NYSUT) blamed the short timeline between adopting curriculum and rolling the tests out and said the tests were not valid measures of teachers' work. "These tests should not be considered a definitive summation of a student's ability or, for that matter, a teacher's effectiveness," Maria Neira, NYSUT vice-president, said in 2013.[10] Later, the union went further, calling for parents and teachers to "opt out" of state testing. The union said it would "vigorously defend" members if their district sought to discipline them for "speak[ing] out against the harmful effects of high-stakes tests."[11] And when the state legislature passed a budget giving the state education department the right to weight test results in teacher evaluation, NYSUT president Karen Magee told members that the union would fight. "Brothers and sisters, we didn't start this war, but with your help, we will end it," she said.[12] New York was an extreme case—the Democratic governor was especially combative with the unions, and the education commissioner built no bridges on the test. It was also one of the first to implement teacher assessment with new tests with all the attendant early adopter glitches and troubles. But if it was the extreme case, the pushback there laid bare the political troubles assessment would face elsewhere in muted tones.

A core purpose of the Common Core was to push instruction and advance education for low-performing students and low-performing schools, a purpose which was impossible without comparable data. A widely cited pro-Common Core blogger, RiShawn Biddle, argued that the commonality of the standards would be largely meaningless unless common assessments could smoke out political favors. "One of the underlying reasons why states banded together through PARCC and Smarter Balanced to develop the tests," he wrote, "is to effectively move proficiency target-setting from state boards of education, which have been prone to setting low cut scores because of pressure to lower expectations from suburban districts, middle-class white suburban households, and affiliates of the National Education Association and the American Federation of Teachers."[13] Mike McShane, an education policy fellow at the American Enterprise Institute (an organization which was ambivalent about the standards), recognized the conflict. "Standards don't really mean anything—they're just words on a page," he said. "It's the assessments that actually make them real. So the thought that you can . . . magically have one without the other . . . I just don't think is possible."[14] The designers of the Common Core recognized this, and it is not for nothing that after leaving the development of the Common Core, David Coleman became president of the College Board. His new position would ensure that at least the SAT would be aligned to the standards. The federal government, too, directly subsidized the development of Common Core–aligned tests by funding the Partnership for Assessment of Readiness for College and Careers (PARCC) and Smarter Balanced Assessment Consortium (SBAC).

Despite critics' displeasure with the Common Core–aligned tests, assessment and accountability predated the standards, and even should they succeed in dismantling the PARCC, SBAC, or any other Common Core–aligned tests, it appeared unlikely that assessment would disappear, particularly teacher assessment. Like the Common Core, teacher assessment had strong bipartisan support. Unlike the evidence linking standards to academic performance, research is definitive that teacher quality drives student academic achievement.[15] But teachers also have a powerful political force in the two national teachers' unions, and the unions were opposed to assessing teachers using student performance. Thus, one explanation for the upsurge in opposition to the Common Core–aligned tests was that the standards had already suffered political damage. Testing opponents sought to capitalize on the Common Core's wounds to roll back a related policy. That was a political strategy, and the close identification of the Common Core with assessment did neither the standards nor the exams any favors.

Still, the combination of these almost universally adopted standards and the annual-testing regimen that the federal government required created a potent and explosive combination for the Common Core itself. As explored in other chapters, the Common Core curriculum framework itself drew criticism for its pedagogical choices, its method of adoption, its exemplar texts, and the shadowy role of the federal government. These arguments were typically too abstract to rally opponents; the tests were not. They are a focal point of the school year and take hours of classroom time. While Common Core–aligned tests were *not* the Common Core, most legislators, lobbyists, and certainly opponents linked the two. In North Carolina, for example, a committee hearing on a bill to replace the state's Common Core–aligned assessment test was dominated by discussion of the Common Core itself.[16] Michigan legislators who supported dropping the SBAC test similarly equated the two. And they have attracted opposition from heavily Democratic teachers' unions, better-off parents, and conservative politicians seeking to undercut the Common Core. The opposition faults the tests for their links to teacher performance, alleged testing overkill, and—again—federal overreach.

First, the tests would be used by many states to evaluate teachers' performance. Like the adoption of the Core, states agreed to use student performance in part when assessing teachers to win points for RTTT. Measuring teachers this way was novel for most of them. For teachers' groups, the affront that testing appears to be was compounded by the limited input teachers had on the design of the Common Core itself. By 2014, both national unions—the AFT and the NEA—had passed resolutions calling for major changes, if not abandonment, of the Common Core Standards as implemented. With the rise of anti-Core union leaders in Chicago, Massachusetts, New Jersey, and New York, the Common Core gained formidable liberal opponents. Like conservatives, teachers' unions have condemned the loss of local curricular input, the invasion of privacy, and "an overreach of federal power." Unlike many conservative organizations, however, teachers' unions and their supporters decried the Common Core's "toxic testing" and especially the use of students' test results to evaluate teachers' classroom performance.[17]

Second, critics tarred the Common Core tests as "testing overkill . . . [from] the same, incompetent, profit-driven companies."[18] They also argued that the tests harm learning rather than promote it. While these critics leveled similar charges at the testing requirements of NCLB and its predecessors, they argued that Common Core tests were typically longer and given more grades than pre-existing state NCLB tests. Better-off parents, too, had taken the lead in opting their children out of the exams. Although districts in New York, New Jersey, and Colorado received a lion's share of media attention, students in many other states also have refused to take the tests. Their objection was only sometimes to the Common Core itself; more often their opposition was to a heightened sense of the "culture of testing." A founder of the parent-organization group New York State Allies for Public Education told a Rockland, N.Y, *Journal News* panel that Common Core testing was demoralizing and served no purpose. "We're not going to opt-in to harmful tests," she said.[19]

Third, politicians, often conservatives, used the exams as another avenue to attack the alleged federal overreach of the Common Core. These critics charged that states and testing companies rushed to meet *political* deadlines, suggesting that test results would be a reflection of poor implementation rather than student learning. They latched on to high-cost overruns, scoring problems, lapses in test security, and computer troubles in many states, including Colorado, Florida, Illinois, Minnesota, Montana, Nevada, New Jersey, North Dakota, and Wisconsin.[20] Elsewhere, district officials publicly argued that their districts could not meaningfully retool for the exams on schedule.[21] Typically, these politicians used these real troubles to call for state-designed tests—and perhaps new, state-designed standards along the way. They used the widespread disenchantment with the exams and the relatively high cost of the exams to undercut the Common Core itself.

These controversies may not threaten the future of the Common Core as a set of standards, but they have seriously damaged one of the pillars of the Core: holding students and teachers accountable for a common set of standards nationwide. Without some common assessment framework, there would be no way to know how well students or teachers were progressing on the Core's standards. Unlike much of the conservative criticism, this strand of opposition has met with some success. Attacks on "Common Core tests" have prompted many states to abandon the federally funded testing consortia—withdrawals abetted by both Republican and Democratic governors. This is bipartisan opposition. Yet, as with other critiques of the Common Core, none of these are unique to the standards. Instead, they reflect a long-standing, deep-seated controversy over the place of the teacher in the classroom and the role of external oversight of schools. Earlier forms of the argument came in the guise of teacher licensure reforms, credit-hour standards, school report cards, and even school choice. The Common Core tests are only the latest iteration.

MEASURING STUDENTS AND TEACHERS

The recent controversy over testing is odd from one perspective. Standardized testing is nearly a century old. The Stanford Achievement Test (for elementary grades and higher, and different than the SAT college-entrance exam) was introduced in 1926 and the Iowa Test of Basic Skills in 1935, and their widespread use in American education began with a push from the federal government for financial accountability and civil rights, and from the states as an indicator of economic competitiveness. Most recently, they became a means to reshape the teacher workforce. The arrival of Common Core–aligned tests drew them into this policy debate.

Students

In the early 1960s, policy makers knew anecdotally that low-income and non-white students did less well in school than their white or higher-income peers, although the causal mechanism was unclear. Federal courts had held that segregation was unconstitutional, but the central case *Brown v. Board of Education* (1954) relied on the apparent sociological effects rather than academic outcomes or school spending. No one *knew* how desegregation or increased spending would affect learning. U.S. Commissioner of Education Francis Keppel, who was later a designer of the Elementary and Secondary

Education Act (ESEA), argued that "American education had not yet faced up to the question of how to determine the quality of academic performance in schools . . . The nation could find out about school buildings or discover how many years children stay in school; [but] it had no satisfactory way or assessing whether the time spent in school was effective."[22] As appropriate for an official on the brink of a landmark expansion of federal intervention in schools, Keppel wanted to have the tools to show federal activity worked. In 1963, Keppel convinced a panel of testing experts including well-known testing expert Ralph Tyler to design a national exam to measure academic and civil rights progress. That exam became the National Assessment of Educational Progress (NAEP). In 1964, Congress followed suit and commissioned the Equality of Educational Opportunity (usually known as the Coleman Report) study in the Civil Rights Act of 1964, which, among other things, administered standardized tests to thousands of children. Policy makers saw standardization as a useful metric to uncover discrimination and disparities in education.

Both the Coleman Report and the NAEP came in for criticism. James Coleman's report was controversial for its conclusion that schools were far less important to education than a student's home and community environment (although some have suggested the data was less pessimistic than the report suggested).[23] Criticism of NAEP, however, was eerily similar to those made by Common Core opponents. Keppel summarized the opposition:

[One] fear is that [NAEP] enables the federal government to control the curriculum. This is . . . a misunderstanding. The objectives to be assessed are those which are accepted by teachers and curriculum specialists as goals toward which they work. They have been reviewed by lay leaders throughout the country so as to include only aims deemed important by public-spirited citizens.

[Another] fear is sometimes raised that this project would stultify the curriculum by not allowing changes over the years in instructional methods and educational goals. It should be made clear that the project will assess what children, youth, and adults have learned, not how they have learned it. Hence, the assessment is not dependent upon any particular instructional methods.[24]

The political pushback from teachers, school administrators, and curriculum specialists was intense. The American Association of School Administrators encouraged members to opt out of tests, and a national English teachers' organization told teachers to "fight" the move to measure education.[25]

The controversy prompted the test's designers to largely abandon its expansive scope. The original design for NAEP included many questions about students' civic values, political activity, and other non-academic aspects of schooling. The test was also to give at least state-level results for comparison.[26] Both the questions and comparisons were scrapped. In 1994, states were encouraged to join NAEP to allow state-level results, and in 2001, states were required to do so.

Yet, in the 50 years since its inception, the NAEP has been the sole nationally representative exam; and even at that level, the NAEP uncovered the persistent race and ethnic performance gap. After 1994, it also found differences in student performance between states. In that, it has fulfilled Keppel's intent: policy makers now know that disparities in American education exist both within and between states. Indeed, the gaps the NAEP identified helped motivate the Common Core. Not only is the exam cited in the Common Core State Standards Initiative's (CCSSI) official materials, but the NAEP also demonstrated that state assessments set very low bars to success.[27] That is, compared with the NAEP, all states except Massachusetts reported much higher rates of student proficiency than did the NAEP, as described in Chapter 2.

To race and income inequality, though, were added other political considerations in the 1970s, especially by governors. America's economic funk and widespread dissatisfaction with the federal government prompted state governors to argue that improved education could be a driver of economic performance. Many governors wanted to retool education to meet business needs, and tests seemed one way to measure it. Some 33 states had some form of competency test before graduation, partly to allay the complaints from businesses that high school graduates were not ready for employment.[28] This narrative became a juggernaut once an obscure federal education commission issued *Nation at Risk* in 1983 pointing to the "rising tide of mediocrity" and noted a "virtually unbroken decline" in standardized test scores since 1963. The "risk" was that poor academic performance threatened "our once unchallenged preeminence in commerce, industry, science, and technological innovation."[29] Governors also sought to show that education spending was *effective*—in 1986, Missouri Governor John Ashcroft told the National Governors Association (NGA) that, "the public has the right to know what it is getting for its expenditure of tax resources. . . . They have a right to know that their resources are being wisely invested and committed."[30] Ohio Governor George Voinovich extended the argument and suggested that education was effective for employment as well. Before his election in 1990, he had been the mayor of Cleveland, where he had successfully brokered financial and academic improvements in the troubled

Cleveland School District with the assistance of business groups in that city. As governor, he sought to use the Ohio Department of Education to tailor the state's ninth-grade proficiency tests to business wishes.[31]

The linking of testing for civil rights and testing for economic development was a powerful political driver. In the decade following the Civil Rights Act of 1964, the use of standardized tests rose by a quarter and 30 percent again by 1980.[32] This political argument prefigured the federal partisan agreement that became NCLB and the subsequent broad acceptance of common standards across the political spectrum—David Coleman, as president of the College Board, suggested that this was one of two education policy areas that were uniquely non-partisan in the 2010s. The other was teacher evaluation.[33]

By the 1990s, the purposes of testing expanded again—this time to ensure that *schools* were using tax dollars efficiently and effectively. Although some governors promoted financially efficient schools, state courts forced the hands of others. A series of state court cases beginning with *Rose v. Council for Better Education* (1989) suggested that (some) state constitutions required educational equity and adequacy. The courts defined adequacy to mean that students *could* meet state standards, and those standards would be measured across the state by state tests. Low-performing schools and districts took this finding to argue that unless and until their students performed better on standardized tests, state legislatures should provide increased financial support.[34] In arguments before the Colorado Supreme Court, for example, the assistant attorney general argued that equal student performance *could* be used as a yardstick to meet a (state) constitutional standard for equity, although the legislature had never used performance this way.[35] The Supreme Court of Ohio explicitly said that the state had to provide money to districts to meet mandates, including those regarding the state's graduation test. The plaintiffs in the case made a specific recommendation: in part, "the cost of an adequate education" would be the sum of money necessary for "75 percent of the eligible students [to pass] each part of the 9th Grade Proficiency Test."[36] The purpose of standardized tests was turned on its head: instead of highlighting *schools or students* that needed improvement, the tests would show where the *state* needed improvement.

By the end of that decade, then, policy makers across the spectrum believed that standardized tests were a valid, reliable, and useful measure of academic outputs. This agreement was a sea change from the 1960s, when stakeholders decried the sacrilege of standardized testing in education. Many saw increased education as one of the few levers for economic advancement, Republicans wanted schools to be accountable for results, and Democrats wanted to ensure that schools did not segregate non-white, non-Asian students into learning-disabled classrooms to boost their scores. The testing requirements of the NCLB Act of 2001 reflect that agreement. Tests seemed to be both an external monitor *and* external motivator.

Teachers

Support for standardized tests for students was widespread by 2001, but their use for evaluating teachers was far more politically controversial. Students did not have political representation, workplace advocates, or national interest groups to represent them; teachers have all three. Still, when these teachers' groups protested the use of Common Core–aligned tests to measure teacher performance, they only revived a long-running debate over the status of teaching. Is a teacher a professional or just a skilled employee? In the mid-20th century, the AFT and the NEA spent substantial political capital, making the argument that "what teachers want is what children need." The unions argued that teachers were professionals, like doctors or lawyers, who were well informed and could make careful and reasonable judgments about students. Because no one knew *how* learning happened—and it certainly seemed to happen different ways—there could be no uniform way to teach. With the right training and credentials, they argued that teachers were uniquely suited to make classroom choices. As a corollary, because teachers could be expected to tailor instruction to individual students, outside supervision was not only disruptive but also harmful to the learning process. The outsiders could not know the folkways of the classroom. The landmark Coleman Report (1966) appeared to confirm this view. Coleman noted that "the quality of teachers shows a stronger relationship to pupil achievement [than school materials], . . . [but] the results are not at all conclusive regarding the specific characteristics of teachers."[37] To protect teachers' independence, unions fought for and won significant job protections and collective bargaining rights.

But by the late 1990s, it had become clear to policy makers that *some* characteristics of teachers correlated with student performance, although no research to date has demonstrated precisely how to *predict* quality teaching.[38] Early reforms focused on teacher training because low-performing students, and especially low-performing non-white students, were more often in classrooms with non-credentialed teachers with few (or no) years of experience.[39] States sought to boost teacher training at the front end by instituting multilevel licenses with periodic review from "master teachers." The federal government, in the Higher Education Act (1998), required colleges of education to test teacher candidates for "knowledge and skills."[40] Some reformers suggested an apprenticeship system.[41]

Teacher preparation was still no magic bullet. Teachers who pursued certification by the rigorous and well-regarded National Board for Professional Teaching Standards (NBPTS) seemed to be better teachers as measured by students' test performance, but the effect was small.[42] Further, studies of those teachers suggest that the quality pre-existed the certification. Washington State, which gave teachers a bonus for becoming so certified, allowed teachers to retake parts of the certification process if they did not meet standards. Students of teachers who had to retake parts of the exam showed *no* difference in test scores as a result of the certification.[43]

This persistent tension between professionalism and variable teacher quality prompted the federal government to adopt a hands-off approach. Perhaps teachers cannot be trained to be uniformly high quality and their quality known in advance, but surely *student results* can weed out weak teachers. Over time, then, the teacher corps would become stronger.

This is the logic of external accountability. State governments can set standards for teachers. High-quality teachers will be able to meet them— even if they, or researchers, cannot tell why or how they can. Although a handful of states had been experimenting with rewarding teachers for students' performance before 2009, Obama's RTTT signaled a new emphasis on the approach. To win points for the competition, states could design teacher evaluation systems to reward (or exit) teachers. The catch was that student score growth was to be a "significant factor." Beginning in 2011, the Obama administration formalized this approach by offering to waive elements of the much-disliked NCLB in return for new teacher assessments (among other policies). That meant that the new Common Core tests, just entering their final development stages, would be used as the evaluation instrument. The connection was not lost on wary teachers.[44]

COMMON CORE TESTS FOR TEACHER QUALITY?

Teachers' and teachers' union concerns with Common Core–aligned tests revolve around three topics: use of testing for the assessment of teachers, lack of resources for teachers to prepare for testing, and lack of local input on the standards and tests.

First, although teachers' unions have raised concerns about the appropriateness of tests for students or for teachers, by far the most controversial aspect of the Common Core tests has been their use in connection with teacher performance. This criticism ranges from concern about the lack of effective evidence, to rushed implementation, to ideological opposition to evaluating teachers. An open letter written in 2012 by New York principals Sean Feeney and Carol Burris is evidence of the first approach. Their letter, signed by 1,525 other principals, emphasized the statistical and practical problems of relying on student test scores for assessment of students, teachers, or principals. They recount research showing that over 85 percent of students' performance can be traced to non-classroom factors, including home life, race, ethnicity, income, and peer group. On that count alone, it would be difficult *not* to penalize teachers with high concentrations of students with low-performing characteristics *despite* teachers' best efforts. Further, they document that average student scores vary significantly from year to year in any given classroom. Although data may point to overall trends, or even to school district trends, they argue that the tests are not designed to measure teachers. "Using them to measure the latter teachers is akin to using a meter stick to weigh a person: you might be able to develop a formula that links height and weight, but there will be plenty of error in your calculations," they write.[45] These concerns prompt them to suggest that if student evaluation must be used, then the scores should be used to create school-wide "score bands." The bands—they suggest "ineffective," "developing," "effective," and "highly effective"—would mitigate unstable test scores and reduce the problem of uncertainty. (Incidentally, these suggestions model the pre-existing requirement of NCLB). This argument was echoed by AFT president Randi Weingarten later that year in a speech calling for a delay in teacher evaluation based on Common Core tests.[46] Among other things, she worried that the tests had simply been imposed "from on high" and called for them to be "field-tested" before any evaluation be linked to the standards.

Second, others suggested that the quick rollout of the Common Core left districts and teachers flat-footed. Because the Common Core was adopted too quickly, "Common Core" material was not available in many districts until well into the school year in which testing was supposed to start. (This was one reason that the Common Core and testing were so closely linked. The tests were meant to measure items from the Common Core, but neither aligned curriculum nor the training was yet finished. The tests depended on Common Core.) George Miller (D-CA), a liberal Democrat and strong supporter of the Common Core, called for a "smart pause" in 2014. "If [the standards] are fully developed, you have something to evaluate," he said. Otherwise, the Common Core would fall prey to the same testing morass that had plagued NCLB, he said.[47] Miller's support for a testing delay was important because he has been a long-time proponent of evaluating teachers and a sharp critic of teacher preparation (at one point calling it a "fraud").[48] In New Jersey, the NEA affiliate successfully won a reprieve on teacher evaluation when Gov. Christie created a special "Study Commission" after vigorous complains about the standards' rollout. Wendell Steinhauser, the union president, called the speedy rollout of the Common Core and related tests "a perfect storm," especially around the limited ability of teachers to appeal their evaluations drawn from student scores. "It is unfair to teachers and students to make high-stakes decisions based on a new test, one that has not had a state-wide field test."[49]

A third group adopted less-measured language to protest the assessment of teaching and learning. Representatives of AFT, NEA, and many other Democrats acknowledged that perhaps the Common Core was rushed, perhaps the tests were not field-tested, and perhaps the measures needed tweaking, but they defended the standards themselves as essentially sound. It was the "implementation," not the "curriculum." But the tests attracted far more strident opposition from a grassroots teacher group known as the Badass Teachers Association (known as BAT). This group began in June 2013 to "erase" poverty and refuse "assessments, tests and evaluations imposed by those who have contempt for real teaching and learning."[50] Although the group is small relative to the teachers' unions (the group claims about 50,000 members), it scored some notable recruitment successes, and it amplified the concerns of teachers who believed that the tests were disconnected from actual classroom practice. The group decried standardized testing as "not objectively reliable" and argued that poor scores point not to schools or teachers but to student poverty. In its place, BAT advocated "a much stronger alternative to this narrow vision of accountability: practice standards and teacher evaluations that are democratically developed by incorporating the voices of the people closest to the real problems of students—classroom teachers, children and their parents."[51] Although BAT has made no secret of its contempt for the tests, the core of their view appeared to be shared by a majority of teachers. In 2012, a survey done by the pro-Core Bill & Melinda Gates Foundation and Scholastic, Inc., found that only 28 percent of teachers thought state-standardized tests were "very important" or "absolutely essential" to measure achievement (a similar number thought the same of district-required tests). Teachers placed much greater faith in their own assignments as 91 percent of teachers said that doing so was "very important" or "absolutely essential" to measure students' preparedness for the next level of education.[52]

In this regard, perhaps one of the most noteworthy BAT successes was the election of Barbara Madeloni as president of the Massachusetts Teachers Association (MTA) in 2014.[53] Massachusetts was widely acknowledged to have the most rigorous academic standards prior to Common Core and a well-regarded state assessment system as well. The outgoing MTA president, Paul Toner, had been a supporter of Common Core and the Massachusetts' assessment system. The change in leadership could not have been more dramatic. Unlike Toner, the *Boston Globe* called Madeloni "pointed, confrontational," and her positions were sharply different than his.[54] Madeloni made no secret of her opposition to the Common Core. Her campaign materials listed eight reasons she opposes the Core, but two indicate her loyalty best. First, the Common Core *assessments* were "imposed" and were invalid because they did not "trust . . . classroom teachers and their professional knowledge" of students' needs. Second, she argued in the same vein that the "Common Core severely limits the voices of educators, their expertise, and their academic freedom."[55] Elsewhere she argued that "teacher development occurs best in the context of autonomy"—something the Common Core limits.[56] She described herself as an "outspoken critic" of tests who "boycotted a Pearson, Inc., field test" when she was an instructor at the University of Massachusetts and encouraged organized protests against testing at a Miami opt-out convention.[57] There was no question that testing, and Common Core testing, was squarely in her sights.

BAT's and Madeloni's opposition to common testing and promotion of teacher autonomy was not new. John Dewey advocated for autonomy in 1903, a call picked up and amplified by American teachers' unions since then. Recent scholars of teaching have also argued the point. Linda Darling-Hammond, a professor of Education at Stanford University and Sen. Barack Obama's education advisor for his 2008 presidential campaign, argued that assessment was inappropriate for teachers. Instead, Darling-Hammond argued, "Developing more-skillful teaching is a *sine qua non* for attaining higher and more equitable achievement for students in the United States."[58] The Common Core did not meet her expectations, and she was "fearful" that the Common Core would be detrimental to teachers, especially because of the "federal insistence on implementing sanctions for teachers." She describes her ideal system as one in which "educators are regularly convened over several years to revise the national or state curriculum expectations . . . unfortunately, this was not the process used to develop and roll out the CCSS."[59] (Even with her concerns, Darling-Hammond agreed to become an advisor to SBAC.)

Other Democrats were less sanguine. Diane Ravitch, a Democrat, had put her partisanship aside to work for high national standards in the George H. W. Bush administration. In her book criticizing testing, she reminisced about the intangible quality of her high school English teacher. Of her teacher, she wrote, "her greatness as a teacher—her ability to inspire students and to change their lives—would go unrewarded because it is not in demand and cannot be measured."[60] She argued that testing myopia would cascade to students: "What is tested may be ultimately less important that what is untested. . . . If we do not treasure our individualists, we will lose the spirit of innovation, inquiry, imagination, and dissent."[61] For her, testing deprived teachers of life.

The lack of teacher input on the tests and the perceived loss of teacher autonomy made the Common Core and its tests increasingly difficult for some Democrats to abide. Indeed, the self-styled "progressive" wing of the party took to attacking Arne Duncan as an unqualified elitist. Joel Spring, a left-leaning textbook author, hashed Duncan: "It's hard to explain Duncan's rapid rise from professional basketball player to head of the Chicago school system after only eight years of running a mentoring program and working in a charter school." He credited ties to Chicago investment banking firms.[62] Dora Taylor, selected as a "featured writer" by *The Progressive*, likened Duncan's time as a "reign of terror" and himself leaving a "slimy trail" from Chicago.[63] But the opposition to standards and testing was deeper than opposition to Duncan. As teachers' unions in Massachusetts, New York, New Jersey, Washington, Colorado, and elsewhere led opt-out movements and complained about the perceived loss of autonomy, the major national unions found it difficult to continue to trumpet the virtues of the Common Core. NEA president Dennis Van Roekel told members that the Common Core's rollout had been "botched." "NEA members have a right to feel frustrated, upset and angry about the poor commitment to implementing the standards correctly," he said—despite the NEA's own large pro-Common Core outreach program, complete with lesson plans.[64] Weingarten of the AFT initially followed suit in softer language, but in early 2015 endorsed teacher "opt-outs" to protest Common Core–aligned assessment. "We believe parents have [the] right to opt-out and teachers should be able to advise parents how," she wrote. If she had children in the public school system, "I'd opt them out of the Pearson (PAARC [*sic*]) test this year."[65]

The Common Core was not made to measure teachers, but it worried some and infuriated others. While this very Democratic constituency was unlikely to roil Republican education plans, it threatened to undermine the bipartisan consensus forged with NCLB. Paul Toner, the former MTA president, was a Democrat, as was his successor. Whereas one argued for working with the Common Core, the other blasted the Democratic president's RTTT. Yet it was undeniable that teachers' unions had become scourges of the exams. The danger to the Common Core was real. Education reform founders when teachers revolt.

COMMON CORE TESTS AS CLASSROOM DISRUPTION?

Although the use of the Common Core–aligned tests generated ire among teachers' groups, the number and length of tests also raised opposition from teachers and parents. Initially, some saw Common Core as a way to reduce the hodgepodge of standards and tests prevailing under NCLB, but the initial steps toward assessing the Core proved disappointing. The PARCC and SBAC tests proved to be at least as numerous, longer, more expensive, and prone to embarrassing technical glitches as previous standardized tests. Secretary of Education Arne Duncan only inflamed matters in November 2013 when he memorialized testing opponents as "suburban white moms" who have discovered their children "aren't as brilliant as they thought they were."[66] That comment was politically tone-deaf, and social media lit up with outrage—from white, suburban moms, but also from others. Suburban moms did indeed comprise some of the opponents of the Core, but Duncan's caricature was too narrow.

Prominent Common Core critic Carol Burris, on the left, noted that "the problem [with Common Core testing] is one of vanity. But it is not the vanity of suburban moms who think too highly of their children. Instead, the problem may be the vanity of those who refuse to admit that they may not be the civil rights heroes they believe themselves to be."[67] Others saw lurking racism in the debate. One, a left-leaning associate professor of Education at Furman University, argued that the Common Core had become political only because "whites" were affected. "Duncan has personified and voiced an education agenda that disproportionately impacts black, brown, and poor children in powerfully negative ways," Paul L. Thomas wrote. "The same urgency witnessed in the responses to Duncan's 'white suburban moms' contrasts significantly from the silence surrounding challenges to Duncan's discourse and policies that are classist and racist, policy designed for 'other people's children.'"[68]

Duncan's comment and its fallout highlighted a political schism that was not partisan but local. Many of these critics argued that federal and especially state bureaucrats were aloof and deliberately ignoring problems and local anger over, not the standards themselves, but testing. Teachers and parents faulted the tests because of the disruption they created to learning. A pro-Core writer at the *Atlantic* in early 2015 still found suburban opposition puzzling, but she did admit that the *national* character of the standards could lead to political disenfranchisement. "Suburban parents who are known for being particularly involved in their kids' education and traditionally enjoy a good deal of influence on district policymaking, are frustrated by not being able to convince their local school boards to alter the standards or testing requirements," the author noted.[69] This feeling of disempowerment in the face of (alleged) federal policy was widespread.

The most visible of these critics were the hundreds of thousands of families who "opted-out" from taking state Common Core exams. These mini-protest movements gained national attention as union leaders like Randi Weingarten and Chicago Teachers Union President Karen Lewis promoted opt-outs and indeed encouraged teachers to resist administering the test.[70] But by and large, parents became the face of "opt outs." When pressed, most gave reasons relating to over-testing, length of the tests, "developmentally inappropriate" exams, or student stress. One parent told Utah Governor Herbert, "Testing results are more often low which negatively (and erroneously) sends students and their families this crushing message: 'You'll never amount . . .' 'Your options are limited!' 'You can't move forward!' 'You're not progressing in school, so you certainly WON'T succeed in college or in life.' Is such REALLY the message Utah wants to send out?" Others simply said that they did not want teachers evaluated with the test results.[71] For others, trust in teachers as professionals was paramount. "These standards cause the educational system to turn into a testing society," one Utah parent said.

> If you can't test it, then you shouldn't be teaching it. Testing and following educational standards will destroy the one thing that makes Americans so special—the passion to learn about the unknown and creativity to make it happen. If you check with China, teaching and learning inside a box is what they've done wrong in the past. They've learned what America has done right in the past and headed for it. Trust the professional educators to teach the passion of what they've done in the past. Forcing them to teach to a test and a standard that they didn't create is mistake that will change America to the worse.

That sentiment was shared by parents in other states as well, as they also made an explicit link between the Common Core and student assessment. Others intimated that the tests were simply another manifestation of the loss of local control, and especially input from local educators. "I do believe this is a historic day in New York State, as we try to regain local control over the education of our kids. These refusals are meant to protest a system that is currently failing our children and educators," one New York City area parent told reporters.[72]

Interest groups and district officials registered similar concerns with the exams, especially regarding their length. This was no surprise; in 2013, the National Center for Fair and Open Testing, a long-time testing critic, claimed that "the Common Core will flood classrooms with even more tests . . . the tests will be longer than current state exams."[73] The numbers in the states bore this out. In Ohio, for example, a student in a typical district would take about five hours of standardized exams over the course of a year prior to the adoption of the Common Core. The PARCC tests in Ohio, however, took approximately 10–13 hours to administer depending on the grade level—more than double the time. A Columbus-area superintendent complained that the tests detracted from learning and organized a local summit to discuss them, saying, "We're losing too much time for instruction. We're creating an atmosphere that is built on testing and not teaching and growing young people."[74] A teacher in Colorado gained national attention when she refused to administer the PARCC tests for much the same reason: "I am watching an onslaught of Common Core curriculum infiltrate our schools, along with additional tests and test prep to add to the test load which permeates every minute of every school day. . . . I refuse to administer the PARCC because I believe that participation in such testing gives the test credibility—of which it has none."[75] Others noted an increase in student stress. A group of New York principals reported that the tests "requir[ed] more stamina for a 10-year-old special education student" than for those taking the SAT, but even so "the time was insufficient for the length of the tests." As a result, the tests seemed to generate widespread "frustration, despondency, and even crying . . . . The extremes were unprecedented: vomiting, nosebleeds, suicidal ideation, and even hospitalization."[76]

Supporters were quick to defend the tests even as they tried to accommodate some of the loudest complaints. They noted that the number of tests that students took *could* remain the same as before the arrival of Common Core assessments.[77] They also showed that the Common Core was not responsible for the "culture of testing"; the majority of tests that students took were required by states or districts instead. In 2012, half of the state required high school exit exams and 15 required end-of-course exams as well.[78] In their study of 14 urban and suburban districts, the Center for American Progress found that K–2 students took three times as many district tests as state tests, while high schoolers took twice as many district tests as state tests.[79] They also found that testing took less than 2 percent of instructional time.[80] Similarly, Teach Plus, a Massachusetts education reform organization, found that testing in schools was driven primarily by local assessments, but the organization found significant variation in both state and district tests. Chicago Public School students took 3.1 hours of district tests and 4.5 of state tests while Cleveland, OH, administered 14.5 hours of district tests and 10.5 of state tests. Overall, "high-testing" districts gave more than three times as many tests as "low-testing" districts, a disparity that belies the political opposition to the Common Core.[81] If districts "overtest," they may themselves be a major part of the problem.[82] Supporters of standardized tests could also take heart; a poll conducted by the

National Opinion Research Center (NORC) in 2013 found that 61 percent of parents agreed that their students took the appropriate number of standardized tests; only 26 percent thought there were too many. This gap is even more favorable to standardized tests among non-white parents.[83] An *Education Next* poll found 66 percent support from parents.[84]

The length of the Common Core–aligned tests was not an accident because both the SBAC and PARCC tests were designed to measure more than rote learning. Secretary of Education Arne Duncan wanted the RTTT competition to privilege tests of higher-order thinking. "It is time to think beyond assessing students with narrowly-focused bubble tests," he told the National PTA. He promised that the replacements would test "the higher-order skills that students need to survive and thrive in the 21st century."[85] Unlike most "bubble tests," these Common Core tests were meant to measure problem solving, and so required students to show their work and write out answers (usually on a computer). Some opposition to the tests was based on a misunderstanding of testing technology. Computer-adaptive tests, which some states used, did not give every student the same questions and were not meant to give a "passing" score, confusing some opponents. How could a test measure standards if each student did not receive the same questions? They wondered. But Duncan was right in that the newer tests were able to measure student learning to a much better degree than bubble tests. As such, proponents of the test argued that these were fundamentally better tests.

Further, they noted that the tests would advance civil rights even better than bubble tests had. A progressive blogger took fellow-travelers to task for rooting for the failure of the tests. Alternet, a progressive Web site, cited an anti-testing principal with approval: "The whole school reform machine falls down without the data." The blogger responded, "Indeed, the school reform movement DOES fall down without the data. So do the movements around climate change, civil rights, public health, banking reform, industrial safety, economic justice and more. It's odd for a progressive outfit like Alternet (which is run by the former publisher of *Mother Jones*) and others to be cheering on the loss of data when it comes to the systematic failure of children of color in our traditional public schools," she wrote.[86]

Still, both state consortia were sensitive to the length of time the tests might take. SBAC cut the number of "performance tasks" (such as writing a short essay) by two-thirds in 2012.[87] Initially, PARCC would have required *three* tests spaced throughout the school year, but the board discarded that as untenable. The SBAC was also scaled back. While disappointing to some, proponents realized the political difficulty of creating a 10-hour exam. "The price point people felt they could manage politically has meant we're doing less than we could have done, and it will not signal as firmly that we want kids to demonstrate their learning," Linda Darling-Hammond, the advisor to SBAC, told *Education Week* in 2014.[88]

This sensitivity did not mollify critics. Lee County, FL, public schools voted to end all Common Core tests and state-required end-of-course exams in 2014 in response to mobilized parents. Parental discontent and complaints from the teachers' union prompted a similar response from the school board of the Colorado Springs, CO, District 11. At a board meeting, the union argued that 30 percent of classroom time was spent on preparing for tests. The board proposed giving only a small random sample of students the PARCC test and eliminating it for the rest.[89] The school board noted their resolution was driven by "local control" and the need for teachers to "adapt to new standards and tests."[90]

In the short run as neither district successfully ended their districts' participation in state tests. Lee County's board rescinded their resolution a week later after their superintendent noted that students could not receive diploma under state law without the tests.[91] The Colorado Springs board's appeal to the state was denied as there was no legal way for a district to opt out of state requirements on behalf of students.[92]

In the long run, however, the tests appeared to be in greater danger as Common Core opponents used both the length of the test and their costs to justify rolling back participation in the name of teacher expertise and local control. Table 5.1 shows both testing consortia membership and the dates of withdrawal for states. PARCC, which only provides Pearson-designed tests, saw the greatest attrition. SBAC member states use tests from a variety of providers.

Ohio provides an instructive example. Legislators there introduced legislation in August 2014 to replace the Common Core with Massachusetts' pre-Core state standards; the bill did not have support from either Gov. John Kasich (R) or many legislators.[93] The bill was significant because it would have *also* allowed districts to opt out of state tests—an issue that continued to fester even as the broader bill failed. Kasich noted that he was ambivalent about the standards themselves, but not the tests. "Is the test good? Well, I don't know . . . If the test is goofy, we'll just throw the test out. I think we have too many tests. . . . What do I care about Common Core? I just want kids to learn," he said. "I don't have any ideological, personal, or emotional commitment to anything other than: Let's make sure our kids do well."[94] But the tests motivated him and the General Assembly to require the Ohio Department of Education to recommend limiting state tests.

The state superintendent did, and recommended cutting time spent on tests almost 20 percent—limiting them to no more than 2 percent of

Table 5.1   Membership and Withdrawal from Multi-State Testing Consortia

PARCC		SBAC	
State	Date of Withdrawal	State	Date of Withdrawal
Colorado		California	
District of Columbia		Connecticut	
Illinois		Delaware	
Maryland		Hawaii	
Massachusetts*		Idaho	
New Jersey		Michigan	
New Mexico		Montana	
Rhode Island		Nevada	
		New Hampshire	
California	May 2011	North Carolina	
Delaware	September 2011	North Dakota	
South Carolina	August 2012	Oregon	
Alabama	January 2013	South Dakota	
Pennsylvania	June 2013	Vermont	
Georgia	July 2013	Washington	
Indiana	July 2013	West Virginia	
North Dakota	July 2013	Wyoming	
Oklahoma	July 2013		
Florida	September 2013	Kentucky	February 2012
Kentucky	January 2014	Colorado	August 2012
Arizona	May 2014	Utah	August 2012
Tennessee	May 2014	Alabama	January 2013
Mississippi	January 2015	Pennsylvania	June 2013
Louisiana	May 2015	Kansas	December 2013
Arkansas	June 2015	Alaska	January 2014
Ohio	June 2015	South Carolina	April 2014
New York	July 2015	Iowa*	August 2014
		Missouri	May 2015
		Maine	June 2015
		Wisconsin	June 2015

Note: States could be members of multiple consortia.

*Massachusetts will use a version combining PARCC with its own state exam. Iowa opted to use an SBAC test in September 2015.

Sources: Education Week, PARCC, and SBAC.

instructional time and only 1 percent of instructional time for test practice. He also recommended careful study of the first year of the PARCC test—a test that had posed numerous technical difficulties for school districts.[95] "Testing this school year was an administrative nightmare for many Ohio school districts," said one Ohio interest group representative, who supported the changes. Shortening the exam would help "make it feasible to administer a test that's more than just filling in bubbles."[96] The legislature also convened a panel to study Ohio's participation in PARCC and the use of other state tests in early 2015—but this was not enough for critics of the test. In May 2015, the Ohio House voted 92–1 to limit testing to three hours per year, an hour shorter than Ohio's former state tests and seven hours less than a typical PARCC administration. The bill also would have ended Ohio's use of the PARCC test entirely.

A week later, PARCC voted to cut its exams a further 90 minutes and eliminate one of its two testing windows in the spring. The consortium's board suggested that it was being politically responsive to the needs of its member states. A member of the board, quoted in the organization's press release, said, "We've listened to the voices of all stakeholders—educators, parents, and students—and are using the lessons learned and feedback to produce a better assessment . . . PARCC serves as an even better tool to help our kids."[97] But it was hard to avoid the impression that the PARCC board was worried. Ohio's lawmakers thought the action was a response to the bill. "I think it's too little, too late," said Andrew Brenner (R), the sponsor of the dump-PARCC bill.[98] A Democratic supporter, Rep. Greta Johnson, argued that the PARCC did not really fill its mission of measuring learning, either. "We need to trust teachers. Teachers know when students are learning," she said.[99] In June, the state's 2015–2017 budget eliminated funding for PARCC.

COMMON CORE TESTS COST TOO MUCH?

Legislators in other states used the tests to take aim at the Common Core without abandoning the standards themselves. Indeed, the length of the tests led to an easier off-ramp from the politicized debate: cost. This argument enabled legislators to take direct and meaningful action against the most disliked part of the Common Core package without ditching the standards. In a way, the anger against the tests gave politicians a way out. Legislators in states including Arkansas, Michigan, Georgia, Wisconsin, Louisiana, North Carolina, and Florida have directed their departments of education to replace PARCC or SBAC tests with something else—with a test either state-designed or from a non-consortium vendor. One legislator in Michigan was particularly blunt about a requirement he put in the state budget to drop SBAC. "While Michigan has not abandoned the harmful Common Core State Standards, the legislature has decided to put a halt on the Smarter Balanced for which I am thankful," he said. "Michigan will be in control of its testing for at least another year, allowing us to watch as Common Core and the nationalization of education falls apart across the country."[100] Michigan eventually used a "blended" test that included locally developed questions combined with those from SBAC.

In Mississippi, local control became an issue with PARCC, but whether PARCC represented local control or suppressed it was unclear. The issue appeared when the state board terminated its contract with PARCC in 2015 after an embarrassing legal setback the previous year. A state contracting board ruled that the state department of education had failed to solicit competitive bids for the test and instead gave it to Pearson, the PARCC test developer.[101] The board complied with the legal finding and issued a request for testing proposals and, as a consequence, announced that it would leave PARCC as well. Neither the state board president nor the state superintendent was pleased, and noted that, contracritics of the Common Core, *Mississippi* teachers had been instrumental in designing the exam. "Hundreds of Mississippi educators had a hand in developing the test items. . . . These tests are the only assessments that have Mississippi's voice and input." But Mississippi Governor Phil Bryant, a Common Core critic, noted that he favored the new tests because they would be developed "without [the] federal interference" of PARCC.[102]

In Wisconsin, the presidential aspirations of Gov. Scott Walker kept Common Core supporters guessing on his true support of the standards (he initially supported them, then opposed them, and the simply said he supported "Wisconsin standards"), but both he and state lawmakers objected to the Smarter Balanced exam that the state used (once) in 2014–2015. The first administration of this computer-adaptive test was plagued with problems, ranging from the failure of the "adaptive" part of the exam, concerns about an overly long exam, to some districts having to give a paper version of the test. The test was also delayed two weeks due to programming problems.[103] More problematic for legislators and Walker, however, were the tests' exorbitant cost overruns—almost 25 percent over budget, or $7.2 million. The state's Department of Public Instruction told legislators that the tests cost $33.64 per student instead of the $26 per student originally estimated. The state's senate education committee chair said, "If we're finding it's now too cost-prohibitive, I don't want to put all these eggs into this basket. I would rather find an alternative to be truly fiscally efficient."[104] The speaker of the state assembly agreed. "We're not going to pay the entire bill" because taxpayers have been "ripped off" by the exam, he said, and noted that the legislature would pass a bill to prohibit the scores from the exam from counting toward any legal accountability requirements in 2015. That law was enacted in May 2015.[105] The legislature also cut any further funding for the SBAC exam. The governor said he favored "Wisconsin-based standards and assessments" in lieu of consortia exams.[106] Supporters of the exam blamed broader national politics for the demise of the SBAC exam. One Milwaukee business-group lobbyist noted that the Common Core debate led "people [to lose] a little bit of faith in the validity and the credibility in that piece of our assessment package."[107]

Other states found that local control pared nicely with the cost argument. Gov. Nathan Deal (R) and state superintendent John Barge (R) announced early—in 2013—that the state would not administer the PARCC test before it was administered the following school year, bypassing many of the financial difficulties met by Wisconsin, Mississippi, and others. They cited the projected $27 million cost to the state, which was greater than its entire current testing budget. Gov. Deal said that Georgia was committed to the same standards and even would work with neighboring states, but the "state could create better value for taxpayers while maintaining the same level of quality." The executives also noted concerns about technological demands and length of the tests, especially for Georgia's less well-off districts. Nevertheless, Barge emphasized that exiting PARCC would give the state greater control over its curriculum and give "educators across the state" more say in the tests.[108] The shout-out to teacher expertise was of special significance in Georgia, where teachers had reacted very negatively to out-of-state assessment tests in the past. Former (elected) state superintendent Werner Rogers lost his re-election bid in 1994 partly due to the rollout of the Georgia Kindergarten Assessment Program, a standards-based test designed by a California company. Rogers sought to salvage the exam, including a video press release in which he said, "It is based on our state Quality Core Curriculum [so] it assesses those things that are already part of the instructional program, and it allows *teachers to observe and document capabilities as your child attains them.*"[109] The PARCC test appeared to fall afoul of the same criterion.

CONCLUSION

By 2010, the use of testing for accountability was thoroughly ingrained in American schools, and its proponents hoped that a journey to Common Core–aligned tests would meet a smooth path. The proponents were disappointed and surprised by the stiff political headwinds they encountered. And, unlike ideological or partisan opposition to the standards, opponents of the tests won some significant skirmishes—states as diverse as Wisconsin, Ohio, Colorado, Maryland, and Mississippi took steps to reduce or replace Common Core–aligned tests, even after existing SBAC or PARCC tests had been developed *and* administered. Critics argued that there were too many tests, that schools were saturated in "test culture," and that the tests are too technologically demanding.

Yet, none of the criticisms is unique to these tests. Anti-testing groups like FairTest had been in existence since 1985, and some critics had no particular opposition to the Common Core State Standards themselves. Instead, the political fracas in which the Common Core found itself proved useful for advancing their broader goal: undermining student and teacher assessment. The Common Core was just a convenient political vehicle. Unfortunately for the standards, they abetted these interest groups by opening a new and more potent political front. In the past, complaints about testing might have been handled between testing vendors and the district or state department of education, but the multi-state nature of the Common Core raised the political bar, and major test designers found themselves testifying to special legislative committees instead.[110] In previous waves of education reform, complaints from parents or educators who thought that students were tested too much could be contained locally—no other state was required to use the same tests. Perhaps inadvertently, the federal RTTT's incentive to join a multi-state testing consortium broadened the base of opposition. Parents and educators who were opposed to the form or rationale for tests could create a reinforcing feedback loop across the country, amplifying opposition in blogs, Facebook groups, and public "out-out" events. In doing so, they intertwined opposition to *assessment* with opposition to the Common Core State *Standards*.

Ironically, although the most visible national opposition to the Common Core came from the right—Republican governors, conservative talk show hosts, and long-time conservative organizations—the greatest threat to the *usefulness* of the Common Core came from teachers and parents. The danger was most apparent with the withering of the two federally instigated testing consortia, the PARCC and SBAC. Despite the initial energy behind them, by 2015, a majority of states were in *neither* of the exam consortia, undermining a central political rationale for common national standards: common comparisons. Chester Finn, a former U.S. undersecretary of education and president of the Thomas B. Fordham Institute, argued the problem would mostly be felt at the state level. "Better for states to drop out in advance than to fake it," he wrote. Unfortunately,

> state tests don't yield comparable results, and discrepant proficiency bars are much of what went wrong with NCLB—so the drop-out states

that devise their own assessments still won't know how their kids and schools compare . . . the go-it-alone states will forfeit one of the major benefits of commonality, and someday perhaps they'll see the error of their ways—or face up to the fact that (like Texas and Virginia) they don't really want to use the Common Core at all.[111]

Losing common tests would be a short-term political cover, but it might be the long-term horizon for the Common Core.

SIX

The Reverie of the Left: Foundations, Think Tanks, and Interest Groups

In 2009, blogger and activist Anthony Cody complained that the Common Core was becoming a second act for No Child Left Behind (NCLB). For him, the rhetoric of high standards from NCLB was already a perversion of quality education, but the lack of input from teachers and educators for this new wave of standards setting was more alarming:

> Didn't the entire No Child Left Behind fiasco teach us what happens when policies are enacted without the active engagement of the professionals expected to carry them out? . . . Heaven forbid "interest groups" such as teachers, parents and students should be given the opportunity to muck up these standards. They do not seem to be asking, but perhaps our first bit of input could be in the form of a collective howl of outrage. After the dismal failure of NCLB, which was caused in no small part by the exclusion of classroom teachers from its design, how can we launch another major reform effort in a similar way?[1]

Calling the Common Core's drafting committees the "secret sixty," Cody predicted that the Core would be nothing more than a "wild goose chase" that allowed politicians to "fixate" on the lack of national standards—the very thing that had "emerged as the biggest excuse for this failure" of NCLB. Cody preferred solutions of social spending, higher teacher pay, and "nurturing communities." Further, he thought Common Core would only enrich testing companies that would "make literally billions of dollars of profit from revamping the curriculum and tests from coast to coast."[2]

Cody's concern represents a core part of the liberal attack on the Common Core. Critics including Diane Ravitch, Mercedes Schneider, and Anthony Cody dressed down the Common Core not so much because they were common standards—Ravitch, for example, was a long-time supporter of national standards—but because they were adopted by non-representative groups. These opponents garnered less attention partly because many staunch liberals and their allied groups were among the standards' chief supporters, including Arne Duncan and Barack Obama at the federal level; liberal Democratic governors like Andrew Cuomo (D-NY), Edmund "Jerry" Brown (D-CA), and Jack Markell (D-DE) in the states; and a wide range of local teachers' unions and Democratic civil rights groups. Conservatives were out of political power at the federal level and *could* complain, especially as the broader political environment became deeply polarized. Political liberals had to explain why they found the Common Core wanting when a panoply of fellow travelers found the standards so appealing, especially the civil rights groups. Although those on the political left shared conservatives' worries about the Core's weak evidence and the potential loss of student privacy on the associated tests, they were at the forefront of criticism over the Core's quasi-public and private foundation sponsors and its "secret" drafting process. From one perspective, liberal critics were right—the Common Core was drafted by a small number of non-elected bureaucrats, university professors, and representatives of testing companies whose identity was not publicly released until long after the process started. From another perspective, however, the Common Core was no secret; and governors across the political spectrum had spent 20 years preaching higher academic standards to legislators and bureaucrats. Even so, *most* public policy is debated among bureaucrats, interest groups, and affected parties in iron triangles or issue networks.[3] The specifics of the Common Core were developed out of the public eye, perhaps; but the motivation and intent were written in blazing print.

FOUNDATIONS OF COMMON CORE

Critics on the left found the *process* of the Common Core damaging to the project. Perhaps the standards were fewer, higher, and better; and perhaps students would learn more with existing education dollars than without, but liberals objected that the foundations and funders behind the Core were in no way representative of the wishes of parents or teachers, nor—in the critics' view—were they particularly concerned about the quality of education. As with the conservative critics, Core opponents wielding the argument ranged from mildly critical to conspiratorial. Anthony Cody complained that only one Common Core standards writer had been a recent classroom teacher; Mercedes Schneider, an anti-Core blogger, cited evidence of a "checkbook vote;" Fenwick English, an academic, foresaw the destruction of public education.

There was no doubt that private groups were heavily invested in the design of the particulars of the Common Core, although the ideas driving the Core were drawn from the very public pronouncements of American governors in the two decades before Gov. James Hunt called together the first informal Common Core meetings in 2007. The private organizations that supported the Common Core illustrated the unusual three-way political alliance that motivated standards and assessment reforms around 2000: business groups seeking economic development; conservatives looking for accountability; and liberals looking to education to bolster civil rights. This alliance led to NCLB in 2001. Those liberal critics in 2001 who had looked askew at the accountability provisions and the involvement of business leveled the same charges against Common Core a decade later.

This is best shown by the transformation of Diane Ravitch, a former federal Department of Education official and educational historian. She was a strong proponent of high national standards through the debacle of the early 1990s and, for a time, was a board member of the Thomas B. Fordham Foundation, a strong standards supporter. But she became thoroughly disenchanted with the business of education politics by 2006 and argued that the motivation behind both NCLB and (later) the Common Core was flawed.[4] "The great hijacking occurred in the mid-1990s when the standards movement fell apart," she argued. "The passage of No Child Left Behind made testing and accountability our national education strategy."[5] NCLB's reliance on market-like incentives and public accountability left school districts to "play[] a shell game with low-performing students, moving them out and dispersing them, pretending they don't exist."[6] NCLB legislators might have imbibed market values (although Ravitch speculates "it is unlikely that many of members of Congress read it thoroughly and fully understood all the eventual consequences"), but Ravitch blasted the rise of private foundations in education policy:[7]

[Venture philanthropies] converged in support of reform strategies that mirrored their own experience in acquiring huge fortunes, such as competition, choice, deregulation, incentives, and other market-based approaches. These were not familiar concepts in the world of education, where high value is placed on collaboration. . . . There is something fundamentally antidemocratic about relinquishing control of the public education policy agenda to private foundations run by society's wealthiest people; when the wealthiest of these foundation are joined in common purpose, they represent an unusually powerful force that is beyond the reach of democratic institutions. . . . The foundations demand that public schools and teachers be held accountable for performance, but they themselves are accountable to no one. If their plans fail, no sanctions are levied against them. They are bastions of unaccountable power.[8]

Despite her own long record of supporting high national standards, she applied much of the same criticism to the Common Core as it became public. She was troubled by the lack of evidence for their success and their rushed adoption, and she worried that the Common Core's associated tests would multiply NCLB's failures. The new standards might "cause a precipitous decline in test scores, based on arbitrary cut scores, and this will have a disparate impact on students who are English language learners, students with disabilities, and students who are poor and low-performing." In response to proponents who thought the scores were indicators of good standards, she queried, "Why so much glee at the prospect of higher failure rates?"[9] In this, she mirrored the criticism of teachers' unions and parent opt-out groups.

More fundamentally, Ravitch recoiled from the influence of non-public groups, just as she had with NCLB. "President Obama and Secretary Duncan often say that the Common Core standards were developed by the states and voluntarily adopted by them," she wrote. "This is not true. They were developed by an organization called Achieve and the National Governors Association, both of which were generously funded by the Bill & Melinda Gates Foundation. There was minimal public engagement in the development of the Common Core. Their creation was neither grassroots nor did it emanate from the states." And she lamented the small coterie that controlled them, and even more the centrality of David Coleman. "Is there not something unseemly about placing the fate and the future of American education in the hands of one man?"[10]

The Common Core was not the product of a single man, but it was drafted by only a handful of key supporters. Ravitch mentions three: the private group, Achieve, Inc.; the quasi-public group, NGA; and the private personal philanthropy of Bill Gates, Microsoft Corporation's founder and former CEO. In reality, the list was longer, but not by much. One group was the official sponsor of the effort; and both were private groups that had public officials as members. A second group of organizations was business groups and foundations. These groups had for 20 years argued that education was central to economic growth or at least preparedness. They provided a link to the central political appeal of the standards: young adults will be more competitive in the world economy. A third group, policy groups on the right, chiefly the Thomas B. Fordham Institute, provided conservatives cover for a nationalizing reform. Since their change of heart in the mid-1990s, national Republicans had sought to bolster the party's education credentials so long as federal money was tied to assessment. These think tanks and interest groups insisted that assessment had little meaning without a common yard-stick. A fourth group, policy groups and foundations on the left, saw NCLB and the Common Core as a way to aid low-income and non-white students who had few resources to "buy" their way out of low-performing schools. They offered cover to liberal Democrats. A final group was led by large, private philanthropists. As noted by Ravitch and countless other critics, the Bill & Melinda Gates Foundation led the list, but others provided funds, too, including the Helmsley Charitable Trust, the Hewlett Foundation, the Charles Stewart Mott Foundation, and the Carnegie Corporation of New York.[11] Critics saw these groups as amplifying the business bias of the Core; others saw them as outside-the-box reformers necessary to break through the lethargy of the "ten thousand democracies" that American school dis-tricts comprise.[12]

Official Sponsors

The two organizations officially responsible for the Common Core were the NGA and the Council of Chief State School Officers (CCSSO). Both the organizations served as forums for public officials, the NGA for governors and the CCSSO for the top state school officers. Both were non-public in the sense that they were not governed by law, and membership in the organ-izations was voluntary. These organizations were—by their very nature—bipartisan; every governor is a member of the NGA, and every state has a representative at CCSSO. But they were not *public* organizations in the sense of being accountable to voters for their activities.

The roles of the NGA and CCSSO were to provide an organizational framework for developing the standards, to conduct research to support them, and to promote a national political message. The framework included convening meetings of state school superintendents, governors, and other school experts and drafting the Common Core Memorandum of Agreement (MOA). The first such meeting was in August 2009 at the Chicago Hilton. Both NGA and CCSSO had research divisions before Common Core to assist states when drafting legislation; many states did not have the funds or personnel to conduct their own, and Common Core was no different. Finally, leaders in both organizations knew that the standards effort of the early 1990s had foundered on federal issues, and so the NGA and CCSSO would serve as a buffer against federal influence.[13]

The NGA and CCSSO also had a long track record of supporting state standards, as discussed in Chapter 2. NGA issued a report in 1986 calling for K–12 and college academic standards, a call repeated in 1989 and 1996 by the organization. CCSSO likewise advocated for standards as early as 1984.[14]

This history did not assuage critics. Instead, critics argued that the mere non-public nature of the organizations, and their ownership of the Common Core copyright, was novel for public education and would make future changes to the standards difficult. Mercedes Schneider, a well-known Core critic based in Louisiana, cited a clause in the Common Core's copyright language indicating prohibited uses, including "recasting [the standards] in a manner that, in the view of NGA Center and CCSSO, changes the meaning or intent of the Common Core State Standards or any part thereof." She interpreted the language this way: "There is nothing stopping the CCSS copyright holders from mandating 100% CCSS adherence once, say, all current legislative sessions are ended. That's right: Laws passed regarding 'modifying' CCSS can be made null by a change in CCSS copyright that requires 100% CCSS adherence. Tricky, but NGA and CCSSO 'own' CCSS. Never forget that."[15]

Schneider's readers saw even more cynical reasons. Agreeing with Schneider's analysis of copyright, one wrote:

Common Core is not even a testing regimen per se nor an educational program—it is an asset in the business portfolios of venture capitalists that are involved in the rapid privatization of yet another public institution. Common Core is merely the latest marketing concept (the hammer to crack open the nut of taking public monies and placing them into private hands) used to manage public opinion and sell the idea that schools need radical restructuring that can only be done by corporate ideology and investment.[16]

The copyright appeared as a tool to guarantee revenue.

It was true earlier versions of state standards had been drafted by state committees working as official government bodies, funded directly by taxes and governed by open records laws. But *model* standards of the past were designed in the private sphere, whether by the National Council of Teachers of Mathematics (NCTM), the National Center for History in the Schools (NCHS), or the National Council of Teachers of English (NCTE). Contemporary state standards often tracked those, and public officials used those private standards to validate the work of public committees. By 1993, for example, 41 states used all or part of NCTM's math standards.[17] Further, state standards of the 1990s were drafted in response to changes to *federal* law rather than to an enlightened and chivalrous interest in education.

The difference, of course, was that despite federal law, states were not bound to adopt NCTM's or any other group's standards; no state signed Memoranda of Understanding with any group. Although the Common Core was not "required," the political reality of Race to the Top (RTTT) was that no other standards were available. And so critics argued that the copyrights were an abridgement of freedom and public debate. There seemed to be no alternatives, and it was certain that there was limited public input (though it was available) during the drafting of the standards.

The CCSSO took exception to this characterization of their organization generally and the copyright in particular. Chris Minnich, CCSSO's executive director, responded that "We're ultimately run by our membership, so the two organizations [CCSSO and NGA] hold the copyright in order to protect the states. . . . If the standards weren't copyrighted, a publisher could've taken the standards and sold them back to the states." In his view, the copyright was the inverse of the anti-democratic charge. Instead of preventing input, it was protecting the states' earlier work on the standards.[18] Minnich also was adamant that the standards were the work of the two groups on behalf of those public officials; elected officials were ultimately responsible for the standards. He specifically singled out Indiana, where the state legislature withdrew from the Common Core but used essentially the same standards. According to Minnich, they were not in violation of the copyright, and instead their action proved that the Common Core was subject to public oversight. "States own their own academic standards," he said.[19] Neither did the NGA nor the CCSSO take action against other states that never adopted or dropped the Common Core even when they adopted standards that were quite similar, such as Missouri or South Carolina.

Still, the political *message* that opponents took from owning a copyright was that these private organizations would allow limited public input.

Business Groups

A second group of non-public groups in support of the Core were the business groups. Their support of standards was not new, and neither was the criticism of their involvement.

The governors' 1989 Charlottesville Education Summit emphasized the economic benefits of standards, and business groups inherited the mantle of education standards reform in the mid-1990s. Groups like the Business

Roundtable, National Alliance of Business (NAB), and the United States Chamber of Commerce (USCC) were quick to tout the "skill-gap challenge" that could be remedied by better, career-focused state standards. At the same time, governors and business groups were calling for "comparable" standards among states, foreshadowing Common Core.[20]

The highest-profile effort to bring in business groups came when Gov. Tommy Thompson (R-WI), the chairman of the NGA in 1995, paired with IBM chairman Louis V. Gerstner to promote a "small, intense meeting that will produce action [and especially to] build on the successes that states have had in developing and implementing school reform," as they said.[21] Gerstner told at the NGA's annual meeting that year that American education needed a "bone-jarring, full-fledged, 100 percent revolution that discards the old and replaces it with a totally new performance-driven system."[22] The following year, 40 governors and 49 business leaders convened a national education summit to "start a national effort to establish high academic standards, assessment and accountability and improve the use of school technology as a tool to reach high standards."[23] This partnership led to the creation of Achieve, Inc., a private organization meant to boost existing state standards and ensure that high school education prepare students for employment—that is, high school education would be aligned to the needs of businesses and colleges. (A follow-up summit in 2001 noted that half of college students took remedial courses in reading or math; and that more than a third of job applicants failed employer literacy or mathematics tests.)[24] Achieve, Inc., boasted a board comprised of both business executives and sitting governors, and so it was not insulated from contemporary political controversies. This quasi-private organization became the primary driver for raising *academic* standards and boosting *academic* achievement. Achieve, Inc., was unequivocally the organizational progenitor of the Common Core, and clearly ahead of NGA or CCSSO.

But Achieve, Inc., was not the only private group behind the Common Core. In line with their commitments at the education summits hosted by Achieve, Inc., business groups also pushed higher state standards, especially for high schools. One such venture was the American Diploma Project (ADP), which was a joint project of Achieve, Inc., Thomas B. Fordham Foundation, The Education Trust, and NAB. The Business Roundtable was also a strong supporter of the ADP.[25] NAB's particular contribution was to help launch the ADP in 2002, an effort that 35 states joined by 2015.[26] The organization interviewed executives from 23 companies to build a set of "skills and knowledge necessary for success . . . once [students] left high school."[27] NAB, founded in the 1960s for workforce preparation, had come to embrace many education reforms by the 1990s, and it had joined the Business Roundtable, the USCC, and the National Association of Manufacturers to advocate teacher performance assessment, state standards-based student assessment, and national teacher licenses.[28] But more striking was that many of the same companies were members of several of these groups. NAB's report quoted Lou Gerstner and the U.S. Secretary of Education Richard Riley approvingly, as well as executives from Intel, State Farm, and Williams—all companies *also* represented on Achieve, Inc.'s board. These businesses and business interest groups were keeping the promise that they made at the two national education summits in the 1990s: they would advocate for radical changes to education.

In many ways, the ADP was a prototype for the Common Core. Its inaugural 2004 report, *Ready or Not*, used the "college and workplace readiness" language that prefigured the Common Core's "college- and career-ready" verbiage. ADP also presented a universalistic standard. The organization claimed that "ADP's college and workplace readiness benchmarks offer the solid foundation upon which states can raise academic expectations and build education systems that will enable students to reach these goals. Without clear academic expectations that have currency beyond 12th grade—as those described in this report do—states' efforts to improve high schools undoubtedly will fail."[29] ADP was convincing; virtually all of the states applying for RTTT funding mentioned their participation in ADP as evidence of their commitment to high standards developed in a "consortium of states" *in addition* to Common Core. For example, Georgia's RTTT grant application touted its early participation in ADP and noted that "Achieve found Georgia to have 'incredible alignment to Achieve's College and Career-ready standards.'"[30] Minnesota's application likewise highlighted praise from Achieve: "The Minnesota K–12 Academic Standards in Mathematics . . . present student learning expectations that are intellectually demanding and well aligned with the ADP Benchmarks, with minor exceptions. If Minnesota students master the state standards, they will likely be well prepared for both workplace and college success."[31] The state also noted that the Common Core standards would be "building upon the work of the ADP effort through Achieve."[32] Other state applications made similar comments.

Business groups had sold the states an economic rationale for education long before the Common Core. Their support was not secret, and Achieve's work on the ADP was central to the development of the Common Core. Politically, the groups drew support from across the spectrum. These groups were just as likely to be headed by Democrats as Republicans, and indeed, President Obama praised them as such. In a 2010 address to the Business Roundtable, Obama said, "Over the last year, we've worked together on a number of issues—from economic recovery and tax policy to education and to health care. And more often than not, we've found common ground . . . education reform is one of those rare issues where both Democrats and Republicans are enthusiastic."[33] The president took business support as a token of broad political support.

But business involvement did little to comfort opponents on the left. Fenwick English, an education professor and well-known curriculum expert, scorched their role in education in an essay detailing the "enemies" of public education. He singled out the Business Roundtable and argued that "neoliberal warriors argue that democratic values be subordinated to economic considerations."[34] Therefore, the project of Common Core was fundamentally flawed because of its connection with the dominant education trend. But English saw deeper flaws, too. He cited Henry Giroux approvingly:

> The ascendancy of neoliberal corporate culture into every aspect of American life both consolidates economic power in the hands of the few and aggressively attempts to break the power of unions, decouple income from productivity, subordinate the needs of society to the market, and deem public services and goods an unconscionable luxury. But it does more. It thrives on a culture of cynicism, insecurity, and despair.[35]

Other critics were less vituperative even as they still found business' involvement disconcerting. Schneider, the Louisiana blogger, believed that "business presence at the 1989 and 1996 education summits was not pushing for the privatization of public schools."[36] But privatization was not her first worry. Like English, she worried about the shift of the rationale of education with business involvement in the run-up to Common Core. "Benchmarking in business is *money-centered*," she wrote:

> This leads to another truth inherent in Achieve's 1998 report [on state standards]: the danger of viewing human beings—in this case, teachers and students—as either assets or liabilities to the school's profit venture. Given that student test scores were becoming the revered and preferred outcome measure of academic success, it is easy to see how the business model of education could easily promote the value of good test-takers over poor ones and high-scoring schools over low-scoring ones.[37]

Beyond treating students as interchangeable parts, Schneider worried that Common Core had escaped "democracy-fostering control," but the issue was that businesses stood to reap substantial profits from Common Core and none more so than Pearson, Inc., a test and curriculum publisher.[38] Pearson and other business organizations had provided money and support to design the Common Core beginning in 2007. As they were *already* producing a vast number of state tests, their interest in the Common Core was not out of line; they *were* the experts. But Schneider was worried about the profit motive. "CCSS is tailor-made for the Pearson philosophy of embedding and acquisition, and like so many organizations involved in the CCSS venture, Pearson is positioned to benefit from its initial 'investment' in CCSS license owner, CCSSO."[39]

Schneider's concerns notwithstanding, Common Core was not the windfall that some on the left expected. Pearson was the test developer for Partnership for Assessment of Readiness for College and Careers (PARCC), but it came in for severe criticism over repeated testing delays and grading errors in 2014. McGraw-Hill Education, a competitor and long-time test provider, sold its testing business in 2015 in part because of the shift to state-controlled testing that had begun under NCLB. The Common Core accelerated the trend as several states pooled testing resources under PARCC and Smarter Balanced Assessment Consortium (SBAC). Because school districts in many states no longer could shop for their own exams, the shift to Common Core meant that fewer tests were needed and that states would dictate the content of exams rather than the publisher. This led to a flatlining of the market rather than exponential growth. States spent almost $1.1 billion on tests in the 2013–2014 school year, a figure almost unchanged from 2008–2009 when it was $1.2 billion.[40]

Business involvement in the Common Core was a boost to the project as legislators in both political parties could argue that the standards could lead to more and better employment prospects for their constituents. Many critics from *within* education, however, found them threatening their rationale for American education.

On the Right

Business groups' wishes appeared to be largely met by the development of the Common Core. The standards were comparable, that is, national curricular standards that explicitly focused on career readiness. But business groups were outsiders to education politics, leaving them to rely on more politically minded groups to convince elected officials that a common curriculum was politically feasible—and safe. Into that gap stepped the Thomas B. Fordham Foundation, a center-right foundation revived in 1997 to focus on the "renewal and reform of primary/secondary education in the United States generally and in Dayton, Ohio, particularly."[41] Its first president was

Chester E. Finn Jr., a former Reagan administration official and long-time public proponent of higher academic standards "known for his fierce defense of his positions," according to the organization.[42] (The foundation created a parallel institute for legal purposes in 2007; from that time, the Thomas B. Fordham Institute published virtually all of its reports and research.)

In line with its mission, Fordham provided politicians and the education press with a steady diet of reports calling for higher standards (in 1997, 2000, 2003, 2005, 2006, 2009, and 2010). The organization commissioned curriculum experts to grade state standards (including Sandra Stotsky, now a Common Core opponent); states like Massachusetts and Indiana frequently led the pack with A's, while Wisconsin, Michigan, Washington, and Florida brought up the rear with F's and D's. The political point of the exercise was less to shame the laggards (although that was part of the plan) than to show that states *could* devise high standards. "It's no secret what causes most jurisdictions to botch the job: over-reliance on faulty national standards; the exclusion of real subject-matter experts from the standards-writing process; an obsession with vast committees and 'stakeholder consensus.' But California, Massachusetts, and Indiana avoided these traps because they had visionary leaders—and bare-knuckled infighters with thick skins—who exploited unique political opportunities to fight for and pass top-flight standards," wrote a Fordham author.[43] These near-annual reports received substantial attention as the Common Core process came together. National standards should *not* be "faulty."

Finn, a former assistant secretary at the U.S. Department of Education, had been an advocate for national standards for more than a decade at that point. In 1989, he told a panel of business leaders that there was a need to "develop a nationwide sense of minimum acceptable standards . . . developed by a consensus-seeking process."[44] He was emphatic that they *not* be "federal" standards but developed by the states. He was also certain that teachers and other school personnel should be left out of the process if they were to be meaningful measures of schools. At the time of the 1996 summit, he wrote:

> Overturning the regnant ideology of a self-contained, self-perpetuating, self-certifying, decentralized, ostrich-like profession, most of whose members have lifetime tenure, seems to me unrealistic. . . . It is not enough, after all, for a school merely to dish up content; it also has an obligation to see that its students consume and digest a decent quantity. Else we'll find ourselves back where those running schools employ only such input measures as per-pupil spending and class size as gauges of "quality"; where the ostriches-on-the-left encounter nothing to

counter their claim that U.S. schools are doing a fine job that could only be enhanced by added resources; where schools are judged by the lushness of their services rather than the achievement of their pupils; and where some educators get away with malpractice precisely because there is no generally accepted—or enforceable—definition of success.[45]

He was certain that standards would improve school quality if only parents and others would know what their children were *supposed* to be learning. The Common Core was near to Finn's dream of national standards, and as he was Fordham's long-time president (1997–2014), it came as no surprise that the Thomas B. Fordham Institute was strongly in favor of the Core. Indeed, the offices of the Common Core State Standards Initiative (CCSSI) in Washington, DC, shared a floor with Fordham. Finn himself, however, worried that there were not enough "incentives" for states to do well. "The adoption went way too fast, and it isn't sincere," he said. "The standards won't matter unless they are implemented conscientiously, and states may not have sufficient incentives to do that carefully."[46]

Fordham was the most visible proponent of better state standards in the run-up to the Common Core, and, as the standards came under attack by conservatives, the organization dispatched its staff to convince legislators to keep the Common Core. In some states, Fordham's appeal was clearly political. In 2013, the organization's executive vice president Michael J. Petrilli recounted his political lineage to legislators in Ohio (he had been an official in the George W. Bush administration) and praised the standards as a "conservative victory" because they encouraged or required fiscal responsibility, accountability, school choice, competitiveness, innovation, and "traditional educational values."[47] Elsewhere, Petrilli said Republicans shared "justifiable outrage at the Obama administration's role in the Common Core. . . . Republicans used to stand for standards. We're confident that once GOP governors and legislators have a chance to give [the Common Core] a look, they will again."[48] Fordham formalized the conservative response by creating a pro-Core group, "Conservatives for Higher Standards," with former Gov. Jeb Bush (R-FL)'s Foundation for Excellence in Education. That group listed high-profile Republican state legislators who supported the Common Core in states like Florida, Louisiana, Pennsylvania, Tennessee, and Utah.[49]

Although Fordham had no role in the design of the actual Common Core standards, it provided talking points and political visibility for conservative supporters. Predictably, its support only irritated unhappiness on the left, as some talked about "right-wing" support for "retrograde policies" contained in President Obama's support of standards and accountability.[50]

Schneider and English both argued that Fordham was a pro-privatization outfit "larded with military and corporate control metaphors."[51] To its credit, Fordham proclaimed its support of standards and assessment publicly; there were no backroom dealings needed for the organization to support Common Core. Here, opposition from the left was baldly political: Fordham was run by two former bureaucrats from Republican administrations; therefore, their positions were toxic.

On the Left

There was no counterpart to the visibility and drive of the Fordham Institute on the left of the political spectrum, although a constellation of groups supported the Common Core. These groups provided Democrats with arguments to support Petrilli's "conservative victory" without capitulating to conservatives. There was less work to do on the left, however, as many of the politically controversial themes of the Common Core had been vetted in Congress in the reauthorization of the Elementary and Secondary Education Act (ESEA) in 1994 and 2001. As a result, the Common Core's universalistic standards and companion student-based academic accountability had already been accepted by major Democrats and civil rights groups as part of the contemporary education landscape.

Groups that supported the Core included the Center for American Progress (CAP)—a think tank like Fordham—and an array of civil rights groups like the Mexican American Legal Defense and Educational Fund, the League of United Latin American Citizens, and the National Association for the Advancement of Colored People (NAACP).[52] These groups largely provided after-the-fact support of the Common Core, assuring their constituents that the standards "promote[d] equity by ensuring all students, no matter where they live, are well prepared with the skills and knowledge necessary to collaborate and compete with their peers in the U.S. and abroad."[53] One group, CAP, hosted pro-Common Core events attended by prominent Democrats.[54] With the civil rights groups, CAP held that the Common Core would help hold states accountable for low-income and non-white students.[55] Two groups, however, were central to the initial impetus that fed the Common Core, The Education Trust and the American Federation of Teachers (AFT).

The Education Trust (usually known as "EdTrust") was founded in 1990 as part of the American Association for Higher Education. Like the Fordham Institute, its explicit focus was higher standards and meaningful academic assessment for all students. Initially, the group was better known for its privately funded college placement programs—indeed, its founder, Kati Haycock, had been an Affirmative Action director in the University of

California system—but it boosted its advocacy in the earlier levels of K–12 education toward the end of the 1990s.[56] Through the 1990s, the group enjoyed a bipartisan reputation, although the group's interests attracted more support from Democrats. One of EdTrust's centerpiece policies, boosting teacher accountability, was championed by a liberal Democrat, Rep. George Miller (D-CA) in the later 1990s, but other Democrats praised EdTrust's work as well. "They have . . . great expertise," according to one Democratic staffer.[57] EdTrust was one of the founding partners of ADP.

Unlike Fordham, EdTrust's primary constituency was non-white, low-income children, although its call for higher standards for all students paralleled Fordham's. It did share a key characteristic, however, with both business groups and with Fordham. It had no patience with teacher-centered, locally designed education policy. "We have no stake in the status quo," Haycock said in 1999.[58] EdTrust did support local decision making but only in concert with real consequences for schools, teachers, and students for poor performance on standards-based assessment made by someone outside the school, and especially if those standards were uniform. The EdTrust was a fan of federal action, but cross-state support was better than nothing. "I have more confidence that the federal government will remain focused on producing more equitable outcomes for poor and minority kids than I do that the 50 states or the 15,000 local school districts will," Haycock said. She still supported the Common Core because it provided leverage for all teachers. "We can't afford to burden teachers with the task of creating really great curricular materials and inventing their lessons every single day. . . . Certainly, we have a unique window now with the Common Core standards and the second-largest teachers' union squarely in support of that," she said.[59] Here, she deliberately echoed the teachers' unions' central reason for supporting the Common Core: the standards would relieve teachers of designing lessons by themselves day to day.

But EdTrust was less interested in the standards themselves than in the college targeting and common assessments. The EdTrust's college-directed focus seemed to be rewarded by the Common Core. The adoption of the standards "marks the first time the K-12 community has stepped up and said, unequivocally, 'College readiness is the goal for all students,'" Haycock said.[60] Elsewhere she noted that, "As long as you have different paths and standards, educators will send poor and minority kids down the lower-level one."[61] If nothing else, the Common Core fused "college and career ready" together in a way that made separate college curriculum difficult, a key tenet of EdTrust and a major reason that the organization was seen as left-leaning. The organization also pushed for college involvement in drafting the standards—if students were to be "college-ready," colleges would have to play a role in their creation—a requirement that seemed to be met as 31 members of the Core work groups (of 101) had university affiliations.

The organization's support of common assessments was received more ambiguously by its fellow partisans, but EdTrust staff argued that the common curriculum was meaningless without common assessments—much like Fordham had on the right. Initially, Haycock had been cautiously skeptical. As the governors were meeting to finalize the Core's framework in the spring of 2009, she said, "Who is going to do the work? . . . Having new standards does us exactly no good until we have curriculum and assessments that go with it [sic]."[62] Yet, after lamenting that textbook publishers had long "chased" different state standards with non-comparable tests, Haycock argued that "common standards across all states give us a chance to do [assessment] right this time."[63] The assessments were secondary to the Common Core, but they became the biggest flashpoint for opposition on the left. EdTrust continued to defend frequent assessments as central to advancing the education for non-white and low-income children. As NCLB came up for possible reauthorization—with potential riders to reduce testing or make it optional—Haycock stood firm: "Removing the requirement for annual testing would be a devastating step backward, for it is very hard to make sure our education system is serving every child well when we don't have reliable, comparable achievement data on every child every year."[64] The Common Core's assessment consortia were the only national-level vehicle for that commonality.

The Education Trust sat in an unusual political position. Because many in the education policy realm identified it with Haycock, criticism on the left tended to focus on her resume, statements, or positions. Leonie Haimson, a blogger on the left, calls Haycock a "privateer."[65] Schneider found fault with Haycock's limited teaching experience. "Kati Haycock is no classroom teacher and certainly no classroom teacher facing the test score-producing pressures of NCLB," she wrote.[66] But others on the left criticized the organization's positions. The single-minded goal of the EdTrust gained the organization the enmity of other liberal educational groups. "The Ed Trust is like the person who killed his parents and begged for mercy as an orphan," wrote John Thompson, a *Huffington Post* blogger.

The Education Trust has long pushed for the most anti-teacher aspects of the Obama administration's "teacher quality" and school turnaround "reforms." . . . The Education Trust seeks value-added teacher evaluations, even though they are systematically unfair to teachers in high-challenge schools and even though they would encourage an out-migration of teaching talent from schools where it is harder to raise test scores. Also, it would sentence students in classes that are not currently subjected to high-stakes tests to more bubble-in accountability. The Ed Trust supports collective punishment, i.e. the mass removal of teachers in turnaround schools.[67]

Yet even Thompson elsewhere noted that the EdTrust was a "liberal" group with ultimately "constructive" ideas about the place of student learning.[68]

Some took issue with Haycock's contention that civil rights groups were "united" in favor of standards and accountability. Haycock had argued that civil rights groups held a "unanimous conviction that our country should not abandon the annual testing that gives parents and teachers a regular objective measure of how well their children are progressing."[69] A board member of a left group, the Network for Public Education, fired back: "Instead of stimulating worthy discussions about over-testing, cultural bias in tests, and the misuse of test data, these activists would rather claim a false mantle of civil rights activism."[70] As with the response from the right, the tests had become the major political flashpoint.

As with Fordham, the face of The Education Trust was a single person, validating some of Anthony Cody's lament about the closed nature of the Common Core. The political framework of the Common Core *was* designed by strikingly few individuals. Business groups, Fordham, and The Education Trust served as idea and advocacy factories, and their testimony was influential in state legislatures and in Congress, especially as education had been linked, seemingly indelibly, to economic competitiveness. Their pervasive influence obscured their minuscule numbers.

Had they been the only supporters, however, the Common Core would have perished in the subsequent political fallout. National standards in the early 1990s, also supported by business groups and governors, failed in the face of public protest and lack of support in the schools. Indeed, one major difference of the Common Core from national standards in the early 1990s was that the teachers' unions were supportive—vigorously on the part of the AFT and mildly on the part of the National Education Association (NEA). The success of the initial *rollout*, if not the implementation, of the Common Core was assured by this, much larger group—a group that was crucial to actual classroom change. The vocal support of the country's second-largest teachers' union, the AFT, solidified the political bargain.

Like The Education Trust, the AFT's support of the Common Core provided Democrats and progressives reasons to support the standards despite their association with controversy over privacy, teacher assessment, and testing. For its part, the AFT had come out early in support of higher academic standards by issuing reports critiquing state standards in beginning in 1995.

Unlike Fordham, AFT's reviews were focused on the ease with which state standards could be used by teachers in the classroom.[71] But, like EdTrust, the AFT saw uniform standards as a way to eliminate tracking. In 2003, the AFT wrote that its former president, Albert Shanker, had "urged states to learn from other high-achieving countries and set high and rigorous standards for all children and do what was necessary to make sure that they all had an opportunity to achieve them. . . . Setting high, clear standards for all students makes it much more difficult to sustain a two-tier education system—with one level of education provided to poor children and another level provided to everyone else."[72] And this all before NCLB required much the same thing. In 2010, union president Randi Weingarten—like Haycock—argued that teachers should not have to "make [curriculum] up every single day," and she praised Finland's educational system, with its "rigorous national standards."[73] In line with this commitment, the AFT provided substantial early feedback on the Common Core before they were public, and it and its locals conducted frequent Common Core teacher workshops on the implementation of standards materials.[74] The union also provided grants to locals to develop Common Core–aligned teacher materials through its Innovation Fund. The union argued that its support was necessary to keep the standards *as* standards because "in the recent past, efforts to set academic standards fell short because they swiftly moved into assessments, bypassing teachers and students."[75]

The union's support was politically crucial for another reason as well: The federal RTTT competition awarded points to states with support from unions. Although the AFT is clearly smaller than its cousin, the NEA, it boasts affiliates in most of the United States' largest school districts, thereby providing ample opportunities for local media coverage. State leaders who deliberately included union representatives into the application process found it easier to generate buy-in for RTTT funds, and AFT president Weingarten highlighted the collaboration of her unions' locals with state leaders in New York, Pennsylvania, Florida, and Illinois as reasons for their RTTT support.[76]

Later, when unions and other left-leaning groups became disenchanted with the Common Core, chiefly due to the associated testing, the AFT held firm. At the behest of Weingarten, the AFT passed a resolution in July 2014 *continuing* to support the Common Core. At the time, AFT president Randi Weingarten said:

We will continue to support the promise and potential of these standards as an essential to tool to provide each and every child an equitable and excellent education while calling on the powers that be in districts and, states and at the national level to work with educators and parents to fix this botched implementation and restore confidence in the standards. And no matter which side of the debate our members were on, there's one thing everyone agreed on—that we need to delink these standards from the tests.[77]

The standards were still gold.

The AFT's commitment contrasts with the decidedly lukewarm support from the larger union, the NEA. In 2009, the NEA was championing its own version of "fewer, higher, better" standards. For the NEA, the "standards" were creative thinking, communication, and technological skills and called them "21st Century Skills" as part of the Partnership for 21st Century Skills (known as P21). At the time, Common Core supporters (including AFT at the time) argued that P21 standards were content free. They said that P21's "approach to teaching those skills marginalizes knowledge." Instead they foreshadowed a key Common Core talking point: "Education policy and practice should be based on sound research and informed by an understanding of what has worked and what has failed in the past. . . . Unless it is fundamentally revised, the program put forth by P21 also will fail. In the meantime, it is undermining the quality of education in America."[78] The NEA eventually warmed to the Common Core and issued a document to help teachers match P21 goals with the Common Core.

Still, the NEA did have some foundational involvement with the Common Core. The organization noted that four of "our teachers" were members of the Common Core Working Groups, and it issued a policy brief in 2010 that said the standards "can lead to better instruction" but that "policy should . . . not rush or neglect any of the various pieces or constituencies."[79] Its further activities were similarly supportive but muted. The NEA created an in-house Common Core Working Group in late 2012 and began issuing a handful of Core-related grants in 2013—some two years after the AFT's Innovation Fund began funding Common Core projects.

NEA president Dennis Van Roekel eventually endorsed the Common Core directly in January 2014, though in ambiguous terms: The Common Core was "our best guess of what students need to know to be successful. . . . If someone has a better answer than that, I'd like to see it."[80] Yet a month later, NEA suggested that the Common Core implementation had been "botched." The union then said that states needed a process to incorporate union input despite earlier input from the union.[81] By that time, several NEA affiliates, including New York's, had passed resolutions or issued statements opposing the Common Core.

Part of the difference between the unions was that the NEA's primary concern was about the Core's effect on *teachers*. As it was a union, this was not earth-shattering news, and NEA lobbyists had argued in the past that standards and assessment were "mechanistic" and secondary to class-size reduction, teacher training, and pay.[82] In 2013, an NEA representative argued that the Common Core could only be done right if implementation "is done in ways that support teachers."[83] Although that was also part of AFT's mission, statements from Weingarten frequently highlighted effects of the standards on students, as had statements from past presidents Sandra Feldman and Albert Shanker. Although the Common Core might have faced less turbulent waters if the NEA had mounted a vigorous defense of the standards, its non-opposition provided the standards with a safe harbor for their initial rollout. Teachers would have to form their own opinions of the standards, but Democrats knew, too, that the teachers' unions would not come after them if they supported the standards.

FUNDING THE CORE THROUGH PRIVATE PHILANTHROPY

The design and implementation of the Common Core State Standards were tests for a new generation of educational philanthropy. Traditional educational philanthropy from the likes of the Ford Foundation, the Carnegie Corporation of New York, and the MacArthur Foundation had long eschewed "political" projects in favor of bolstering existing teachers and institutions; they certainly contributed to favored schools and teaching methods—and their research work led to a spate of lawsuits challenging the constitutionality of school funding—but they kept due respect for the norms of the education profession.[84] Such an approach was thought to create greater buy-in from teachers and administrators.

Walter Annenberg's 1993 "challenge to the nation" marked the last major gift in this tradition of educational philanthropy. The billionaire's record-breaking $500 million gift to over 2,400 American public schools was widely heralded as a "dream." Although Annenberg's grants had goals—smaller, innovative schools; greater local control; higher academic standards; and increased public–private partnership—Annenberg continued the hands-off tradition of other foundation donors.[85] Different schools could pursue different projects and the implementation would be left to teachers and administrators inside the existing system. But a decade later, most philanthropies saw the grants as a failure. Although some schools and students benefited immensely, the grants had not fundamentally changed American schooling. A new generation of philanthropists were disappointed by the limited return on investment from Annenberg and struck out on a new path.

They would not trust the "experts."

Instead, these "venture philanthropists" would set clear goals, fund research to support those goals, and keep their fingers in the implementation. The explosive growth of open enrollment and charter schools combined with the politically successful introduction of private school vouchers in the 1990s challenged the value of working from within.[86] These policies *all* implied that traditional school politics were unresponsive to the needs of students and wishes of parents. And because they were politically successful—all three reforms came through state legislatures or Congress—venture philanthropists saw a political opening. They would not have to work through the system, either.

In this new world, Bill Gates played an outsized role. Although his foundation was not the only major private funder of education reform policies—others were the Broad Foundation, the Walton Family Foundation, Ewing Marion Kauffman Foundation, and the Laura and John Arnold Foundation—the Bill & Melinda Gates Foundation was a core funder for virtually all of the pro-Common Core organizations. The Gates Foundation was formed in 2000 from a handful of smaller Gates-related foundations, and had $42.9 billion in endowments in 2015.[87] It had made a high-profile foray into education with an initiative beginning in March 2000 that emphasized small high schools; hundreds of districts took up the foundation's goals and its money. Despite the money and energy, by 2009, the results of that effort were ambiguous at best. In Bill Gates' annual report letter, he noted, "The hope was that after a few years they would operate at the same cost per student as before, but they would have become much more effective. Many of the small schools that we invested in did not improve students' achievement in any significant way."[88]

But Gates' interest in education was not deterred. In addition to poverty, hunger, and health, the Foundation had an abiding interest in boosting high school education. Even as its small high schools were not working quite as expected, the Foundation was funding work to improve state standards or to align standards with college or career expectations. Gates' interest in improving academic standards lines up neatly with the goals of the national education summits of the previous decade. Those summits *were* about raising standards, but they were also focused on improving data collection and using technology to improve teaching. In 1996, IBM was taking the lead on teaching technology (and Gates' Microsoft was not listed as a participant), but by 2001, Gates' Microsoft was on board and the Foundation provided funds to support the National Education Summit of that year. Technology—and the ability to use technology to improve teaching—was the link to the standards for Gates. The major difference between Gates and the many other business executives who supported higher standards was that the Gates Foundation had substantial cash to promote them.

The best evidence of this link for Gates was his trope that American education was "obsolete" and in need of measurement. Gates praised the Common Core in 2009 because it would lead to better measurement for the public and for teachers. "Without measurement, there is no pressure for improvement," he said.

> We need longitudinal data systems that track student performance and are linked to the teacher; and we need fewer, clearer, higher standards that are common from state to state. The standards will tell the teachers what their students are supposed to learn, and the data will tell them whether they're learning it. These two changes will open up options we've never had before. . . . When the tests are aligned to the common standards, the curriculum will line up as well—and that will unleash powerful market forces in the service of better teaching. For the first time, there will be a large base of customers eager to buy products that can help every kid learn and every teacher get better.[89]

He echoed some of these statements in a speech to the AFT in 2010, as he announced the foundation's efforts to better measure effective teaching though technology. "We have to make sure that teachers get the evaluations, training, standards, curriculum, assessments, and the student data they need to improve their practice. . . . The chief goal is to work with teachers—using technology, data and research—to develop a system of evaluation that teachers believe is fair and will help them improve," he said.[90]

If teachers and curriculum at single schools could not "improve students' achievement," perhaps changing the standards for those schools could. The Gates Foundation and its predecessor foundations sweetened the pot for Common Core in 1999 with a $1.0 million grant to Achieve, Inc., "to support comprehensive benchmarking and review of academic standards and assessments between states." In 2005, another $2.1 million grant to that organization was meant "to help states align secondary school math expectations with the demands of postsecondary education and work." The ADP received a $12.6 million grant in 2008. The Education Trust received multiple grants for operating support; the Thomas B. Fordham Institute received money to grade state standards; the Education Commission of the States received money to build "awareness" of the "rationale" for Common Core; and the NGA received money to work on "implementation of the Common Core State Standards." By 2015, the Gates Foundation listed 208 grantees in all who received money to support Common Core specifically, which does not include any related pro-standards work.[91]

Gates was not the only one, of course, and several foundations banded together as the Collaborative for Student Success, including the Broad Foundation, the Carnegie Corporation of New York, the Hewlett Foundation, and the ExxonMobil Foundation. This organization made grants to local organizations to provide a "fact based about the Common Core . . . that accurately represents the . . . teachers and academic experts who have contributed to the creation and implementation of high standards across the country."[92] These activities included drafting letters to place in newspapers, forming political coalitions among higher-education officials, and issuing pro-Common Core press releases.[93]

Even though foundations like Gates only grant a fraction of what the U.S. Department of Education does on an annual basis (itself a fraction of state government monies), school districts and organizations are exceedingly eager for outside funds. Foundations *can* have tremendous impact. One scholar notes the breadth and depth of reforms that foundation grants made in New York City and Los Angeles (including some from Gates), and that these foundations are increasingly important to federal education policy: "The federal government draws talent and ideas from the philanthropic sector. Simultaneously, the Department of Education is relying on foundations as partners and supporters to advance aspects of the administration's agenda. . . . Elements of the reforms that have already occurred in New York City and Los Angeles are becoming part of an emerging national education agenda led by public and private actors."[94]

The appearance of collusion created unease on the left. Foundations of the past shied away from political controversy—they were philanthropic, after all—and even Bill Gates sought to distance himself from the fray in a tense interview with a Washington Post reporter. "These are not political things," he replied when asked about the policy positions of his foundation's grantees. "These are where people are trying to apply expertise to say, 'Is this a way of making education better?'"[95] But when the Democratic Administration seemed to partner with self-identified conservative organizations and indisputable billionaires to advance the Common Core, liberals smelled a rat. Critics on the left saw the Common Core's connection with philanthropy and private sector ground in general as an end-run around democratic accountability. "CCSS is glaringly undemocratic and stands as a lesson for what can happen when one man has enough money to enforce his opinion via 'checkbook vote,'" wrote Schneider.[96]

As in all politics, money is a route of influence, and many on the left saw philanthropy as "buying" officials and policy. The phrase "Gates-funded" appeared frequently in blog posts and comments as shorthand to suggest that results from a study or comments from an author were "bought." For example, Carol Burris, a prominent opponent of Common Core from New York, sought to destroy the credibility of a Common Core supporter this way:

> Mr. Sigmund is the director of High Achievement New York, a group funded by the Bill and Melinda Gates Foundation, the Helmsley Charitable Trust and the Robin Hood Foundation to promote and defend the Common Core. Mr. Sigmund is also an advisor to a group which advocates for renovations of New York and New Jersey airports, a favored project of Governor Cuomo. There is no indication that Mr. Sigmund has a background in teaching or learning.[97]

Jack Hassard, a self-identified progressive blogger, argued that Gates took criticism of the Common Core as an attack on his investments rather than concerns for educating students. "Why is Bill Gates so concerned about those that have taken on Achieve's Common Core State Standards?" he wrote. "The answer is that the Gates Foundation has invested about $2.3 billion into the Common Standards and related efforts. . . . As we've seen, someone with a lot of money can influence organizations in ways that ordinary classroom educators cannot."[98] Ravitch went further to suggest that Barack Obama, too, had been bought. "Almost every consequential education group was funded by the Gates Foundation to study or promote the Common Core standards. . . . What made the Gates' coup possible was the close relationship between the Gates Foundation and the Obama administration."[99]

Others took a more conspiratorial tone. The problem, in this view, was that philanthropy money was tainted by a "corporate agenda" fundamentally incompatible with critics' conception of American education. The most visible purveyor of this view was the vocal Badass Teachers Association. In addition to opposition to the Common Core, it was opposed to any educational policy attached to foundation money. Its Web site published an open letter to New York State's commissioner of education that suggested that foundation money itself was pecunia non grata. The letter claimed that "here in [New York State], anything associated with the Bill & Melinda Gates Foundation and education is unacceptable. If you follow the money trail, it all leads to privatization of our public schools. . . . Without hesitation you [Commissioner of Education MaryEllen Elia] are a proponent of the Gates-funded Common Core State Standards."[100] Others took this view to further extreme and suggested that private money went hand in hand with a scheme to "privatize" education. Fenwick English, the university professor, wrote that foundation money "sloshed behind the scenes to elect or select candidates who 'buy' the . . . corporate agenda." Those funded by such money "polemicize . . . in support of neoliberal policies."[101] Though he does not mention Common Core in name, English derides common curriculum and lists three figures central to the Common Core—Arne Duncan, Chester Finn, and Lou Gerstner—as "enemies" who "want to take public education down a road where it will not perform any better, or even possible worse, than it does today, and in the process substantially degrade or destroy . . . 'civic virtue.'"[102] And Diane Ravitch memorably titled a chapter in one of her books on education reform as "The Billionaire Boys' Club."[103]

CONCLUSION

As with criticism of Common Core from the right, criticism of the standards from the left took on a grassroots quality with ample support from the blogosphere and social media. But unlike criticism on the right, no prominent politicians on the left voiced opposition to the Common Core. Combined with the settled support from Democrats for major elements of the Core's goals, critics on the left tended to see furtive motives behind the Common Core as a chief threat *rather* than the standards themselves.

This is most apparent in progressives' treatment of private funding. It was unquestionable that foundation money from Gates and other organizations was instrumental in promoting the Common Core. But the critique from the left seemed fixated on a single foundation despite the broader foundation support. In 2012, an education philanthropy group reported that 24 percent of education-related philanthropies were funding or were planning to fund Common Core-themed activities. Fully 33 percent of these were place-based foundations (tied to a particular city or school district), and these were the largest category. Some 24 percent were private foundations, 21 percent were corporate, and 14 percent were family foundations.[104] The report also noted that most of this money went toward improving teacher implementation of the Common Core, in line with the wishes of some liberal groups, including the NEA and AFT. It was also notable that, while the Gates Foundation did provide significant funds to Common Core–related activities, it did not conduct *any* of the reports or research that led to the Common Core, and it was notably absent from the initial discussions about curriculum and standards in the 1990s and early 2000s.

The broad support from civil rights groups seemed to lay to rest this critique. Gates' strong support of the Common Core may well have dovetailed with a concern that non-white and poor American children needed better standards across the board. Perhaps The Education Trust advocated unpopular teacher assessment measures, but even the organization's critics granted that it was concerned with needy students first. And Democrats at the state level often expressed as strong support for the Common Core as the president of the United States had.

The Common Core *did* find something in common. Despite the withering public glare to which the standards were subject in 2014 and 2015, opponents on the left, as on the right, had difficulty finding traction against the standards. The process angered the critics, but the product pleased many in the states.

SEVEN

Through a Glass Darkly: The Way Forward

The Common Core left the realm of shadows in 2009. The dream of national standards, so close in 1994, was ushered from dream to reality through a fortuitous political opening that year. No Child Left Behind (NCLB) was in political disarray, the Republican administration was unpopular even among fellow partisans, and the incoming president campaigned on transformational change. The policy window was cracked open, and the Common Core flew through it. The Core was easily, eagerly adopted—Kentucky did so before the standards were final—and proponents relished their successes.

Supporters *did* have cause for jubilation. The Common Core did what 20 years of trying had not. Governors and President George H. W. Bush tried to promise their way to higher standards at Charlottesville in 1989; Clinton tried to legislate them from Washington in 1994; Achieve, Inc., tried to leverage business influence; and a coalition of interest groups tried the bureaucratic route with the American Diploma Project (ADP). Each attempt had some successes—especially the Diploma Project—but none succeeded in transforming state standards, driving curriculum, or aligning teacher assessment as the Common Core State Standards Initiative (CCSSI) did.

ACCOMPLISHMENTS OF THE COMMON CORE

What has the Common Core accomplished?

First, it dramatically raised state standards in almost every state. Massachusetts and Indiana had reason to complain that their standards were equal to or better than the Common Core, but 43 *other* states that adopted the new, better standards. Standards themselves do not raise student achievement or guarantee success (the effect of standards alone is ambiguous at best), but standards are an explicit promise to students, parents, colleges, and employers. A diploma's text might read, "This student has met the standards for graduation." Implied in that statement is a promise that those standards guarantee competence if not excellence. It is not for nothing that hospitals flaunt *their* compliance to standards. For the first time in American history, the Common Core built a public edifice promising a meaningful set of skills and body of knowledge in any state that adopted the standards. Combined with the ADP, the arrival of the Common Core meant that colleges *and* employers could expect that high school students would have been exposed to a known set of material—wherever they lived. This fulfilled an often-made dream of governors and others who, like Gov. Bill Clinton, were given to saying that students' education should not depend on whether they lived in Massachusetts or Mississippi. It was also a boon to America's mobile society as children moving in the middle of the school year—especially common among lower-income students—would face the same standards wherever they attended.

Second, the Common Core destroyed "the proficiency illusion" that many states had projected since standards and accountability swept public education in the 1990s. Prior to the Common Core, federal laws in the form of the Improving America's Schools Act (1994) and the NCLB Act (2001) had prodded the states to write standards, and NCLB required states to show that students met them. States become notorious for both slipshod standards *and* extremely rosy interpretations of their assessments of them. Kevin Carey, an education policy writer, faulted states for their Panglossian view of the world:

> When states have the opportunity to define the terms of their own success, many will make themselves look better than they really are. The inclination of state education officials to overstate academic progress is understandable. Most chief state school officers report directly to elected officials and one-third are elected themselves. In providing educational results to the public, they're essentially reporting on their own performance as education leaders. They have every incentive to report—and create—good news.[1]

And states were taking that opportunity. The concepts and skills for "proficiency" in reading were vastly different in Mississippi than they were in Massachusetts. In 2005, the state of Mississippi claimed that 89 percent of its fourth-grade students were proficient in reading. In Massachusetts, the number was just 50 percent. Yet, the National Assessment of Educational Progress (NAEP), which uses the same standard across the country, found that only 18 percent of Mississippi fourth-graders met its proficiency level, while 44 percent of Massachusetts' did.[2] The tests measured different standards, but the discrepancy between student performance on state standards and national standards gave policy makers pause. The Thomas B. Fordham Institute argued in 2007 that "standards-based reform hinges on the assumption that one can trust the standards, that they are stable anchors to which the educational accountability vessel is moored. If the anchor doesn't hold firm, the vessel moves—and if the anchor really slips, the vessel can crash against the rocks or be lost at sea."[3] The Common Core did not directly establish the second part of the equation, assessment, but it did guarantee that students in Mississippi and Massachusetts were *expected* to learn the same concepts in the same grades. A student moving from one state to another would find compatible academic expectations. Policy makers, too, could expect that state exam results *should* be comparable to national exam results. Mismatches would guarantee that there was a game afoot.

Third, the Common Core established a new, common rationale for public education. Schools would train students for college and career, and not primarily for citizenship, local priorities, social life, cultural appreciation, exploration of children's interests, or any number of other goals. The political force of this is hard to deny. On his blog in 2015, Fordham's Petrilli asked Republican presidential contenders, "Do you mean that you oppose standards that aim to get young people ready for college or a good-paying career? Do you think that's too high a standard? What standard would you prefer?"[4] Although politicians and activists postulate other purposes with some frequency (especially that school should "rectify inequality"), publicly dismissing college readiness or "good-paying" careers would be politically suicidal. This rhetoric is pervasive in contemporary politics in both major political parties. In his 2015 State of the Union address, the Democratic president claimed that "by the end of this decade, two in three job openings will require some higher education." New York Governor Andrew Cuomo (D) likewise dismissed other claims for education. Unions and parent groups in that state had publicly questioned what they saw as a testing regime, but Cuomo turned the question back. "Now 38 percent of high school students are college ready," he said. "How can 38 percent of students be ready, but 98 percent of the teachers be effective? . . . Who are we kidding, my friends? The problem is clear and the solution is clear."[5] For him, if 98 percent of teachers were effective, 98 percent of students should be college ready. College and career readiness would be central to American education policy.

These policy shifts were no superficial change. *Both* Democratic and Republican politicians easily adopted the verbiage of the Common Core, if not the title. All major national civil rights organizations supported the standards. Both major teachers' unions spent considerable political capital defending the standards, and substantial financial resources promoting implementation in their members' schools and districts. School districts themselves had taken millions of dollars from private philanthropies to improve and implement aspects of the Common Core, boosting local buy-in. The National Parent Teacher Association was on board. Each group had reservations about aspects of the Common Core, but all believed that "fewer, higher, better" was a dramatic improvement on American education in the era of NCLB.

In other words, while the ultimate *goal* of national education policy remained unchanged, the theory of action to get it changed. American education policy would still seek to remedy inequality among students, but the inequality would not be rectified necessarily by increasing spending, bolstering school choice, or catering to students' diverse interests. Instead, schooling would rectify inequality of *economic* opportunity through standardizing *content*. Certainly, other policies would continue, and teachers' unions, in particular, were quick to ask for more and better teacher training and pay, but the method had shifted. All major stakeholders agreed: Economic opportunity and educational equity was to be achieved through better standards. It seemed the stars were aligned.

COMMON CORE'S POLITICAL PITFALLS

The easy political success proved a mirage. Grumbling on the left about back-room dealing merged with anger about federal control on the right. The cross-talk from disgruntled partisans and activists might have remained so much static if Barack Obama had not quickly and visibly taken credit for the standards. Although his fingerprints were absent from the Common Core, his endorsement of them destroyed their bipartisan appeal. To critics on the right, Obama's support transformed these new educational standards, endorsed by such Republican stalwarts as Mitch Daniels (R-IN) and Jeb Bush (R-FL), into yet another example of narcissistic, progressive high-handedness by the president. The Common Core did not escape the visceral polarization of American politics across the president's two terms.

Likewise, some Democrats began to take issue with the apparent extension of corporate power into the Common Core. Why should *every* Core-related project—in the schools, in the states, at the think tanks, by the

Council of Chief State School Officers (CCSSO), in the American Federation of Teachers (AFT)—seem to be bankrolled by Bill Gates? Why was test giant Pearson given a plethora of state testing contracts with little effective competition from (much smaller) firms like the American Institutes for Research? Why was there little public input on the standards? Why were legislators almost entirely absent from the initial debates?

Even with the president's attention and Republicans' stunning political gains in the states in 2010 and 2014, the Common Core as a *standard* is unlikely to fail. Perhaps Common Core was "incentivized" by the federal government, but it was clearly developed away from Washington, DC. It was just as obviously sponsored by the state-led organizations National Governors Association (NGA) and CCSSO. The political ire on the right was driven by the actions of a particular president in a particular context. Outside that context, "ObamaCore" would no longer have the same political bite. In that same way, the left's concerns rang hollow as teachers' unions came under (successful) attacks in many states by Republicans and some Democrats, and conservatives wondered how liberals could criticize the Common Core's adoption after the legal and procedural gymnastics Democrats took to pass the still-unpopular Affordable Care Act. They also wondered how they could criticize the president, one of the most liberal presidents in American history. He was clearly one of their own.[6] But the Common Core's long-term success does not depend on these shifting political skirmishes—especially *after* its widespread adoption. Even in Louisiana, Gov. Jindal's successor dropped all remaining lawsuits against the U.S. Department of Education. The train has left the station.

The standards are also unlikely to fall under the weight of controversy about educational methods, book lists (or the lack thereof), or even criticism of overdrawn evidence. These controversies dogged earlier educational reforms, too. Rhetorical wars over reading and mathematics raged in the 1920s, 1960s, and 1990s. Boosters of many reforms offer "evidence," but in the world of education, evidence is all but nonexistent; and programs continue with fervent supporters even when evidence is *against* them. The federal Head Start Program, which funds preschool education and social programs, has no observable long-term effects despite the sincere desire of advocates for the program.[7] Supporters troop on. Reducing class sizes has mixed (though generally positive) evidence. A fabled study of Tennessee classroom sizes (the STAR study) was restricted to a specific set of conditions. It was not clear whether students benefited each year from smaller classes or whether the considerable cost of small classrooms justified the academic results.[8] But both of these education favorites offer hefty political benefits in spite of evidence. Evidence is unlikely to bring down the Common Core, which also enjoyed considerable political benefits. It is at least as well supported by evidence as other political favorites.

In these circumstances, the Common Core is likely to survive. The standards will be rebranded as in Indiana, South Carolina, and Utah; they will be extended in other states like Massachusetts; and they may even be renegotiated, as in Missouri. But the explicit support of the bipartisan NGA and CCSSO gave the Common Core an imprimatur of acceptability from governors and bureaucrats, and those same governors and bureaucrats were unwilling to reopen Pandora's box. For example, Oklahoma Governor Mary Fallin (R) only reluctantly repealed her state's participation in the Common Core. Even though Oklahoma, unlike other states, adopted clearly different academic standards after repeal, *Politico* magazine had rated Fallin as a "wildcard" in Common Core politics.[9] In late 2013, she issued an executive order clarifying that the federal government had not written the Common Core, and that the state was ultimately responsible for the standards.[10] But the governor still touted the Common Core as a political *accomplishment*! The governor "raised academic standards" by "implementing exit exams and new Common Core standards," her Web site read in 2014.[11] She was not a true critic.

The standards are threatened instead by deep political and philosophical questions that appeal to partisans across the spectrum. The first: While the *content* of the standards has been the subject of some criticism and late-night TV comedians, the substantial—and existential—debate has focused on the politics of control. The fundamental political critique of the Common Core is that schools are primarily local affairs. The critics argue that local decision making is more democratic and therefore superior to elite-driven, closed-door, expert-made, or federally required mandates. Some on the left made this argument in relation to the Common Core, but the critique has a long pedigree in American politics on the right and on the left. The second: The Core philosophical threat concerns the purpose of American education. The breakthrough for the Common Core came because Republican and Democratic governors *agreed* on the central purpose of schooling, to wit, preparation for college education or gainful, purposeful employment. It is not certain that parents or teachers agree. As with local control, the purposes of American education have been contested since the country's founding. Are they to prepare moral citizens for public life and services? To explore natural interests and proclivities? Or to prepare students for adult work? The Common Core has an answer, but the standards' political survival hinges on whether the public embraces their raison d'être.

THREATS TO THE COMMON CORE

The Common Core State Standards *are* national standards. Even though supporters of higher state standards had been burned by the term "national" in the 1990s, the broad national coverage and majority of states (and children) who are now covered by them leaves no other interpretation. In that, the first major challenge to the Core is whether national standards actually deprive local schools of real political control, or, more politically, whether parents, teachers, and politicians *think* the Common Core actually deprives schools of real political control.

Conservatives have been quick to oppose the Common Core because it struck at local, or at least state, control of education. Joy Pullman, a prominent conservative critic, highlighted this as the greatest threat. For her, the Common Core was just another centralized "curriculum mandate" that would perpetuate poor-quality education. "The answer to the destructive unintended consequences of central planning is not more central planning and mandates on ordinary folks from elitist bureaucrats who will never meet their test subjects. It is to realize that central planning disempowers average folks and advantages the well-connected, and in the process destroys quality," she wrote.[12] Scores of Utah Governor Herbert's constituents made reference to local control. One said, "National standards are a threat to freedom. Even rigid state standards do not allow for the flexibility local school districts [need]." Another told the governor, "Personal responsibility, liberty, and local accountability will breed success far better than any broad, far-reaching standard ever could. We can be the light of hope, shining brightly on the hill, inspiring the rest of the Union to pursue a better path." Herbert was forced to seek an opinion from his attorney general regarding Common Core's effect on local control. The attorney general was blunt: "There was no acquiescence of [local] educational control or state sovereignty at the time of [Common Core] adoption."[13]

"Local control" of education is something of a quixotic endeavor in contemporary American school districts as states supply an increasing share of money, building requirements, and, yes, academic standards to schools. If by "local control" proponents mean robust public input and local elections, they may be chasing the wind. Although some have found that school districts follow public opinion to an extent, public participation in local school politics is minuscule. In a typical year, fewer than 15 percent of registered voters participate in school elections.[14] Collective bargaining between school boards and teachers' unions further constrain local control. Some states prohibit teachers' contracts from specifying "curriculum" issues, but the length of the school day, time spent planning for lessons,

teacher evaluation, and overall workload *can* be. Those issues place meaningful limitations on what curriculum is adopted and how it is used. In practice, local control is little more than the local teachers' association or union
and local school board circling scarce school dollars with little public input.

Despite the limited reality of local control, most Americans place great
stock in their local schools. For the last 15 years, the Gallup Poll consistently found that 75 percent of parents were somewhat or completely satisfied with their children's school, even as 50–55 percent of the general public
was somewhat or completely dissatisfied with K–12 education as shown in
Figure 7.1.[15] Although a minority of Americans, parents, and teachers support the opt-out movement, the initial waves of opting out showed a distinct pattern: districts with higher socioeconomic status had substantially
more parents opting their children out of exams. These are warning shots;
the same parents are far more likely to be politically involved than others.
In Colorado, New Jersey, and New York, parents were able to hamstring
state accountability systems—despite threats from the state government and
the federal government that schools might lose money.[16] One opt-out organizer said if state officials "think parents are unhappy with them now, just
wait until they take money away from school districts."[17] Those opting out

Figure 7.1   Approval Rating of American Schools, 1999–2015

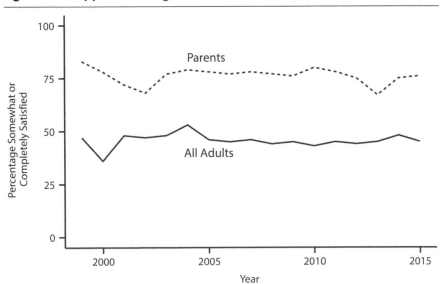

Question for parents: How satisfied are you with the quality of education your oldest child is receiv-
ing? Question for all adults: Overall, how satisfied are you with the quality of education students receive
in kindergarten through grade 12 in the U.S. today? *Source:* Gallup, Inc.

suggested that they were protesting the takeover of local schools. "Parents have been lobbying the governor, the Board of Regents, the legislature, demanding a reduction in high-stakes testing, demanding to have their classrooms be returned," one opt-out parent leader in New York told *CNN*. "We've been ignored, and enough is enough." Another parent argued that the Common Core was "all about money and out kids are pawns" of the state and testing companies.[18] Should the very parents who are politically active see the Common Core as thwarting local schools, the Common Core's long-term viability will be in danger.

Part of the disconnect on local control—obvious in the opt-out participation rates—is that the Common Core was meant to boost the achievement for the neediest students, but the Common Core affects *all* students. Unlike most federal programs for low-income students, the effects of the national (not federal) Common Core are obvious in all classrooms, not just in low-income areas. Secretary of Education Arne Duncan might have accurately diagnosed that "white, suburban moms" were disgruntled about the Common Core, but not for the reasons he thought. Those moms had children who were not likely to see the need for more attention to college readiness; their children were *already* more likely to go to college than the average American student.[19] They only saw the less salutary aspects of the standards and assessment dream: testing. The Common Core itself might not have required assessments, but assessments were clearly part of the package. Virtually all of the supporters of the Common Core *also* supported some form of testing. One need not look farther than David Coleman, the architect of the Common Core, who went from there to the nation's most influential testing company, the College Board. The Fordham Institute was up front, too. "Much else needs to happen before one's education system can reach that destination. One important element is development of strong assessments that are aligned with the standards. . . . This is potentially a bigger deal than the Common Core itself, because 'what's on the test' is the real standard, for better or worse," Petrilli and Finn wrote.[20] The Common Core was sold as a benefit for struggling, non-white, low-income students; the point of the exercise was lost for less-needy families. And they were politically active.[21]

Testing companies were slow to respond. In a fit of hubris, Common Core–aligned tests were also touted as "higher and better," complete with high failure rates to match. There is no doubt that hours-long tests produce more, and more detailed, information about students' progress in school, but they also focus attention on the tests rather than the content. In Florida, for example, Common Core–aligned tests waltzed into an already politically fractious debate about the role of testing in education; even the most ardent supporters of the Common Core in Florida had to announce sharp cuts to the testing schedule.[22] If those failure rates hit the same politically active families with college- and career-bound children, the Common Core will falter.

There was some evidence of this in 2015 as members of Congress worked on the Every Student Succeeds Act, the much-maligned law that helped spawn Common Core's initial success. Although serious differences emerged between the parties on school choice, block grants, and other predictable issues, a major roadblock emerged over the role of state standards and federally required testing. The House of Representatives passed a bill including a right for parents to opt their children out of state tests. The Senate version of the same bill would have abolished multi-state testing requirements (à la PARCC or SBAC), and it specifically prohibited the federal government from requiring or promoting Common Core or any multi-state academic assessments.[23] Democrats staunchly defended testing, and it remained; but Common Core supporters were few. Instead, they and Republicans would only require "challenging academic content standards" as defined by each state.[24] These positions threatened the loss of a common testing framework and granted *explicit* permission from the federal government to abandon the Common Core.

In sum, the Common Core's supporters, and the testing companies, need to attend to the politically active parents who see little need for the Common Core. They might not object to new standards—Common Core might be safe—but the tests they cannot abide. To the extent that Common Core is identified with the tests, then the risk to the standards is great. The testing highlights the (apparent) loss of local control and, with it, local political support. Local decisions may privilege the status quo, but they by definition have political support. If, as boosters of the Common Core allege, existing state standards were hodgepodge, overbroad, and required very little effort to satisfy, they may systematically disadvantage children whose life chances are already limited. But if the Common Core is indeed a distant mandate, it may undermine the confidence of teachers and parents in the public, tax-funded school system. It will create strong incentives to shirk or cheat the system. The tests were too much, and they threaten the standards.

These were the same incentives that undercut NCLB and made its accountability system laughable for its rosiness.

The politics of control are more likely to sidetrack the Common Core in the short term, but the common standards face a deeper threat from a persistent, lurking philosophical debate. What *is* the purpose of school? Governors and business leaders for 30 years have argued that education is for employment (and maybe college). Since governors' own electoral prospects are contingent on economic performance, their support is not hard to explain. Business leaders, too, are rightly interested in the quality of new hires. It is expensive to train employees, and even in times of high unemployment, recruiters reported difficulty hiring, in part due to the low quality of job applicants.[25] Even the Senate version of the 2015 ESEA reauthorization bill, despite its put-down of Common Core, included several clauses supporting "college and career readiness." That victory may be temporary; American education has only recently been driven by academic performance or job prospects. If the American public rejects this narrative, the philosophical reason for Common Core will collapse, and the bipartisan political coalition with it.

The Common Core has some affinities with what is called "essentialist" education, a view often associated with Theodore (Ted) Sizer.[26] Essential schools emphasize that all student must meet a school's standards, and they typically promote practical application of basic skills to real-world problems so that students can contribute positively to society. Similarly, "essential" education promotes *less* topic coverage so that students can better handle a few tasks. (Sizer's model also emphasized tailored, individual instruction, something that the Common Core does not do.) The Common Core, like essential schools, meant to train students in a few, practical basics well.

But this is only one philosophy of education. Sizer's own "Coalition of Essential Schools" was a relatively small, voluntary network of schools; the Common Core gave elements of essentialism a national audience. The Core's version of essentialism toppled the reigning progressivist philosophy with a potent left–right coalition in the late 1990s, but progressive supporters remained, knowing that there is no such thing as a permanent coalition in American politics. The progressive view, most associated with John Dewey, sought to develop the "whole child," whereby students would experiment and learn with guidance, but not answers, from teachers. Problem solving rather than content was given pride of place. Importantly, progressivism explicitly downplayed preparation for adulthood; instead, the social, emotional, physical—and intellectual—needs of children came first. Educators should "recognize the distinctive talents that individual children possess and to create an environment that actualizes those potentialities. . . . We are interested in helping children become who they are."[27] Although political progressives certainly have held this view, it is not exclusive to the domain of left-wing politics; Catholic and other private schools frequently adopt elements of whole-child learning. Even the pro-Common Core Catholic Identity Curriculum Integration group acknowledged this: Catholic schools would be "going beyond those [Common Core] standards to educate the whole child. Catholic schools cherish each child by giving each child the knowledge, skills, and understanding needed to transform the world in the light of Gospel values."[28]

This vision for schooling has not gone quietly. Among the loudest (and most superficial) manifestation of this protest of the Common Core—as standards, *not* as curriculum—was that the Core elevated "informational texts" far above literature. Christel Swasey, the Common Core blogger, argued that "Imagination makes children read and helps them to love books. No little child is motivated to read because he/she is concerned about college and career, years from now. The child reads because the story is interesting. Period."[29] In a similar vein, another conservative critic noted that children understand stories better than "information"—and so the Common Core would undermine the whole understanding of culture: "This is the reason we love fiction: it plunges us into the midst of history, and awakens our eyes and minds to its reality. You can tell a student to read news articles about the Cold War—or you can tell them to read *A Day in the Life of Ivan Denisovich*. Which, do you think, will be more compelling?"[30]

Others argued that "informational texts" subverted the purpose of the Common Core *because* they artificially divided human experience into "fiction" and "non-fiction," denying that education *had* to be holistic. One blogger asked, "Did the folks who put together these 'standards' actually think that literary works never present arguments, make claims, use reasoning of varying degrees of validity, nor present evidence of varying degrees of relevance and sufficiency? . . . It's Philistine to divide the world up into the literary and the informational. Are Plato's dialogues literary or informational?"[31] Some English teachers, understandably, found the standards offensive because fiction was relegated to "not for college or career." They argued that the works, like the child, had to be understood in totality:

So, you see, [the Common Core] really only use[s] literature in the classroom as a sort of bucket to carry in little nuggets of concept and skill. The literature doesn't really have any intrinsic value of its own. Why read the whole novel when we only really care about (aka test) a couple of paragraphs on page 142? If we were hoping to pick up some metaphor-reading skills along the way, why not just read a page of metaphor examples? . . . Literature lets students experience people and places and feelings and ideas that they do not encounter in their own world, and it lets them encounter things exactly like what they experience in their own, and it lets them experience both in ways that open the experience up to new understanding and expression. . . . Reading literature is part of the process of growing and advancing and becoming more fully human.[32]

Common Core supporters bristled at this particular critique. In a post faulting both Sandra Stotsky's and Diane Ravitch's obsession with "informational texts," Kathleen Porter-Magee returned fire: "In an irony so rich even Alanis Morissette would correctly label it, at this point the debate over Common Core implementation has become so heated that opponents of the standards are publicly and repeatedly misrepresenting what the standards require in ways that will actually lead these standards to be implemented in ways that run contrary to both what they actually require and these critics' own deeply held beliefs," she wrote.[33] The standards themselves acknowledged that most informational reading would likely take place outside of English classrooms.

But that is missing the point. The critics see the Common Core's failure as a failure of imagination.

Beyond the standards themselves, harsher critics saw the Common Core as emblematic of a troubled crusade that emphasizes efficiency, competition, and docility above all. Some of them questioned the Common Core's fundamental assumption and asked whether the focus of schooling *should* be college or career. These critics adhered to another philosophy of education, one that saw schools as a means to reconstruct society, whether through multiculturalism, socialism, or egalitarianism. For them, the schools were fundamentally *not* about learning facts or skills, but about eliminating what they saw as inequity in society.

Although Diane Ravitch, the blogger and former federal education official, was not supportive of the Common Core State Standards, she spared them from much of her withering criticism. That was not the case for the philosophy underlying the standards, however. Ravitch's 2013 book *Reign of Error* was sharply critical of the college and career goals of the Common Core and similar education reforms. She also doubted that career education was truly the key to better economic chances in America: "We know what the Gates Foundation wants: It wants a workforce that is prepared to compete with workers in other nations. Leave aside for the moment whether we are losing jobs because of better-educated competitors or because American workers expect to be paid more than workers in China and Bangladesh; businesses outsource where the costs are lowest."[34] For her, the problem was not curriculum, it was American job expectations. Others extended her critique by arguing that the Common Core was demeaning to jobs with lower academic requirement. "We aren't serving anyone well by sending kids this message that college is a requirement for success and happiness in America," one blogger noted. "We need truck drivers and plumbers and carpenters too—all of which are worthwhile and potentially fulfilling professions, especially when they are performed in a culture that values all its workers."[35]

Others saw an overt cultural bias in the Core's expectations. Anthony Cody, the blogger from the left, argued that the Common Core, in fact, would worsen some students' life prospects *because* the standards were "higher." He argued, "We use the Common Core to create an artificial and arbitrary set of barriers to employment, and declare that anyone who is unable to surmount those barriers is too lazy or stupid to succeed in the modern competitive world. . . . It is a sorting mechanism, and a system to justify subjugation and abandonment of the poor and disadvantaged."[36]

These critiques are deeper than the political critique because they hold that the Common Core—and contemporary American schooling—perverted the highest and best use of schooling. These critics typically argued that schools should fulfill a higher calling than college or career. That calling is democratic "struggle." Because "public schools themselves are sites of cultural production," one prominent exponent of this view noted, they are crucial to forming future democratic citizens. "Schools can be democratic public spheres that can foster critical consciousness, democratic dispositions, and habits of engaged citizenry. . . . Public schooling has also been open to ongoing experimentation, tinkering, and response to intellectual movements across the political spectrum including good ones like progressivism and bad ones like scientific management."[37] The Common Core would seem to foreclose *both* democratic discourse in local schools and intellectual experimentation.

More extreme proponents of this view charged that the Common Core was simply corporate collusion with ascendant politicians. The standards and attendant reforms exalted certain corporate standards, in these critics' view. That philosophy, one argued, idealized "upward individual economic mobility (the promise of cashing in knowledge for jobs) and the social ideals of global economic competition. . . . [The] thesis has infected educational thought as the only questions on reform agendas appear to be how to best enforce knowledge and curriculum conducive to national economic interests and the expansion of a corporately managed model of globalization as perceived from the perspective of business."[38]

These critics are harsh, and they are unlikely to overthrow the Common Core on their own. Jobs and college are the fabric of American educational politics, and no halcyon representation of education past (or Marxist future) is likely to fray it. But they do offer a warning should the Common Core not deliver on its promises of better college access or career success. In the not-so-distant past, American education was led by a different piper, one whose tune called students to other paths. Jonathan Goodlad wrote that American educators, parents, and politicians expected schools to shoulder as many dreams as Americans. They wanted athletics, affirmation, citizenship, career training, social services, and democracy. These other goals of schooling continue in the public mind, even if they have taken second place to college and career. The Common Core's lease on their imagination will hold if the standards allow space for other American dreams.

WAKING FROM THE DREAM

The Common Core State Standards Initiative was an outstanding policy success, and it was a testament to the tenacity of American governors that, after 20 years, they succeeded in enacting the "World Class Standards" they promised in Charlottesville, Virginia. The Common Core also exemplifies the power of institutional politics in the United States. Governors, their state superintendents, and their state boards of education pulled off a standards coup largely without legislative input. Opponents of the standards, and especially legislators, were livid that the standards bypassed the rough-and-tumble of legislative politics—even though standards would not normally have gone through the legislature—but neither the NGA nor the CCSSO wanted a public airing. Public input would thwart the Core goals of standards coherence, "few," and likely "high." Officers at NGA and CCSSO *knew* that state executive branches had broad discretion regarding state standards, and state curriculum standards are in the legal domain of either the state board of education or state superintendent in every state. Some argued that state school boards offered public feedback and openness to the process, but governors, not voters, appoint most state school board members and many state superintendents. (State boards are entirely elected in only seven states—and those states experienced some of the strongest opposition to the Common Core: Alabama, Colorado, Kansas, Michigan, Nebraska, Texas, and Utah. Nebraska and Texas refused to adopt the Common Core.)[39] Common Core supporters knew this political avenue was legal and open when the normal legislative process had proven tortuous.

The strategy was genius, but these institutional politics were the 21st-century equivalent of the smoke-filled rooms of the 19th. Small wonder that legislators and hoi polloi, who were absent from the deliberations, were troubled, angered, or apoplectic over what they *perceived* to be a power grab by a cabal of bureaucrats, testing companies, and well-heeled funders. (Legislators struck back in 2014 with bills designed to quash future revisions to state standards without public [or their] input.)[40] The public would have given the standards scant notice had they not been a sharp departure from the vague, aspirational standards present in many states in 2009. If the Common Core were to have an effect, its supporters would have to run the gauntlet of public accountability.

The Common Core State Standards *were* vast improvements over many states' standards, and the aligned tests promised to remedy widespread, and sometimes deliberate, ignorance over the pace of learning in many American schools. They are good and needed things. Learning gaps in schools are stubborn; willful ignorance in education by teachers, administrators, and politicians perpetrates a fraud on American schoolchildren, especially the neediest. The Common Core is a step to bolster the odds of these children's success in life, not only in college or career, but as productive, active citizens. The standards cannot do it alone—parents, teachers, and peers have far greater influence than any multiplication strategy—but building a solid base, a Core, surely places these children on better footing. Supporters were right to argue that, for all its dross, the substance of the effort was gold.

Despite the noise over the exotic math strategies suggested by the standards and the limited attention they gave to literature, the political *process* was the Common Core's great weakness. The standards are unlikely to be genuinely abandoned by any state, and the dominant college- and career-philosophy of education continues its reign. But try as supporters like to find the way; the plain and clear dream of *common* national standards is fleeting. With the passage of the Every Student Succeeds Act in December 2015, Congress all but gave permission to eject the standards, and the simmering discontent over the aligned tests prompted the practical collapse of *both* federally funded common testing consortia, the SBAC and PARCC. The moral of the Common Core, then, is not that they are a failure. They are not. Instead, they illustrate the root purpose of education in a free society. Education *must* be political because its primary purpose is not reading and writing. Its purpose is to reflect the politics of American democracy. And American democracy is not some textbook ideal, but a messy, divisive, and incremental process. American education is a messy and divisive melee. Could Common Core be any other way?

Appendix A: Key Organizations

NOTABLE ORGANIZATIONS DESIGNING OR ADVOCATING THE COMMON CORE STATE STANDARDS

Achieve, Inc.

Achieve, Inc., had grown out of the frustration with the failure of national standards in the early 1990s, and it was the immediate descendant of a 1996 "National Education Summit" of business leaders and governors led by IBM Chairman Louis "Lou" V. Gerstner.

American Diploma Project

Achieve, Inc., launched the American Diploma Project (ADP) in 2005 to prepare students for the workforce and college. The initiative emphasized school–business collaboration, and it advocated common, higher standards for high school diplomas. Most states mentioned the ADP in their Race to the Top (RTTT) grant applications. The ADP was a pre-cursor to the Common Core.

American Federation of Teachers

The second-largest U.S. teachers' union was very supportive of the Common Core Standards Initiative. The national union was also supportive of the affiliated tests despite strong opposition from several large locals. By 2015, however, it changed its position on the tests due to the link with teacher evaluation.

Bill & Melinda Gates Foundation

A tax-exempt foundation for "impatient optimists" that has a special interest in global health threats like malaria and pneumonia, economic development worldwide, and college- and career-readiness in the United States. In 2014, the foundation had assets in excess of $40 billion.

Collaborative for Student Success

An organization that funded pro-Common Core activity by business groups, teachers, and others.

Council of Chief State School Officers

A private non-profit organization that provides a forum for elected and appointed state superintendents to discuss and advocate for particular educational policies. CCSSO also provides technical and policy expertise to members. All 50 states and the District of Columbia are currently members. It was a major sponsor of the Common Core along with the National Governors Association (NGA).

The Education Trust

A non-profit organization founded by Kati Haycock that advocates for policies to improve academic achievement for low-income and non-white students. The organization helped gain Common Core support from other civil rights interest groups.

Hunt Institute

An education reform policy institute founded by former North Carolina Gov. James B. Hunt (D) in 2001. The organization sponsors governors' workshops on standards, economic development, and academic achievement. The Hunt Institute held informal discussions in 2006 about what would become the Common Core.

Thomas B. Fordham Foundation (and Institute)

A foundation re-founded in 1997 as a pro-education-reform think tank. The organization is notable for its commissioned education research, advocacy of charter schools, and staunch support of high academic standards, including the Common Core. The Thomas B. Fordham Institute was created in 2007 in parallel to the Foundation. After that, the Institute became the public face of the organization's research and advocacy.

NOTABLE ORGANIZATIONS OPPOSED TO THE COMMON CORE

Badass Teachers Association

An organization of teachers who advocate a strong form of teacher control of education, including assessments and curriculum. Opposed to the Common Core largely because it was not teacher-designed or adopted by teacher consent.

FreedomWorks

A non-profit conservative "grassroots" organizer against a broad range of bills, politicians, and policies, including the Affordable Care Act, the Common Core, and Barack Obama. An election-driven organization rather than a policy-driven organization.

Network for Public Education

A group founded by blogger Anthony Cody that advocates for traditional public schooling. It is strongly opposed to Common Core and test-based academic accountability as currently used.

Parents Against Common Core

A loosely knit umbrella group for anti-Common Core parents' groups including Hoosiers Against Common Core, which successfully rolled back Indiana's official participation in the effort. The organization helps coordinate anti-Core messages.

Pioneer Institute

A Massachusetts-based think tank advocating for limited government and market-based public policy. It published sustained attacks on the Common Core and later engaged prominent Core critics to write policy pieces. The organization does not conduct research.

Appendix B: Timeline

1892

Committee of Ten recommends standardizing high school curriculum and lists concepts to which students should be introduced.

1958

National Defense Education Act appropriates funds for states willing to increase math, science, and foreign-language preparation in elementary and secondary schools, as well as colleges and universities.

1965

Elementary and Secondary Education Act commits the federal government to improving racial disparities in educational spending.

1966

Coleman Report finds widespread disparities in educational resources, preparation, and achievement by race and geography.

1983

Nation at Risk issues, suggesting that a "rising tide of mediocrity" threatened the future economic competitiveness of the United States. Likens the crisis to an "act of war."

1989, SEPTEMBER

George H.W. Bush calls an education summit in Charlottesville, VA.

1990, JULY

National Education Goals Panel created, chaired by a governor.

1991

Marshall S. Smith and Jennifer O'Day suggest that state standards spell out what and how students should learn.

1991, APRIL

America 2000 introduced.

1992, OCTOBER

America 2000 filibustered in the Senate; bill dies.

1994

The *Improving America's Schools Act* reconfigures the NAEP to allow state-by-state comparisons of educational performance.

1994, MARCH

Bill Clinton signs *Goals 2000: Educate America Act*. The bill establishes the National Education Standards and Improvement Council (NESIC).

1995, MAY 15

The House votes to repeal NESIC. U.S. Secretary of Education suggests that Goals 2000 will work without it.

1996

Congress passes, and President Clinton signs, a budget eliminating NESIC and Opportunity-to-Learn standards.

1996, MARCH 26–27

IBM Chairman Lou V. Gerstner and Gov. Tommy Thompson (R-WI) convenes the National Education Summit with business leaders and governors in search of "high academic standards, assessment and accountability and improve the use of school technology as a tool to reach high standards."

2001, OCTOBER 9–10

Achieve, Inc., holds a "National Education Summit" that later results in the creation of the American Diploma Project (ADP), one purpose of which was to "identify the 'must-have' knowledge and skills most demanded by higher education and employers."

2002, JANUARY 8

The No Child Left Behind Act (NCLB) is signed, requiring states to participate in NAEP and detailing academic performance for all students.

2005, APRIL 7

Margaret Spellings offers to waive some NCLB requirements if states show achievement *growth* rather than meeting an absolute level.

2006, MAY 15

Education Sector releases Kevin Carey's *Hot Air: How States Inflate Their Educational Progress under NCLB*.

2006, JUNE

Former North Carolina Governor James B. Hunt convenes closed-door meeting of like-minded policy makers in Raleigh, N.C. to discuss national standards.

2006, SEPTEMBER

Alliance for Excellent Education president Bob Wise convenes a second closed-door meeting of education-policy think-tank leaders, including the Aspen Institute, the Education Trust, and the Thomas B. Fordham Foundation.

2006, SEPTEMBER

Thomas B. Fordham Foundation releases *To Dream the Impossible Dream*, proposing ways that national standards could work.

2007

David Coleman and Jason Zimba write "Math and Science Standards That Are Fewer, Clearer, Higher to Raise Achievement at all Levels," a document that prompts the Common Core State Standards Initiative to invite both to participate in drafting the standards.

2007, NOVEMBER

Council of Chief State School Officers' (CCSSO) Annual Policy Forum promotes the idea of common state standards to state superintendents.

2008, JANUARY

The National Research Council holds a two-day workshop at the request of the Hunt Institute, titled "Assessing the Role of K-12 Academic Standards in States."

2008, MARCH

The National Research Council holds a second workshop on state academic standards.

2008, DECEMBER

NGA, CCSSO, and Achieve, Inc., publish *Benchmarking for Success*, which echoes *Nation at Risk* by emphasizing education's ties to economic competitiveness.

2009, MARCH 7

The U.S. Department of Education releases parameters for the Race to the Top (RTTT) competition, which had been authorized in the American Recovery and Restoration Act in February.

2009, APRIL 17

National Governors Association and CCSSO agree to develop national standards and set a 2012 deadline for adoption. They note that the federal government may "incentivize this effort."

2009, JUNE 1

The Common Core State Standards Initiative is formally announced by the National Governors Association.

2009, SEPTEMBER 21

NGA and CCSSO release first public draft of the Common Core State Standards. A grade-by-grade standards draft is released in November.

2010, JANUARY 19

Deadline for states to submit first-round RTTT grant applications. Forty states and the District of Columbia do so.

2010, MARCH 10

Second draft of the Common Core State Standards released.

2010, MARCH 29

Winners for the first phase of RTTT announced. The U.S. Department of Education awards funds only to Delaware and Tennessee.

2010, JUNE 1

Second-round RTTT grant applications due.

2010, JUNE 2

Final Common Core State Standards for English and mathematics unveiled in Suwanee, Georgia. Three states have adopted the Common Core as of this date.

2010, AUGUST 2

Initial deadline set by the U.S. Department of Education for adopting the Common Core State Standards for RTTT competition. Thirty-five states have adopted them by this deadline, including 12 that adopt them less than four weeks before the deadline.

2011, APRIL 7

U.S. Department of Education proposes new student privacy rules. These affect data sharing for testing purposes.

2011, SEPTEMBER 23

Obama administration announces waivers from NCLB requirements to states in return for certain education reforms.

2011, SEPTEMBER 25

Former Gov. Jeb Bush (R-FL) praises Obama and Duncan for pressuring states to improve standards at an NBC event.

2012, JANUARY 3

Revised FERPA regulations become effective.

2012, AUGUST

Utah and South Carolina withdraw from the Smarter Balanced Assessment Consortium (SBAC) and the Partnership for Assessment of Readiness for College and Careers (PARCC), respectively. They are the first states to leave all federally supported testing consortia.

2012, SEPTEMBER 5

Democratic National Committee releases party platform crediting Obama for the Common Core.

2012, OCTOBER

NEA creates a Common Core Working Group to support teachers.

2013, APRIL 12

Republican National Committee votes to oppose the Common Core.

2013, APRIL 16

Arne Duncan tells Chamber of Commerce to step up pro-Common Core political advocacy.

2013, JUNE 25

Arne Duncan tells American Society of News Editors that "the Common Core has become a rallying cry for fringe groups."

2013, NOVEMBER 15

Arne Duncan says "white, suburban moms" oppose the Common Core because it shows their children are not "brilliant."

2013, NOVEMBER 16

Alabama withdraws from the Common Core initiative but does not revise its Common Core-linked state standards.

2014, JANUARY 10

NEA President Dennis Van Roekel endorses the Common Core.

2014, MARCH 21

Popular media begins to mock Common Core. Jeff Severt, a North Carolina parent, posts a "Common Core" math problem to Facebook. The problem is picked up by Glenn Beck as unnecessarily complicated. In the weeks following, comedians Louis CK and Stephen Colbert continue the meme.

2014, MARCH 24

Gov. Mike Pence signs legislation to opt out of the Common Core, although it does not prohibit using the Common Core in future Indiana standards.

2014, MAY 30

Gov. Nikki Haley signs a bill prohibiting the implementation of Common Core or participation in multi-state testing consortia. New standards must be approved by the state legislature rather than the state school board and Education Oversight Committee.

2014, JUNE 5

Gov. Mary Fallin (R-OK) signs a bill withdrawing Oklahoma from the Common Core.

2014, JULY 14

Gov. Pat McCrory (R-NC), a Common Core supporter, agrees to sign a bill requiring North Carolina to review and replace part of all of the Common Core State Standards.

2014, JULY 14

Gov. Jay Nixon (D-MO) signs a bill requiring his state to replace the Common Core State Standards by 2016.

2014, JULY 22

Television personality Glenn Beck hosts a national anti-Common Core event.

2014, AUGUST

Gov. Bobby Jindal (R-LA) files a lawsuit alleging that the Department of Education had unlawfully "nationalize[d] education policy." He later loses the lawsuit.

2015, MARCH 30

NYSUT president calls for mass testing opt-out. Some districts experience refusal rates above 50 percent; other states, including Colorado, New Jersey, Ohio, and Oregon, experience higher-than-average refusal rates, although not so high as New York.

2015, JULY 8

The House of Representatives passes a reauthorization of the federal Elementary and Secondary Education Act (ESEA) which explicitly forbids the U.S. Department of Education to require any particular state standards, including the Common Core.

2015, JULY 16

The Senate passes an ESEA reauthorization which requires "challenging" state standards, but prohibits the Department of Education from requiring any particular standards, including the Common Core.

2015, AUGUST

Education Next reports that 37 percent of parents support the "Common Core," although 47 percent supported them if they are tied to school accountability.

2015, DECEMBER 10

Pres. Barack Obama signs the Every Student Succeeds Act (ESSA), the ESEA reauthorization that passed both the House and Senate earlier in December. The Act curtails the U.S. Department of Education's role in standards and assessment, and forbids federal influence on state standards.

2016, FEBRUARY 4

Louisiana Governor John Bel Edwards, Bobby Jindal's successor, announces that the state will drop its anti-Common Core lawsuit against the U.S. Department of Education.

Notes

CHAPTER 1: THE IMPOSSIBLE DREAM

1. Stephen Sawchuk, "More Than Two-Thirds of States Adopt Core Standards," *Education Week*, August 11, 2010, http://www.edweek.org/ew/articles/2010/08/06/37standards.h29.html.

2. Sean Cavanagh, "Draft Common Standards Hit the Internet—UPDATED," *Education Week*, July 22, 2009, http://blogs.edweek.org/edweek/curriculum/2009/07/draft_of_common_standards_gets.html.

3. Catherine Gewertz, "State Adoptions of Common Standards Steam Ahead," *Education Week*, July 14, 2010, http://www.edweek.org/ew/articles/2010/07/09/36standards.h29.html.

4. Blake Neff, "Bush Avoids Common Core Pratfall," *The Daily Caller*, August 7, 2015, http://dailycaller.com/2015/08/06/bush-avoids-common-core-pratfall.

5. Legislators in a handful of other states, including Missouri and North Carolina, enacted bills to "review" the Common Core.

6. David Coleman and Jason Zimba, "Math and Science Standards That Are Fewer, Clearer, Higher to Raise Achievement at All Levels" (Carnegie-IAS Commission on Mathematics and Science Education, 2008), http://opportunityequation.org/standards-and-assessments/math-science-standards-are-fewer.

7. Robert Rothman, *Something in Common: The Common Core Standards and the Next Chapter in American Education* (Cambridge, MA: Harvard Education Press, 2011), Appendix.

8. Chester E. Finn, Michael J. Petrilli, and Gregg Vanourek, "The State of State Standards," Fordham Report (Washington, DC: Thomas B. Fordham Institute, July 1998), http://files.eric.ed.gov/fulltext/ED423267.pdf, 7.

9. Sheila Byrd Carmichael et al., *The State of State Standards–and the Common Core–in 2010* (Thomas B. Fordham Institute, 2010), http://eric.ed.gov/? id=ED516607, 125, 351.

10. Sarah Garl, "The Man Behind Common Core Math," *NPR.org*, December 29, 2014, http://www.npr.org/blogs/ed/2014/12/29/371918272/the-man-behind-common-core-math, emphasis added.

11. Common Core State Standards Initiative, "Read the Standards," 2009, http://www.corestandards.org/read-the-standards, Standards W.3.1A and RL.8.4.

12. Ibid., Standards 3.OA.A.1 and 8.EE.C.8.A.

13. Ibid., Introduction.

14. David Coleman, "Bringing the Common Core to Life" (New York State Department of Education, Albany, NY, April 28, 2011), http://usny.nysed.gov/rttt/docs/bringingthecommoncoretolife/fulltranscript.pdf, 10.

15. National Center on Education and the Economy, "What Does It Really Mean to Be College and Work Ready? The Mathematics and English Literacy Required of First Year Community College Students" (Washington, DC: National Center on Education and the Economy, 2013), http://www.ncee.org/wp-content/uploads/2013/05/NCEE_MathReport_May20131.pdf. This report suggests that high school mathematics should substantially increase attention to probability and statistics if students were to be even community-college ready.

16. Coleman, "Bringing the Common Core to Life," 7.

17. Rothman, *Something in Common: The Common Core Standards and the Next Chapter in American Education*, x–xi.

18. Associated Press, "Bennett Offers a Mixed Report on Schools in U.S." *The New York Times*, February 11, 1987, sec. U.S., http://www.nytimes.com/1987/02/11/us/bennett-offers-a-mixed-report-on-schools-in-us.html.

19. A phrase borrowed by the Fordham Foundation for a report about creating national standards and tests, which borrowed it from the 1965 Don Quixote-inspired musical *Man of La Mancha*.

20. Rothman, *Something in Common: The Common Core Standards and the Next Chapter in American Education*, 56.

21. U.S. Supreme Court, San Antonio Independent School District v. Rodriguez, 411 U.S. 1, 50 (1973).

22. The academic content, especially the mathematics, have also frustrated parents, but few of the "insider" critics target the academics.

23. Chester E. Finn Jr, Liam Julian, and Michael J. Petrilli, "To Dream the Impossible Dream: Four Approaches to National Standards and Tests

for America's Schools." *Thomas B. Fordham Foundation & Institute*, 2006, http://eric.ed.gov/?id=ED493854, 34.

24. Ibid.

25. Rothman, *Something in Common: The Common Core Standards and the Next Chapter in American Education*, p. 61.

26. Sheila Byrd Carmichael et al., "Stars By Which to Navigate? Scanning National and International Education Standards in 2009. An Interim Report on Common Core, NAEP, TIMSS and PISA." *Thomas B. Fordham Institute*, October 8, 2009, http://eric.ed.gov/?id=ED506714, 4.

27. Ibid., 21, 39.

28. Carmichael et al., *The State of State Standards–and the Common Core–in 2010*, 3.

29. Proponents invoked the process for the U.S. Constitution, appropriately, as it was also written by elites in a closed-door meeting.

30. National Governor Association and Council of Chief State School Officers, "Common Core Standards Memorandum of Agreement," May 2009, http://idahoansforlocaleducation.com/wp-content/uploads/2013/02/Common-Core-Standards-Signed-MOA-May-09.pdf, 2.

31. Ibid., 3.

32. Finn Jr, Julian, and Petrilli, "To Dream the Impossible Dream," 3.

33. In 2015, a Missouri judge ruled that one of the Common Core-aligned testing consortia was an unconstitutional compact. Daniel R. Green, *Sauer v. Nixon* (Circuit Court of Cole County, MO 2015).

34. U.S. Department of Education, "Technical Review Form" (Washington, DC: U.S. Department of Education, 2009), 2.

35. Jean-Daniel Gabriel LaRock, "The Race to the Top Fund: A Case Study of Political and Institutional Dynamics in Massachusetts" (Ed.D., Harvard Graduate School of Education, 2014), 3.

36. Michele McNeil, "States Scramble for Coveted Dollars," *Education Week*, July 24, 2009, http://www.edweek.org/ew/articles/2009/07/24/37racereact.h28.html.

37. Alaska, North Dakota, Texas, and Vermont did not apply for funds.

38. Stephen Sawchuk, "NEA at Odds With Obama Team Over 'Race to the Top' Criteria," *Education Week*, September 2, 2009, http://www.edweek.org/ew/articles/2009/08/25/02nea.h29.html.

39. State of Illinois, "Illinois Race to the Top Application for Initial Funding," January 19, 2010, http://www2.ed.gov/programs/racetothetop/phase1-applications/illinois.pdf, 2.

40. State of Tennessee, "Race to the Top Application for Initial Funding," January 18, 2010, http://www2.ed.gov/programs/racetothetop/phase1-applications/tennessee.pdf, 12. Colorado made similar claims about bipartisanship.

41. State of Delaware, "Race to the Top Application for Initial Funding," January 19, 2010, http://www2.ed.gov/programs/racetothetop/phase1-applications/delaware.pdf, A-11. Minnesota's application also mentioned support from the Democratic Party.

42. Commonwealth of Virginia, "Race to the Top Application for Initial Funding," January 15, 2010, http://www2.ed.gov/programs/racetothetop/phase1-applications/virginia.pdf, 46.

43. Ibid., 48.

44. Ibid., 49.

45. U.S. Department of Education, "Reviewer Comments on Virginia Race to the Top Application," 2010, http://www2.ed.gov/programs/racetothetop/phase1-applications/comments/virginia.pdf, 19–20.

46. U.S. Department of Education, "States' Applications for Phase 2 - Race to the Top Fund," Programs; Reports; Reference Materials; Pamphlets, (February 15, 2012), http://www2.ed.gov/programs/racetothetop/phase2-applications/index.html.

47. Fred Lucas, "Bill Clinton Calls for 'Rebuilding Our Education System' with a 'Common Core'," *The Blaze*, August 28, 2013, http://www.theblaze.com/stories/2013/08/28/bill-clinton-calls-for-rebuilding-our-education-system-with-a-common-core.

48. David J. Hoff, "Clinton Gives Top Billing to Education Plan," *Education Week*, February 12, 1997, http://www.edweek.org/ew/articles/1997/02/12/20clint.h16.html.

49. Caitlin Emma, "Jeb Bush: Debate on Common Core 'Troubling'," *Politico*, November 20, 2014, http://www.politico.com/story/2014/11/jeb-bush-troops-education-reform-113060.html.

50. Some of these watered down their support as political controversy emerged.

51. Jeffrey R Henig, *The End of Exceptionalism in American Education: The Changing Politics of School Reform* (Cambridge, MA: Harvard Education Press, 2013), 46.

52. Quoted in ibid., 37.

53. Paul Manna, *School's In: Federalism and the National Education Agenda* (Georgetown University Press, 2006), 96.

54. Henig, *The End of Exceptionalism in American Education*, 40.

55. Arnold F. Shober, *Splintered Accountability: State Governance and Education Reform* (Albany, NY: SUNY Press, 2010).

56. "Save Our Schools," *Fortune*, May 28, 1990, http://archive.fortune.com/magazines/fortune/fortune_archive/1990/05/28/73597/index.htm.

57. Jay P. Greene, "Buckets into the Sea: Why Philanthropy Isn't Changing Schools, and How It Could," in *With the Best of Intentions*, ed.

Frederick M. Hess (Cambridge, MA: Harvard Education Press, 2005), 49–76, 53.

58. Leslie Lenkowsky, "The 'Best Uses' of Philanthropy for Reform," in *With the Best of Intentions*, ed. Frederick M. Hess (Cambridge, MA: Harvard Education Press, 2005), 77–104.

59. Richard Lee Colvin, "A New Generation of Philanthropists and Their Great Ambitions," in *With the Best of Intentions*, ed. Frederick M. Hess (Cambridge, MA: Harvard Education Press, 2005), 21–48, 25.

60. Vartan Gregorian et al., "Rethinking America's Schools," *Philanthropy*, 2005, http://www.philanthropyroundtable.org/topic/excellence_in _philanthropy/rethinking_americas_schools.

61. Colvin, "A New Generation of Philanthropists and Their Great Ambitions," 31.

62. Annenberg Foundation, "The Annenberg Challenge: Lessons and Reflections on Public School Reform," March 2002, http://www .annenberginstitute.org/sites/default/files/product/252/files/Lessons _Report.pdf, 28, 32.

63. Bill Gates, "Remarks on Education," February 26, 2005, http:// www.gatesfoundation.org/media-center/speeches/2005/02/bill-gates -2005-national-education-summit.

64. Shober, *Splintered Accountability: State Governance and Education Reform*.

65. Achieve, Inc., "National Education Summit Briefing, 1996" (Washington, DC: Achieve, Inc., 1996), http://www.achieve.org/files/1996National EducationSummit.pdf, 3.

66. Achieve, Inc., "Achieve, Inc. Announces 13-State Coalition to Improve High Schools," February 27, 2005, http://www.achieve.org/achieve -inc-announces-13-state-coalition-improve-high-schools.

67. Ibid.

68. Carter Wood, "Business Leaders Back Common Core State Standards," *Business Roundtable*, April 19, 2013, http://businessroundtable.org /media/blog/business-leaders-back-common-core-state-standards.

69. Jesse Hessler Rhodes, "Progressive Policy Making in a Conservative Age? Civil Rights and the Politics of Federal Education Standards, Testing, and Accountability," *Perspectives on Politics* 9, no. 03 (September 2011): 519–44, doi:10.1017/S1537592711002738.

70. *Green v. New Kent County* (1968), 436.

71. Gerald Ford, "Remarks and a Question-and-Answer Session at the White House Conference on Domestic and Economic Affairs in Peoria, Illinois" (Press Conference, Peoria, IL, August 19, 1975), http://www.presidency .ucsb.edu/ws/?pid=5178.

72. Gerald Ford, "The President's News Conference" (Press Conference, Columbus, OH, May 26, 1976), http://www.presidency.ucsb.edu/ws/index.php?pid=6061.

73. Harold Berlak, "Academic Achievement, Race, and Reform: Six Essays on Understanding Assessment Policy, Standarized Achievement Tests, and Anti-Racist Alternatives" (Author, 2001), 17.

74. "National News Roundup," *Education Week*, January 19, 1983, http://www.edweek.org/ew/articles/1983/01/19/03040009.h02.html; Blake Rodman, "U.S. Claims Texas Teachers' Skills Test Is Legal," *Education Week*, October 16, 1985, http://www.edweek.org/ew/articles/1985/10/16/06260038.h05.html; Art Levine, "Dallas Program for Gifted Students Thwarts Desegregation, Group Says," *Education Week*, October 5, 1981, http://www.edweek.org/ew/articles/1981/10/05/01050091.h01.html.

75. M. Suzanne Donovan and Christopher T. Cross, *Minority Students in Special and Gifted Education* (Washington, DC: National Academic Press, 2002).

76. Martin Carnoy and Susanna Loeb, "Does External Accountability Affect Student Outcomes? A Cross-State Analysis," *Educational Evaluation and Policy Analysis* 24, no. 4 (2002): 305–31.

77. Diana Jean Schemo, "New Law Is News to Many," *The New York Times*, October 15, 2002, sec. U.S., http://www.nytimes.com/2002/10/15/us/new-law-is-news-to-many.html.

78. Education Trust, "More Than 25 Civil Rights Groups and Education Advocates Release Principles for ESEA Reauthorization: 'The Federal Role Must Be Honored and Maintained'," January 11, 2015, http://edtrust.org/press_release/more-than-20-civil-rights-groups-and-education-advocates-release-principles-for-esea-reauthorization-the-federal-role-must-be-honored-and-maintained.

79. Mexican American Legal Defense and Educational Fund, "MALDEF Calls on Community Leaders, Parents to Advocate for Equity in Implementation of Common Core State Standards," May 11, 2011, http://www.maldef.org/news/releases/common_core.

80. National Conference of State Legislatures, "2014 - College and Career State Standards: State Legislation Update," November 11, 2014, http://www.ccrslegislation.info/legislation-by-year/2014.

81. Valerie Strauss, "Colbert's 'Common Core Confusion'," *The Washington Post*, April 9, 2014, http://www.washingtonpost.com/blogs/answer-sheet/wp/2014/04/09/colberts-hilarious-common-core-confusion.

82. Frederick M. Hess, "Common Core's Five Big Half-Truths," *National Review Online*, September 3, 2014, http://www.nationalreview

.com/article/386911/common-cores-five-big-half-truths-frederick-m
-hess.

83. Vaishali Honawar, "NEA Opens Campaign to Rewrite Federal Education Law," *Education Week*, July 12, 2006, http://www.edweek.org/ew/articles/2006/07/12/42nea.h25.html.

84. Colvin, "A New Generation of Philanthropists and Their Great Ambitions."

85. Rothman, *Something in Common: The Common Core Standards and the Next Chapter in American Education*, p. 67.

86. Some states, including Maine and Oklahoma, required legislative approval, but both of these state legislatures passed bills to approve the standards or empower others to approve them in their stead. Gewertz, "State Adoptions of Common Standards Steam Ahead."

87. Andrew DeMillo, "Griffin: Changes Needed to Common Core Standards," *Education Week*, July 28, 2015, http://www.edweek.org/ew/articles/2015/07/28/griffin-changes-needed-to-common-core_ap.html.

CHAPTER 2: A VISION OF EQUITY, EXCELLENCE, AND ASSESSMENT

1. Robert A. Margo, *Race and Schooling in the South, 1880–1950* (Chicago: University of Chicago Press, 1990), 21.

2. *Rodriguez v. San Antonio* (1973), 35.

3. *McInnis v. Shapiro* (1968), 335.

4. *Rodriguez v. San Antonio* (1973), 36, 50.

5. *Milliken v. Bradley* (1974), 741.

6. Patrick J. McGuinn, *No Child Left Behind and the Transformation of Federal Education Policy, 1965–2005* (Lawrence, KS: The University Press of Kansas, 2006), 29.

7. Lyndon B. Johnson, "State of the Union" (Washington, DC, January 8, 1964).

8. See Paul Manna, *School's In: Federalism and the National Education Agenda* (Georgetown University Press, 2006).

9. Hugh Davis Graham, *The Uncertain Triumph: Federal Education Policy in the Kennedy and Johnson Years* (Chapel Hill: University of North Carolina Press, 1984), 204.

10. Ruby Martin and Phyllis McClure, "Title I of ESEA: Is It Helping Poor Children?" (Washington, DC, and New York: Washington Research Project and NAACP Legal Defense and Education Fund, 1969), 6–8.

11. Michael W. Kirst and Richard Jung, "The Utility of a Longitudinal Approach in Assessing Implementation: A Thirteen-Year View of Title I,

ESEA," *Educational Evaluation and Policy Analysis* 2, no. 5 (September 1980): 17–34.

12. Quoted in Manna, *School's In*, 107.

13. Marshall S. Smith and Jennifer O'Day, "Systemic School Reform," in *The Politics of Curriculum and Testing*, ed. Susan Fuhrman and Betty Malen (New York: The Falmer Press, 1991), 233–67.

14. Arnold F. Shober, *Splintered Accountability: State Governance and Education Reform* (Albany, NY: SUNY Press, 2010), 66.

15. Ohio State Board of Education, *Milestones: A History of the State Board of Education of Ohio, 1956–1989* (Columbus, OH: Author, 1989), 84–86.

16. Daniel P. Resnick, "Minimum Competency Testing Historically Considered," *Review of Research in Education* 8 (1980): 3–29.

17. Shober, *Splintered Accountability: State Governance and Education Reform*, 135.

18. National Commission on Excellence in Education, "Nation at Risk: The Imperative for Educational Reform" (Washington, DC: Author, 1983), http://www.ed.gov/pubs/NatAtRisk/risk.html.

19. Lawrence C. Stedman and Marshall S. Smith, "Recent Reform Proposals for American Education," *Contemporary Education Review* 2, no. 2 (1983): 85–104.

20. Benjamin Michael Superfine, *The Courts and Standards-Based Education Reform* (New York: Oxford University Press, 2008), 25.

21. United States Department of Education, "America 2000: An Education Strategy Sourcebook" (Washington, DC: Author, May 1991), http://eric.ed.gov/?id=ED327985, 5.

22. Ibid., 15.

23. Ibid., 15, 31.

24. Ibid., 11, 5.

25. Ibid., 22. Later, the 12th-grade target was changed to 10th.

26. McGuinn, *No Child Left Behind and the Transformation of Federal Education Policy, 1965–2005*, 63.

27. Quoted in Maris A. Vinovskis, *The Road to Charlottesville* (Washington, DC: National Education Goals Panel, 1999), 40.

28. Michael K. Frisby, "Bush Education Program is Criticized," *Boston Globe*, April 24, 1991.

29. Lynn Olson, "Plain-Speaking and Fast-Learning, Romer Rides Herd on Goals Process," *Education Week*, October 2, 1991, http://www.edweek.org/ew/articles/1991/10/02/05romer.h11.html.

30. Christine Todd Whitman and James B. Hunt, "To the Honorable William F. Goodling," May 10, 1995, 3.

31. James B. Stedman and Wayne C. Riddle, "Goals 2000: Education America Act Implementation Status and Issues," Congressional Research Service (Washington, DC: Congressional Research Service, February 17, 1998), 20.

32. Julie A. Miller, "Reform Measure Dies–Except as Campaign Issue?" *Education Week*, October 7, 1992, http://www.edweek.org/ew/articles/1992/10/07/05omni.h12.html.

33. H.R. 1804, 103rd Cong., Section 319(b).

34. Julie A. Miller, "Behind 'Love' of Clinton, Unease Over Policy," *Education Week*, August 5, 1992, http://www.edweek.org/ew/articles/1992/08/05/40clinto.h11.html.

35. Stephen Sawchuk, "NEA's Delegates Approve Obama Endorsement, Dues Increase," *Education Week—Teacher Beat*, July 4, 2011, http://blogs.edweek.org/edweek/teacherbeat/2011/07/neas_delegates_approve_obama_e.html.

36. "Politics, N.E.A. Style," *Education Week*, August 5, 1992, http://www.edweek.org/ew/articles/1992/08/05/40note.h11.html.

37. Deborah L. Gold, "Clinton Outlines 1989 School Agenda," *Education Week*, October 19, 1988, http://www.edweek.org/ew/articles/1988/10/19/08430005.h08.html; Julie A. Miller, "With a Track Record on Education, Campaigner Clinton Speaks With Authority," *Education Week*, February 5, 1992, http://www.edweek.org/ew/articles/1992/02/05/20clintn.h11.html.

38. Motoko Rich, "G.O.P. Bill on Schools Would Set Fewer Rules," *The New York Times*, June 6, 2013, sec. Education, http://www.nytimes.com/2013/06/06/education/gop-bill-on-schools-would-set-fewer-rules.html.

39. Olson, "Plain-Speaking and Fast-Learning, Romer Rides Herd on Goals Process."

40. Mark Pitsch, "Picture Mixed for Education, Clinton Team," *Education Week*, January 26, 1994, http://www.edweek.org/ew/articles/1994/01/26/18clint.h13.html.

41. Ibid.

42. Quoted in McGuinn, *No Child Left Behind and the Transformation of Federal Education Policy, 1965–2005*, 91.

43. Mark Pitsch, "Pitched Battle Over Clinton Plan to Shift Chapter 1 Aid Seen," *Education Week*, September 22, 1993, http://www.edweek.org/ew/articles/1993/09/22/03esea.h13.html.

44. Lynne V. Cheney, "The End of History," *Wall Street Journal*, October 20, 1994. The phrase "greed and rapacity" comes from Diane Ravitch and Arthur M. Schlesinger Jr., "The New, Improved History Standards," *Wall Street Journal*, April 3, 1996.

45. Ibid.

46. Cheney, "The End of History."

47. United States Senate, *S. R. 66*, 1995.

48. Sean Wilentz, "Don't Know Much About History," *New York Times Book Review*, November 30, 1997, http://www.nytimes.com/books/97/11/30/reviews/971130.30wilentt.html.

49. Gary B. Nash, "Lynne Cheney's Attack on the History Standards, 10 Years Later," *History News Network*, November 8, 2004, http://history newsnetwork.org/article/8418.

50. Robert B. Schwartz and Marian A. Robinson, "Goals 2000 and the Standards Movement," in *Brookings Papers on Education Policy*, ed. Diane Ravitch (Washington, DC: Brookings Institution Press, 2000), 173–214, 202.

51. Miller, "Reform Measure Dies–Except as Campaign Issue?"

52. Dick Brewbaker, "Why Alabama Rejected Goals 2000," *What Goals 2000 Means to the States* (Author: Washington, DC, February 12, 1997).

53. Whitman and Hunt, "To the Honorable William F. Goodling," 2.

54. Thomas V. O'Brien, *The Politics of Race and Schooling: Public Education in Georgia, 1900–1961* (Lanham, MA: Lexington Books, 1999).

55. McGuinn, *No Child Left Behind and the Transformation of Federal Education Policy, 1965–2005*, 101.

56. United States Department of Education, "America 2000," 21–22.

57. James D. King and Jeffrey E. Cohen, "What Determines a Governor's Popularity?" *State Politics & Policy Quarterly* 5, no. 3 (September 21, 2005): 225–47.

58. Whitman and Hunt, "To the Honorable William F. Goodling," 2.

59. Lamar Alexander, William J. Bennett, and Daniel R. Coats, "Local Options: Congress Should Return Control of Education to States, School Boards—and Parents," *National Review*, December 19, 1994.

60. Ibid.

61. Mark Pitsch, "Education Seen Key to Forging Clinton Legacy," *Education Week*, November 13, 1996, http://www.edweek.org/ew/articles/1996/11/13/11prez.h16.html.

62. Ibid.

63. Joetta L. Sack, "Clinton-Hill Accord Would Hike Ed. Funding," *Education Week*, May 14, 1997, http://www.edweek.org/ew/articles/1997/05/14/33budgt.h16.html.

64. Christina Wolbrecht and Michael T. Hartney, "'Ideas About Interests': Explaining the Changing Partisan Politics of Education," *Perspectives on Politics* 12, no. 3 (September 2014): 603–30, 622.

65. Joetta L. Sack, "Republicans Offer 'Straight A's' Plan for Easing Regulation," *Education Week*, July 14, 1999, 26.

66. Bill Clinton, "State of the Union," Washington, DC, January 27, 2000.

67. Jesse Rhodes, *An Education in Politics: The Origins and Evolution of No Child Left Behind*, 1 edition (Ithaca, N.Y: Cornell University Press, 2012).

68. Christopher L. Jencks and Phillips, eds., *The Black-White Test Score Gap* (Washington, DC: Brookings Institution Press, 1998).

69. James S. Coleman et al., "Equality of Educational Opportunity" (Washington, DC: U.S. Department of Health, Education, and Welfare, Office of Education, 1966), 22.

70. The initial controversy around this finding proved to be justified, as a later analysis of Coleman's data showed that school effects *did* account for some, though not all, variation in academic achievement. See Geoffrey D. Borman and Maritza Dowling, "Schools and Inequality: A Multilevel Analysis of Coleman's Equality of Educational Opportunity Data," *Teachers College Record* 112, no. 5 (May 2010): 1201–46.

71. Laurie Reynolds, "Uniformity of Taxation and the Preservation of Local Control in School Finance Reform," *UC Davis L. Rev.* 40 (2006): 1835.

72. That did not mean the court raised spending. As it happened, California voters passed Proposition 13 in 1978 which severely crimped the ability of the legislature or school districts to raise local taxes. The result was equal spending—but only after a sharp reduction in spending. Lori L. Taylor, "Comparable Wages, Inflation, and School Finance Equity," *Education Finance and Policy* 1, no. 3 (2006): 349–71.

73. *Rose v. Council for Basic Education*, 580.

74. Eric A. Hanushek and Alfred A. Lindseth, *Schoolhouses, Courthouses, and Statehouses* (Princeton, NJ: Princeton University Press, 2009).

75. Richarde W. Donelan, Gerald A. Neal, and Deneese L. Jones, "The Promise of Brown and the Reality of Academic Grouping: The Tracks of My Tears," *The Journal of Negro Education* 63, no. 3 (1994): 376–87; M. Suzanne Donovan and Christopher T. Cross, *Minority Students in Special and Gifted Education* (Washington, DC: National Academic Press, 2002).

76. Quoted in McGuinn, *No Child Left Behind and the Transformation of Federal Education Policy, 1965–2005*, 172.

77. Martin Carnoy and Susanna Loeb, "Does External Accountability Affect Student Outcomes? A Cross-State Analysis," *Educational Evaluation and Policy Analysis* 24, no. 4 (2002): 305–31; Eric A. Hanushek and Margaret E. Raymond, "Lessons About the Design of State Accountability Systems," in *No Child Left Behind? The Politics and Practice of*

Accountability, ed. Paul E. Peterson and Martin R. West (Washington, DC: Brookings Institution Press, 2003), 172–51.

78. *CQ Weekly*, May 5, 2001.

79. Joetta L. Sack, "Bush Unveils Education Plan," *Education Week*, January 23, 2001, http://www.edweek.org/ew/articles/2001/01/23/19bush_web.h20.html.

80. Peter Baker, "An Unlikely Partnership Left Behind," *The Washington Post*, November 5, 2007, http://www.washingtonpost.com/wp-dyn/content/article/2007/11/04/AR2007110401450_pf.html.

81. Paul Manna, *Collision Course: Federal Education Policy Meets State and Local Realities* (Washington, DC: CQ Press, 2011), 39.

82. Government Accountability Office, "Title I: Education Needs to Monitor States' Scoring of Assessments" (Washington, DC: Author, April 1, 2002), http://www.gao.gov/assets/240/233938.pdf.

83. Puerto Rico and the District of Columbia are also covered by Title I. Puerto Rico had a three-year extension by 2002; the District had none.

84. Chester E. Finn, Michael J. Petrilli, and Gregg Vanourek, "The State of State Standards," Fordham Report (Washington, DC: Thomas B. Fordham Institute, July 1998), 6.

85. Michael Petrilli and Chester E. Finn, "The State of State Standards" (Washington, DC: Thomas B. Fordham Institute, August 2006), 12.

86. Ibid., 12.

87. American Federation of Teachers, "Sizing Up State Standards 2008" (Washington, DC: Author, March 2008), http://www.aft.org/sites/default/files/sizingupstandards0308.pdf, 5.

88. Victor Bandeira de Mello, "Mapping State Proficiency Standards Onto the NAEP Scales" (Washington, DC: National Center for Education Statistics, August 20, 2011), http://nces.ed.gov/nationsreportcard/pdf/studies/2011458.pdf.

89. Kevin Carey, "Hot Air: How States Inflate Their Educational Progress Under NCLB," *The Education Sector*, 2006, http://www.mikemcmahon.info/nclbstate.pdf, 1, 5.

90. Andrew Rotherham, "Not So Different At All," *Eduwonk*, July 1, 2008, http://www.eduwonk.com/2008/07/not-so-different-at-all.html.

91. United States Department of Education, "Cross-Cutting Issues From the Peer Panel on Differentiated Accountability" (Washington, DC: U.S. Department of Education, June 2008), http://www.ed.gov/admins/lead/account/differentiatedaccountability/prsummary.doc, 1.

92. Edward M. Kennedy, "How to Fix 'No Child'," *The Washington Post*, January 7, 2008, sec. Opinions, http://www.washingtonpost.com/wp-dyn/content/article/2008/01/06/AR2008010601828.html.

93. Alyson Klein, "Races for Congress Have Sparse Debate on Education Issues," *Education Week*, October 29, 2008, http://www.edweek.org /ew/articles/2008/10/29/10congress.h28.html.

94. Bob Schaffer and Peter Hoekstra, "Educational Freedom in the Wake of No Child Left Behind," *The Heritage Foundation*, February 28, 2007, http://www.heritage.org/research/lecture/educational-freedom-in-the -wake-of-no-child-left-behind.

95. Ibid.

96. National Education Association, "New Policy Statement on Teacher Evaluation and Accountability—Adopted as Amended," *NEA*, July 5, 2011, http://www.nea.org//grants/46326.htm.

97. Mexican American Legal Defense and Educational Fund, "MALDEF Recognizes Fifth Anniversary of No Child Left Behind Act," January 8, 2007, https://maldef.org/news/releases/nclb_010807/index.html.

98. Josef Lukan, "Strengthening Accountability to Ensure Latino Success," October 2009, http://www.nclr.org/images/uploads/publications/file _Strengthening_Accountability_FNL_1.pdf; Avi Salzman, "N.A.A.C.P. Contests Connecticut Lawsuit," *The New York Times*, January 31, 2006, sec. New York Region, http://www.nytimes.com/2006/01/31/nyregion/31schools .html.

99. Kennedy, "How to Fix 'No Child'."

100. Andrew J. Rotherham, " 'Let's Not Weaken It': An Exclusive Interview with George W. Bush on NCLB," *Time*, January 12, 2012, http://ideas .time.com/2012/01/12/lets-not-weaken-it-an-exclusive-interview-with -george-w-bush-on-nclb.

101. Michele Mcneil, "Minnesota Governor Struggles to Keep Seat," *Education Week*, November 1, 2006, http://www.edweek.org/ew/articles /2006/11/01/10minn.h26.html, Michele Mcneil, "Governors Cite Education Records," *Education Week*, December 19, 2007, http://www.edweek.org/ew /articles/2007/12/19/16govs.h27.html.

102. Bob Schaffer, "Colorado Must Lead in Federal Education Reform," *Bob Schaffer—The Best Choice for Better Schools*, 2006, http://www .bobschaffer.org/colorado_must_lead_in_federal_education_reform.html.

103. Alyson Klein, "Senate Democrats to Unveil NCLB Reauthorization Bill," *Education Week—Politics K-12*, June 4, 2013, http://blogs.edweek .org/edweek/campaign-k-12/2013/06/embargoed_do_not_publish.html.

104. Lyndsey Layton, "Plans to Replace 'No Child' Law Bring Dueling Visions of Federal Role in Education," *The Washington Post*, June 6, 2013, http://www.washingtonpost.com/local/education/dueling-visions-of -the-federal-role-in-education/2013/06/06/405277c2-ceda-11e2-8f6b -67f40e176f03_story.html.

CHAPTER 3: THE CONSERVATIVE IMAGINATION: STATES, EVIDENCE, AND PARTISANSHIP

1. J. Cameron Henry, Jr., "JindalLetter.pdf," September 20, 2013, https://drive.google.com/viewerng/viewer?url=http://jcameronhenry.com/wp/wp-content/uploads/2013/09/JindalLetter.pdf.

2. Bobby Jindal, "Gov. Jindal: Leave Education to Local Control," April 23, 2014, http://www.usatoday.com/story/opinion/2014/04/23/common-core-louisiana-gov-bobby-jindal-editorials-debates/8071863.

3. Bobby Jindal, "Jindahl V. Duncan Complaint," August 26, 2014, https://www.heartland.org/sites/default/files/jindal_final_complaint_1.pdf, 7–8.

4. Julia O'Donoghue, "U.S. Chamber Releases Video Touting Bobby Jindal's Support of Common Core on the Day He Backs Away From It," *Times-Picayune*, April 3, 2014, http://www.nola.com/politics/index.ssf/2014/04/us_chamber_releases_video_tout.html.

5. Others include Scott Walker (R-WI) and Rick Scott (R-FL). See Lydia Mulvany, "Walker Backs Changing Common Core Standards," *Journal Sentinel*, January 24, 2014, http://www.jsonline.com/news/education/scott-walker-backs-changing-common-core-standards-in-wisconsin-b99191158z1-241851461.html; Rita Giordano, "Possibility of Compromise Slows Action on Common Core," *Philadelphia Inquirer*, July 6, 2014, http://articles.philly.com/2014-07-06/news/51094135_1_parcc-compromise-task-force; Kathleen McGrory, "Common Core Creates Political Balancing Act for Gov. Rick Scott," *Tampa Bay Times*, September 7, 2014, http://www.tampabay.com/news/politics/stateroundup/debate-over-common-core-presents-political-balancing-act-for-gov-rick-scott/2196364.

6. Nikki Haley, "We Have Been Trying to Repeal Common Core," January 11, 2014, https://www.facebook.com/NikkiHaley/posts/10201743558924447.

7. Andrew Ujifusa, "South Carolina Gov. Haley Vows State Will Ditch Common Core," *Education Week*, January 17, 2014, http://blogs.edweek.org/edweek/state_edwatch/2014/01/south_carolina_gov_haley_vows_state_will_ditch_common_core.html.

8. Allie Bidwell, "Oklahoma, South Carolina Governors Repeal Common Core Standards—US News," *US News & World Report*, June 5, 2014, http://www.usnews.com/news/articles/2014/06/05/oklahoma-south-carolina-governors-repeal-common-core-standards.

9. Lauren Camera, "Okla., La. Center Stage in Common-Core Battle—Education Week," *Education Week*, September 10, 2014, http://www.edweek.org/ew/articles/2014/09/10/03pushback.h34.html.

10. Lyndsey Layton, "Oklahoma Wins Back Its No Child Left Behind Waiver," *The Washington Post*, November 24, 2014, http://www.washing tonpost.com/blogs/local/wp/2014/11/24/oklahoma-wins-back-its-no -child-left-behind-waiver.

11. Andrew Seidman, "Christie's Nominee for Education Department Moves Forward," *Philadelphia Inquirer*, December 13, 2014, http://articles .philly.com/2014-12-13/news/56993778_1_hespe-common-core-state -standards-education-department.

12. Susan Berry, "Twitter Campaign Targets Gov. Pence on Common Core Standards," *Breitbart*, August 30, 2014, http://www.breitbart.com /big-government/2014/08/30/twitter-campaign-targets-gov-pence-on -common-core.

13. Michael Pence, "2014 State of the State Address" (Indianapolis, IN, January 14, 2014), http://www.in.gov/gov/2014stateofstate.htm.

14. Barb Berggoetz, "Gov. Mike Pence Signs Bill to Ditch Common Core," *Indianapolis Star*, March 24, 2014, http://www.indystar.com/story /news/education/2014/03/24/gov-mike-pence-signs-bill-ditch-common-core /6829927.

15. Susan Berry, "Governor Mike Pence Hints Indiana May Drop Common Core," *Breitbart*, January 16, 2014, http://www.breitbart.com/big -government/2014/01/16/governor-mike-pence-hints-indiana-may-drop -common-core.

16. Kathleen Porter-Magee, "Indiana's Potemkin Standards?" *Common Core Watch*, April 16, 2014, http://edexcellence.net/commentary/education -gadfly-daily/common-core-watch/indiana%E2%80%99s-potemkin -standards.

17. Ben McGrath, "The Movement," *The New Yorker*, January 25, 2010, http://www.newyorker.com/magazine/2010/02/01/the-movement.

18. Peter Wallsten and Lyndsey Layton, "Tea Party Groups Rallying Against Common Core Education Overhaul," *The Washington Post*, May 30, 2013, http://www.washingtonpost.com/politics/tea-party-groups-rallying -against-common-core-education-overhaul/2013/05/30/64faab62-c917 -11e2-9245-773c0123c027_story.html.

19. Stanley Kurtz, "Tea Party Revives to Fight Common Core," *National Review Online*, May 31, 2013, http://www.nationalreview.com/corner /349808/tea-party-revives-fight-common-core-stanley-kurtz.

20. Howard Fischer, "Common Core Name Changes, Standards Remain," *Arizona Daily Star*, September 21, 2013, http://tucson.com /news/local/education/common-core-name-changes-standards-remain /article_7a97e40c-bdbf-579f-960c-cbad2db9e9c4.html.

21. Wallsten and Layton, "Tea Party Groups Rallying Against Common Core Education Overhaul."

22. Lyndsey Layton, "Common Core Foes Spreading Misinformation, Duncan Says," *The Washington Post*, June 25, 2013, http://www.washingtonpost.com/local/education/common-core-foes-spreading-misinformation-duncan-says/2013/06/25/332e9574-ddc8-11e2-948c-d644453cf169_story.html.

23. Valerie Strauss, "Arne Duncan Tells Newspaper Editors How to Report on Common Core," *The Washington Post*, June 25, 2013, http://www.washingtonpost.com/blogs/answer-sheet/wp/2013/06/25/arne-duncan-tells-newspaper-editors-how-to-report-on-common-core; Fawn Johnson, "The Very Last Thing Republicans Have to Fight About," *Www.nationaljournal.com*, March 4, 2014, http://www.nationaljournal.com/magazine/the-very-last-thing-republicans-have-to-fight-about-20140304; U.S. Chamber of Commerce, "Common Core Is Common Sense for Business," October 20, 2014, https://www.uschamber.com/blog/common-core-common-sense-business.

24. Mary Ann Zehr, "The Ed Department's Mike Smith Talks About 'Common Standards'," *Education Week—Curriculum Matters*, March 16, 2009, http://blogs.edweek.org/edweek/curriculum/2009/03/the_ed_departments_mike_smith.html.

25. Diane Rufino, "'Common Core' or 'Rotten to the Core'—You Decide," *The Beaufort Observer*, May 13, 2013, http://www.beaufortobserver.net/Articles-COLUMNS-c-2013-05-13-266807.112112-COMMON-CORE-Common-Core-or-Rotten-to-the-Core-You-Decide.html.

26. Ibid.

27. Ibid.

28. Glenn Beck, *Conform: Exposing the Truth About Common Core and Public Education* (New York: Threshold Editions, 2014), 76.

29. Quoted in Johnson, "The Very Last Thing Republicans Have to Fight About."

30. Brad McQueen, *The Cult of Common Core: Obama's Final Solution for Your Child's Mind and Our Country's Exceptionalism* (Brad McQueen, 2014), 14.

31. Anthony Cody, "Is the Tea Party Right About the Common Core?" *Education Week—Living in Dialogue*, June 1, 2013, http://blogs.edweek.org/teachers/living-in-dialogue/2013/06/is_the_tea_party_right_about_t.html.

32. Michael J. Petrilli, "Petrilli Testimony on Common Core in Ohio," *Education Next*, November 20, 2013, http://educationnext.org/petrilli-testimony-on-common-core-in-ohio.

33. Education, "The Federalist Debate: Pullman vs. Petrilli On Common Core," April 16, 2014, http://thefederalist.com/2014/04/16/the -federalist-debate-pullman-vs-petrilli-on-common-core.

34. Robert Rothman, *Something in Common: The Common Core Standards and the Next Chapter in American Education* (Cambridge, MA: Harvard Education Press, 2011), xi.

35. Craig D. Jerald, "Benchmarking for Success: Ensuring US Students Receive a World-Class Education." *National Governors Association*, 2008, http://eric.ed.gov/?id=ED504084, 7.

36. Jean-Daniel Gabriel LaRock, "The Race to the Top Fund: A Case Study of Political and Institutional Dynamics in Massachusetts" (Ed.D., Harvard Graduate School of Education, 2014), 3.

37. Michele Mcneil, "NGA, CCSSO Launch Common Standards Drive," *Education Week*, April 16, 2009, http://www.edweek.org/ew/articles /2009/04/16/29standards.h28.html; Joy Resmovits, "How The Common Core Became Education's Biggest Bogeyman," *The Huffington Post*, January 30, 2014, http://www.huffingtonpost.com/2014/01/10/common-core _n_4537284.html.

38. Lyndsey Layton, "Rethinking the Classroom: Obama's Overhaul of Public Education," *The Washington Post*, September 20, 2012, http:// www.washingtonpost.com/local/education/rethinking-the-classroom -obamas-overhaul-of-public-education/2012/09/20/a5459346-e171-11e1 -ae7f-d2a13e249eb2_story.html.

39. U.S. Department of Education, "Race to the Top: Technical Review Form," March 2010, http://www2.ed.gov/programs/racetothetop/tier1 -technical-review.pdf.

40. New York Race-to-the-Top Application, 10.

41. Utah Race-to-the-Top Application, 26.

42. Common Core State Standards Initiative, "Myths vs. Facts," 2015, http://www.corestandards.org/about-the-standards/myths-vs-facts.

43. Ibid.

44. The Wisconsin Legislative Council is an official non-partisan agency serving legislators' legal research requests.

45. Wisconsin Legislative Council, "To Senator John Lehman," July 25, 2014, http://media.jrn.com/documents/commoncorememo.pdf, 4.

46. Peter Barca, "Representative Barca Statement on Gov. Walker Call to Repeal Common Core," July 17, 2014, http://legis.wisconsin.gov/assem bly/barca/pressreleases/Pages/Representative%20Barca%20Statement %20on%20Gov%20Walker%20Call%20to%20Repeal%20Common%20 Core.aspx.

47. Tony Evers, "Action Alert," February 19, 2014, http://dpiconnected
.dpi.wi.gov/sites/default/files/imce/dpi-connected/pdf/2014-02-19-evers
-action-alert.pdf.

48. Berry, "Twitter Campaign Targets Gov. Pence on Common Core
Standards."

49. Sean D. Reyes, "Common Core Standards Legal Analysis" (Utah
Attorney General's Office, October 7, 2014), 4.

50. Matthew Boyle, "Exclusive—Rand Paul to Prospective 2016
Field: If You Support Common Core, You Will Lose GOP Primary," *Breitbart*, October 6, 2014, http://www.breitbart.com/big-government/2014
/10/06/exclusive-rand-paul-to-prospective-2016-field-if-you-support
-common-core-you-will-lose-gop-primary.

51. Joy Pullman, "7 Things Politicians Will Say So You Think They
Oppose Common Core," December 16, 2014, http://thefederalist.com/2014
/12/16/7-things-slick-politicians-will-say-to-make-you-think-they-oppose
-common-core.

52. Stanley Kurtz, "Obamacore: The White House Takes the Schools,"
National Review Online, December 3, 2012, http://www.nationalreview
.com/corner/334645/obamacore-white-house-takes-schools-stanley-kurtz.

53. Phyllis Schlafly, "Like ObamaCare, Obama Core Is Another Power
Grab," *Eagle Forum*, October 10, 2012, http://www.eagleforum.org/publi
cations/column/obama-core-is-another-power-grab.html.

54. Wilson, "The Whole Story on Common Core," *Glenn Beck*, April 8,
2013, http://www.glennbeck.com/2013/04/08/the-whole-story-on-common
-core.

55. Valerie Strauss, "Common Core Standards Attacked by Republicans," *The Washington Post*, April 19, 2013, http://www.washingtonpost
.com/blogs/answer-sheet/wp/2013/04/19/common-core-standards-atta
cked-by-republicans.

56. Michael J. Petrilli, "The RNC on the CCSSI, OMG!" April 17,
2013, http://edexcellence.net/commentary/education-gadfly-daily/flypaper
/2013/the-rnc-on-the-ccssi-omg.html.

57. Strauss, "Common Core Standards Attacked by Republicans."

58. Thomas Beaumont, "In Iowa, Jeb Bush Defends Common Core
School Standards," *Boston Globe*, March 7, 2015, https://www.bostonglobe
.com/news/nation/2015/03/06/iowa-jeb-bush-defends-common-core
-school-standards/7hjTNu6uqmbN7kFzaNTXUK/story.html.

59. Jason Noble, "Huckabee: I Don't Support Common Core," *Des
Moines Register*, January 24, 2015, http://www.desmoinesregister.com
/story/news/elections/presidential/caucus/2015/01/24/mike-huckabee
-iowa-freedom-summit/22294049.

60. Shane Vander Hart, "Common Core Taken to Task at Iowa Freedom Summit," *Caffeinated Thoughts*, January 27, 2015, http:// caffeinatedthoughts.com/2015/01/common-core-taken-task-iowa-freedom -summit.

61. Beth Reinhard, "Common Core Supporters Run Ads in Iowa," *Washington Wire*, March 4, 2015, http://blogs.wsj.com/washwire/2015/03 /04/common-core-supporters-run-ads-in-iowa.

62. Jonathan Oosting, "Michigan Gov. Rick Snyder Signs 'Solid' $49.5 Billion Budget Short on Money for Medicaid Expansion," *Grand Rapids Press*, June 13, 2013, http://www.mlive.com/politics/index.ssf/2013/06 /michigan_gov_rick_snyder_signs_3.html.

63. Brian Smith, "Common Core Approval Sails Through Michigan Senate on Voice Vote," *Grand Rapids Press*, October 24, 2013, http://www .mlive.com/education/index.ssf/2013/10/common_core_approval_sails _thr.html.

64. Don Gonyea, "Conservatives Heckle Jeb Bush on Education, Immigration," *Weekend Edition* (NPR, February 28, 2015), http://www.npr .org/2015/02/28/389706253/conservatives-heckle-jeb-bush-on-education -immigration.

65. Jeffrey M. Jones, "Obama Ratings Historically Polarized," *Gallup Poll*, January 27, 2012, http://www.gallup.com/poll/152222/Obama-Ratings -Historically-Polarized.aspx.

66. *Squawk Box*, 2009, https://www.youtube.com/watch?v=bEZB4 taSEoA.

67. Jeffrey M. Jones, "Obama's Approval Most Polarized for First-Year President," January 25, 2010, http://www.gallup.com/poll/125345/Obama -Approval-Polarized-First-Year-President.aspx?version=print; Gallup, Inc., "Presidential Job Approval Center," January 8, 2015, http://www.gallup .com/poll/124922/Presidential-Approval-Center.aspx.

68. Democratic Party, "2012 National Platform" (Author, September 5, 2012), http://assets.dstatic.org/dnc-platform/2012-National-Platform.pdf, 5.

69. Layton, "Rethinking the Classroom."

70. Barack Obama, "Remarks by the President in the State of the Union Address" (Washington, DC, February 12, 2013), https://www.whitehouse .gov/node/197846.

71. Andrew Ujifusa, "Arne Duncan Urges Business Leaders to Defend Common Core," *Education Week*, April 16, 2013, http://blogs.edweek.org /edweek/state_edwatch/2013/04/arne_duncan_urges_business_leaders_to _defend_common_core.html.

72. Strauss, "Arne Duncan Tells Newspaper Editors How to Report on Common Core."

73. Valerie Strauss, "Is the Common Core Standards Initiative in Trouble?" *The Washington Post*, April 24, 2013, http://www.washingtonpost.com/blogs/answer-sheet/wp/2013/04/24/is-the-common-core-standards-initiative-in-trouble.

74. Catherine Gewertz and Liana Heitin, "A 2014 Recap, and Common-Core Headlines You Probably Won't See in 2015," *Education Week—Curriculum Matters*, December 29, 2014, http://blogs.edweek.org/edweek/curriculum/2014/12/end_of_year_posts.html.

75. *SDP Beyond the Numbers Convention: David Coleman* (Cambridge, MA, 2013), https://www.youtube.com/watch?v=IPoUmSfTTNI, at 10:59.

76. Ibid. at 24:42.

77. Alex Leary, "Jeb Bush's Bond with Barack Obama on Education Poses 2016 Challenge for Him," *Tampa Bay Times*, January 30, 2015, http://www.tampabay.com/news/politics/stateroundup/jeb-bushs-bond-with-barack-obama-on-education-poses-2016-challenge-for-him/2215805.

78. U.S. Department of Education, "Statement by U.S. Secretary of Education Arne Duncan," February 23, 2012, http://www.ed.gov/news/press-releases/statement-us-secretary-education-arne-duncan-4.

79. Shane Vander Hart, "Jeb Bush Wasn't Against Federal Involvement in Common Core in 2011," *Caffeinated Thoughts*, March 23, 2015, https://caffeinatedthoughts.com/2015/03/jeb-bush-wasnt-against-federal-involvement-in-common-core-in-2011.

80. Education Next, "Jeb Bush Speaks Out: Talking Education Policy with Florida's Former Governor," *Education Next*, November 12, 2014, http://educationnext.org/jeb-bush-speaks-interview.

81. SDP Beyond the Numbers Convention, at 5:00.

82. Jerald, "Benchmarking for Success," 7.

83. Ibid., 6.

84. Nora Fleming, "Common Core Stacks Up Well Vs. Other Respected Standards; Study Finds Content Alignment, Depth," *Education Week*, November 2, 2011, http://www.lexisnexis.com/lnacui2api/api/version1/getDocCui?lni=5480-8T61-F09T-N004&csi=270944,270077,11059,8411&hl=t&hv=t&hnsd=f&hns=t&hgn=t&oc=00240&perma=true.

85. Maine Department of Education, "Governor Signs Rigorous Education Standards into Law," *Maine DOE Newsroom*, April 4, 2011, http://mainedoenews.net/2011/04/04/common-core.

86. Arne Duncan, "Back to School," *The New York Times*, October 19, 2010, sec. Opinion, http://www.nytimes.com/2010/10/19/opinion/19iht-edduncan.html.

87. Frederick M. Hess, "Common Core's Five Big Half-Truths," *National Review Online*, September 3, 2014, http://www.nationalreview

.com/article/386911/common-cores-five-big-half-truths-frederick-m
-hess.

88. Richard Locker, "Analysis: Alexander Doesn't Talk Much About His
Role in National School Standards," *Commercial Appeal*, October 13, 2014,
http://www.commercialappeal.com/news/state/analysis-alexander-doesnt
-talk-much-about-his-role-in-national-school-standards_43693225.

89. Amanda Paulson, "What Have States Actually Done in Crusade
Against Common Core?" *Christian Science Monitor*, September 10, 2014,
http://www.csmonitor.com/USA/DC-Decoder/2014/0910/What-have
-states-actually-done-in-crusade-against-Common-Core-video.

90. SDP Beyond the Numbers Convention, at 11:30.

91. Sandra Stotsky, "Wanted: Internationally Benchmarked Standards
in English, Mathematics, and Science," *Pioneer Institute*, May 8, 2013,
http://pioneerinstitute.org/news/wanted-internationally-benchmarked
-standards-in-english-mathematics-and-science; Lorraine M. McDonnell
and M. Stephen Weatherford, "Evidence Use and the Common Core State
Standards Movement: From Problem Definition to Policy Adoption," *American Journal of Education* 120, no. 1 (November 1, 2013): 1–25, 16; Lorraine M. McDonnell and M. Stephen Weatherford, "Organized Interests and
the Common Core," *Educational Researcher*, November 13, 2013, 8.

92. Hess, "Common Core's Five Big Half-Truths."

93. Common Core State Standards Initiative, "Myths vs. Facts."

94. Ibid.

95. The comparable ELA document—Appendix A—lists no obvious
international comparisons in its bibliography, but does note that "the writing team consulted numerous international models." David Coleman also
glosses over ELA evidence in a May 2013 talk. *SDP Beyond the Numbers
Convention* at 11:33.

96. Gilbert A. Valverde and William H. Schmidt, "Greater Expectations: Learning from Other Nations in the Quest for 'World-Class Standards' in US School Mathematics and Science," *Journal of Curriculum
Studies* 32, no. 5 (September 2000): 651–87.

97. Alan Ginsburg and Steven Leinwand, "Informing Grades 1–6
Mathematics Standards Development: What Can Be Learned From High-Performing Hong Kong, Korea and Singapore?" (Washington, DC: American Institutes for Research, December 2009), http://www.air.org/files/Math
Standards.pdf, 3.

98. William H. Schmidt, Hsing Chi Wang, and Curtis C. McKnight,
"Curriculum Coherence: An Examination of US Mathematics and Science
Content Standards from an International Perspective," *Journal of Curriculum Studies* 37, no. 5 (September 2005): 534.

99. Ginsburg and Leinwand, "Informing Grades 1–6 Mathematics Standards Development: What Can Be Learned From High-Performing Hong Kong, Korea and Singapore?" 8.

100. Common Core State Standards Initiative, "Criteria" (Author, September 17, 2009), http://www.corestandards.org/assets/Criteria.pdf, 9.

101. Sheila Byrd Carmichael et al., *The State of State Standards–and the Common Core–in 2010* (Thomas B. Fordham Institute, 2010), http://eric.ed.gov/?id=ED516607, 357.

102. Ibid.

103. Andrew Porter et al., "Common Core Standards: The New U.S. Intended Curriculum," *Educational Researcher* 40, no. 3 (April 1, 2011): 103–16.

104. Carmichael et al., "Stars," p. 9.

105. Gene Wilhoit, *Improving Our Competitiveness: Common Core Education Standards* (Washington, DC, 2009), http://www.gpo.gov/fdsys/pkg/CHRG-111hhrg53732/pdf/CHRG-111hhrg53732.pdf, 43.

106. For example, Patrick J. Wolf, "The Comprehensive Longitudinal Evaluation of the Milwaukee Parental Choice Program" (Fayetteville, AR: School Choice Demonstration Project, University of Arkansas), http://www.uaedreform.org/the-comprehensive-longitudinal-evaluation-of-the-milwaukee-parental-choice-program; Edward W. Wiley, Eleanor R. Spindler, and Amy N. Subert, "Denver ProComp: An Outcomes Evaluation of Denver's Alternative Teacher Compensation System" (Boulder, CO: School of Education, University of Colorado at Boulder, 2010); Matthew G. Springer et al., "Teacher Pay for Performance: Experimental Evidence from the Project on Incentives in Teaching" (Nashville, TN: National Center on Performance Incentives, Vanderbilt University, 2010); and Martin Carnoy et al., *The Charter School Dust-up: Examining The Evidence On Enrollment And Achievement* (Washington, DC; New York: Teacher College Press & Economic Policy Institute, 2005).

107. Common Core supporters tried. One attempt, by William Schmidt and Richard Houang, expanded Schmidt's earlier work to compare the as-adopted Common Core standards with the A+countries' composite standard in William H. Schmidt and Richard T. Houang, "Curricular Coherence and the Common Core State Standards for Mathematics," *Educational Researcher* 41, no. 8 (November 1, 2012): 294–308. They found that the Common Core appears to be as "coherent" as the A+standard, although they admitted that they measured congruence and performance in a "novel" and "exploratory" way (302, 303).

108. Russ Whitehurst, "Don't Forget Curriculum," Brown Letters on Education (Washington, DC: Brookings Institution, October 2009), http://

www.brookings.edu/~/media/research/files/papers/2009/10/14-curriculum
-whitehurst/1014_curriculum_whitehurst.pdf; Don McLaughlin et al.,
"Comparison Between NAEP and State Mathematics Assessment Results:
2003" (Washington, DC: Institute of Education Sciences, U.S. Department
of Education, January 2008), https://nces.ed.gov/pubs2008/2008475_1
.pdf; Tom Loveless, "The 2012 Brown Center Report on American Education" (Washington, DC: Brookings Institution, February 16, 2012), http://
www.brookings.edu/research/reports/2012/02/16-brown-education.

109. Whitehurst, "Don't Forget Curriculum," 7.

110. Ibid., 7.

111. Loveless, "The 2012 Brown Center Report on American Education," 13.

112. Ibid., 8.

113. It should also be noted that the lack of relationship between standards and performance could be an artifact of having state standards *not*
aligned with the expectations of the NAEP. In this case, students might show
different levels of performance, but the tests would not show any simply
because the test was asking questions students were not *supposed* to know
how to answer. This would not help Core supporters, however—part of their
argument was that state standards *should* be more like those for the NAEP.

114. Porter et al., "Common Core Standards: The New U.S. Intended
Curriculum," 114. The countries were Finland, Japan, New Zealand, Ontario,
Canada, Singapore, and Sweden.

115. See especially Adam Gamoran, Andrew C. Porter, John Smithson,
and Paula A. White, "Upgrading High School Mathematics Instruction:
Improving Learning Opportunities for Low-Achieving, Low-Income Youth,"
Educational Evaluation and Policy Analysis 19, no. 4: 325–38: "Low achieving high school students are capable of learning much more than is typically
demanded of them. The key is to provide a serious, meaningful curriculum:
'hard content for all students'." (336); Whitehurst, "Don't Forget Curriculum."

116. Office of Governor Gary Herbert, "Utah Common Core
Standards—Standards Panel," October 6, 2014, http://demo.utah.gov
/governor/priorities/education.html. They found that they were Benjamin
Wood, "Governor's Common Core Advisers Like the Controversial New
Education Guidelines," *The Salt Lake Tribune*, January 15, 2015, http://www
.sltrib.com/home/2049853-155/governors-common-core-advisers-like-the.

117. Wilhoit, *Improving Our Competitiveness: Common Core Education Standards*, 53.

118. McDonnell and Weatherford, "Evidence Use and the Common
Core State Standards Movement," 12.

119. Ibid.

120. Ibid., 16.

121. Kevin Carey, "Hot Air: How States Inflate Their Educational Progress Under NCLB," *The Education Sector*, 2006, http://www.mikemcmahon .info/nclbstate.pdf.

CHAPTER 4: A SEMBLANCE OF IDEOLOGY: PARENTS, PRIVATE SCHOOLS, AND PRIVACY

1. Glenn Beck, *Conform: Exposing the Truth About Common Core and Public Education* (New York: Threshold Editions, 2014), 103.

2. Ellwood Patterson Cubberley, *Changing Conceptions of Education* (Boston, MA: Houghton Mifflin Co., 1909), 15.

3. Ibid., 63.

4. John Dewey and Evelyn Dewey, *Schools of To-Morrow* (Mineola, NY: Dover Publications, 1915), 32.

5. Quoted in Diane Ravitch, *Left Back: A Century of Failed School Reforms* (New York: Simon & Schuster, 2000), 208.

6. Quoted in ibid., 288.

7. Oddly, recent scholarship has suggested that the Common Core's "fewer, higher, and better" ELA standards are lower than the academic standards represented by the McGuffey readers. See David A. Gamson, Xiaofei Lu, and Sarah Anne Eckert, "Challenging the Research Base of the Common Core State Standards: A Historical Reanalysis of Text Complexity," *Educational Researcher* 42, no. 7 (October 2013): 381–91.

8. U.S. Congress, "National Defense Education Act," http://www .visitthecapitol.gov/exhibition-hall/archives/images/2370.

9. Ravitch, *Left Back*, 287.

10. David Coleman and Jason Zimba, "Math and Science Standards That Are Fewer, Clearer, Higher to Raise Achievement at All Levels" (Carnegie-IAS Commission on Mathematics and Science Education, 2008), http://opportunityequation.org/standards-and-assessments/math-science -standards-are-fewer, 2.

11. Beck, *Conform: Exposing the Truth About Common Core and Public Education*, 90.

12. Lyndsey Layton, "Common Core State Standards in English Spark War Over Words," *The Washington Post*, December 2, 2012, http://www .washingtonpost.com/local/education/common-core-state-standards-in -english-spark-war-over-words/2012/12/02/4a9701b0-38e1-11e2-8a97 -363b0f9a0ab3_story.html.

13. Glenn Beck, "I Will Not Conform," June 20, 2014, http://wewill notconform.com.

14. Common Core State Standards Initiative, "Mathematics Standards" (Washington, DC: Common Core State Standards Initiative, 2010), http://www.corestandards.org/wp-content/uploads/ELA_Standards.pdf, 15.

15. McGraw-Hill's mathematics book website noted, "We fully support the initiatives of the Common Core because they share our long-standing commitment to providing a progression of learning experiences that result in a mastery of knowledge and skills for the 21st century." McGraw-Hill Education, "Common Core State Standards," 2015, http://www.commoncoresolutions.com/math_common_core_solutions.php.

16. Rebecca Klein, "Louis C.K. Has a Lot to Say About the Common Core," *The Huffington Post*, April 28, 2014, http://www.huffingtonpost.com/2014/04/28/louis-ck-common-core_n_5228947.html.

17. Phyllis Schlafly, "Parents and Teachers Object to Common Core," *Eagle Forum*, December 11, 2013, http://www.eagleforum.org/publications/column/parents-teachers-object-common-core.html. The particular line appeared on a fifth-grade worksheet designed by Pearson, Inc. Perry Chiaramonte, "Common Core Lessons Blasted for Sneaking Politics into Elementary Classrooms," *FoxNews.com*, (November 10, 2013), http://www.foxnews.com/us/2013/11/10/common-core-lessons-blasted-for-sneaking-politics-into-elementary-classrooms.

18. Phyllis Schlafly, "Like ObamaCare, Obama Core Is Another Power Grab," *Eagle Forum*, October 10, 2012, http://www.eagleforum.org/publications/column/obama-core-is-another-power-grab.html.

19. Michelle Malikin, "Rotten to the Core (Part 2): Readin', Writin' and Deconstructionism," *MichelleMalkin.com*, January 25, 2013, http://michellemalkin.com/2013/01/25/rotten-to-the-core-part-2-readin-writin-and-deconstructionism.

20. Kyle Olson, "Michelle Malkin Shreds Jeb Bush, Common Core and 'John Dewey/Saul Alinsky-Marinated Progressives'—Kyle Olson—Page 1," *Townhall.com*, May 1, 2014, http://townhall.com/columnists/kyleolson/2014/05/01/michelle-malkin-shreds-jeb-bush-common-core-and-john-deweysaul-alinskymarinated-progressives-n1831812.

21. Beck, *Conform: Exposing the Truth About Common Core and Public Education*, 95.

22. The Common Core's literature examples were 50–50. Common Core State Standards Initiative, "English Language Arts Standards" (Washington, DC: Common Core State Standards Initiative, 2010), http://www.corestandards.org/wp-content/uploads/ELA_Standards.pdf, 32, 58.

23. Sandra Stotsky, "Common Core Standards' Devastating Impact on Literary Study and Analytical Thinking," *The Heritage Foundation*, December 11, 2012, http://www.heritage.org/research/reports/2012/12

/questionable-quality-of-the-common-core-english-language-arts
-standards.

24. Sandra Stotsky, "An English Language Arts Curriculum Framework for American Public Schools: A Model" (Fayetteville, AR: Author, February 2013), http://www.uaedreform.org/wp-content/uploads/2000/01/Stotsky-Optional_ELA_standards.pdf, 60–65.

25. Common Core State Standards Initiative, "English Language Arts Standards," 32.

26. Catholic schools enrolled 42.5 percent of all private students, and Lutheran, Baptist, and non-denominational Christian schools enrolled 21 percent. U.S. Department of Education, "Characteristics of Private Schools in the United States: Results From the 2007–08 Private School Universe Survey" (Washington, DC: Author, March 2009), 7, http://nces.ed.gov/pubs2009/2009313.pdf.

27. United States Conference of Catholic Bishops, "Common Core State Standards FAQs," April 21, 2014, http://www.usccb.org/beliefs-and-teachings/how-we-teach/catholic-education/common-core-state-standards-faqs.cfm.

28. Martin Luther, *Book of Concord* (Minneapolis, MN: Augsburg Fortress, 2000), 406.

29. Ephesians 6:4, English Standard Version.

30. Catholic Identity Curriculum Integration, "Frequently Asked Questions," September 2, 2014, http://cici-online.org/images/Resources/FAQ/faq-revised-09-02-14.pdf, 2.

31. Penny Starr, "Panelist at Podesta Think Tank on Common Core: 'The Children Belong to All of Us'," *CNS News*, February 3, 2014, http://cnsnews.com/news/article/penny-starr/panelist-podesta-think-tank-common-core-children-belong-all-us.

32. Karen Jeffers, "Common Core Supporter: 'The Children Belong to All of Us'," *Daily Signal*, February 4, 2014, http://dailysignal.com/2014/02/04/common-core-supporter-children-belong-us; Melissa Harris-Perry, "Why Caring for Children Is Not Just a Parent's Job," *MSNBC*, April 9, 2013, http://www.msnbc.com/melissa-harris-perry/why-caring-children-not-just-parent.

33. David Freedlander, "Melissa Harris-Perry and the Firestorm Over 'Collective' Parenting," *The Daily Beast*, April 11, 2013, http://www.thedailybeast.com/articles/2013/04/11/melissa-harris-perry-and-the-firestorm-over-collective-parenting.html.

34. Susan Berry, "Panelist Defends Common Core at Center for American Progress Forum: 'The Children Belong to All of Us'," *Breitbart*,

February 3, 2014, http://www.breitbart.com/big-government/2014/02/03 /center-for-american-progress-panelist-on-common-core-the-children -belong-to-all-of-us.

35. Jerome E. Listecki, "Response-Letter-1.pdf," June 9, 2014, http:// catholicsforclassicaled.com/wp-content/uploads/2014/06/Response -Letter-1.pdf.

36. Steve Becker and Abby Figi, "Letter to Archbishop Listecki," June 16, 2014.

37. Jerome E. Listecki, "Milwaukee Press Club: Archbishop Jerome Listecki" (Milwaukee Press Club, Milwaukee, WI, September 3, 2014), http://www.wiseye.org/Programming/VideoArchive/EventDetail.aspx ?evhdid=9007 at 23:32.

38. Toledo Catholics Against Common Core, "Toledo Catholics Against Common Core: Home," 2015, http://www.toledocatholicsagainstcommon core.com.

39. Sarah Perry, "Common Core State Standards: FRC Position," April 22, 2014, http://www.frc.org/issuebrief/common-core-state-standards -frc-position.

40. Anonymous, "Common Core Catholic Identity Initiative," September 2, 2014, 10.

41. Jim O'Donnell, "Guest Column: Common Core Standards Promote Student Achievement in Parochial and Public Schools Alike," *Grand Rapids Press*, September 16, 2014, http://www.mlive.com/opinion/index .ssf/2014/09/guest_column_common_core_stand.html.

42. United States Conference of Catholic Bishops, "Common Core State Standards FAQs."

43. Beck, *Conform: Exposing the Truth About Common Core and Public Education,* 95.

44. Ibid., 159.

45. Erick Erickson, "The Common Core and the 2016 Republican Candidates," *RedState*, http://www.redstate.com/2015/01/28/the-common -core-and-the-2016-republican-candidates, at 3:36.

46. U.S. Department of Education, "Enrollment in Educational Institutions, by Level and Control of Institution: Selected Years, 1869–70 Through Fall 2021," *Digest of Education Statistics, 2012*, January 2013, http://nces .ed.gov/programs/digest/d12/tables/dt12_003.asp.

47. Sheri McDonald, "Christian Schools and the Common Core," *CSE* 17, no. 1 (2013): 20–29, http://pubs.royle.com/article/Christian+Schools +and+the+Common+Core/1497092/173903/article.html, 20.

48. Ibid., 21.

49. United States Conference of Catholic Bishops, "Common Core State Standards FAQs."

50. Listecki, "Milwaukee Press Club: Archbishop Jerome Listecki," at 23:59.

51. Ronald D. Fussell, Jr., "Dear Catholic School Parent," November 3, 2014, http://www.catholicnh.org/assets/Documents/Education/Schools /CommonCore-ParentLetter.pdf.

52. Carol Thomas, "The Common Core: Why Some Private Schools Are Signing On," *Education Week*, August 7, 2013, http://www.edweek .org/ew/articles/2013/08/07/37thomas.h32.html.

53. Anne Hendershot, "Buying Catholic Support for the Common Core," *Crisis Magazine*, November 7, 2013, http://www.crisismagazine .com/2013/buying-catholic-support-for-the-common-core.

54. Catholic Identity Curriculum Integration, "In Support Of," 2013, http://cici-online.org/resources/in-support-of.

55. e.g., Jim Rigg, "Superintendent Addresses Common Core Concerns," May 2013, http://www.thecatholictelegraph.com/superintendent -addresses-common-core-concerns/14336; O'Donnell, "Guest Column."

56. United States Conference of Catholic Bishops, "Common Core State Standards FAQs."

57. Gerard V. Bradley, "Letter to Catholic Bishops on Common Core," October 16, 2013, 2.

58. Cardinal Newman Society, "10 Facts Every Catholic Should Know About the Common Core" (Author, 2014), http://www.cardinalnewman society.org/Portals/0/Mail/Renewal%20Report/pdf%20for%20web%20 Final.pdf, 3–4.

59. Ibid., 2–3.

60. A Beka Book, "A Beka Book and Common Core," 2015, https:// www.abeka.com/Resources/CommonCore.aspx.

61. Bob Jones University Press, "Maintaining Academic Excellence: BJU Press and Common Core Standards," January 26, 2015, https://www .bjupress.com/resources/common-core-standards.

62. David A. Zubik, "Dear Sisters and Brothers in Christ," March 21, 2014, http://diopitt.org/node/7479.

63. Valerie Strauss, "Arne Duncan Tells Newspaper Editors How to Report on Common Core," *The Washington Post*, June 25, 2013, http://www .washingtonpost.com/blogs/answer-sheet/wp/2013/06/25/arne-duncan -tells-newspaper-editors-how-to-report-on-common-core.

64. Kevin Carey, "Hot Air: How States Inflate Their Educational Progress Under NCLB," *The Education Sector*, 2006, http://www.mikemc mahon.info/nclbstate.pdf.

65. Michele McNeil, "Arne Duncan on NCLB, Race to the Top, and a Second Stimulus," *Education Week*, November 30, 2009, http://blogs .edweek.org/edweek/campaign-k-12/2009/11/arne_duncan_on_nclb_race _to_th.html.

66. Sheila Byrd Carmichael et al., *The State of State Standards–and the Common Core–in 2010* (Thomas B. Fordham Institute, 2010), http://eric .ed.gov/?id=ED516607.

67. Aimee Rogstad Guidera, "From Building Systems to Using Their Data," in *A Byte at the Apple* (Washington, DC: Thomas B. Fordham Institute, 2008), 250.

68. U.S. Department of Education, "Fact Sheet—Statewide Longitudinal Data Systems," Pamphlets, (July 30, 2009), http://www2.ed.gov/programs /slds/factsheet.html.

69. Natasha Singer, "Deciding Who Sees Students' Data," *The New York Times*, October 5, 2013, http://www.nytimes.com/2013/10/06/business /deciding-who-sees-students-data.html.

70. Brad McQueen, The Cult of Common Core: Obama's Final Solution for Your Child's Mind and Our Country's Exceptionalism (Brad McQueen, 2014).

71. Sarah D. Sparks, "ED Urges States to Make Data Systems More Open," *Education Week—Inside School Research*, July 20, 2012, http://blogs .edweek.org/edweek/inside-school-research/2012/07/ed_urges_states_to _make_data_s.html.

72. Strauss, "Arne Duncan Tells Newspaper Editors How to Report on Common Core."

73. Christel Swasey, "Six Things the Department of Education Did to Deprive Your Child of Privacy," *What Is Common Core*, October 15, 2013, https://whatiscommoncore.wordpress.com/2013/10/15/six-things-the-us -dept-of-education-did-to-deprive-your-child-of-privacy.

74. U.S. Department of Education, "Education Data Model (National Forum on Education Statistics). Strategies for Building Education Software Systems." July 2010, http://nces.ed.gov/forum/datamodel/eiebrowser /techview.aspx?instance=studentElementarySecondary.

75. Maureen Downey, "The Legacy of Beverly Hall: Did Former APS School Chief Care More About Scores Than Students?" *Get Schooled*, March 3, 2015, http://getschooled.blog.ajc.com/2015/03/02/former-atlanta -superintendent-beverly-hall-dies.

76. Richard Fausset, "Trial Opens in Atlanta School Cheating Scandal," *The New York Times*, September 29, 2014, http://www.nytimes.com /2014/09/30/us/racketeering-trial-opens-in-altanta-schools-cheating -scandal.html.

77. Valerie Strauss, "Why Not Subpoena Everyone in D.C. Cheating Scandal—Rhee Included? (Update)," *The Washington Post*, April 12, 2013, http://www.washingtonpost.com/blogs/answer-sheet/wp/2013/04/12/why -not-subpoena-everyone-in-d-c-cheating-scandal-rhee-included.

78. Carey, "Hot Air: How States Inflate Their Educational Progress Under NCLB," 3.

79. Victor Bandeira de Mello, "Mapping State Proficiency Standards Onto the NAEP Scales" (Washington, DC: National Center for Education Statistics, August 20, 2011), http://nces.ed.gov/nationsreportcard/pdf /studies/2011458.pdf.

80. Marci Kanstoroom, Robert D. Muller, and Eric C. Osberg, "Forward," in *A Byte at the Apple*, ed. Marci Kanstoroom and Eric C. Osberg (Washington, DC: Thomas B. Fordham Institute, 2008), x.

81. Bill Tucker, "Putting Data into Practice: Lessons from New York City" (Washington, DC: Education Sector, 2010), http://www.schoolturn aroundsupport.org/sites/default/files/resources/Putting%20Data%20 Into%20Practice_RELEASE.pdf, 12.

82. Achieve, Inc., "P-20 Data Systems," 2014, http://www.achieve.org /print/P-20-data-systems.

83. Coleman and Zimba, "Math and Science Standards That Are Fewer, Clearer, Higher to Raise Achievement at All Levels," 5.

84. *SDP Beyond the Numbers Convening: David Coleman* (Cambridge, MA, 2013), https://www.youtube.com/watch?v=IPoUmSfTTNI at 25:13.

85. New York State Allies for Public Education, "Resolution to Support the 'I Refuse' Movement," *NYS ALLIES for Public Education*, http:// www.nysape.org/resolution-to-support-the-ldquoi-refuserdquo-movement .html.

86. Laura McKenna, "What Happens When Students Boycott a Standardized Test?" *The Atlantic*, April 9, 2015, http://www.theatlantic.com /education/archive/2015/04/what-happens-when-students-boycott-a -standardized-test/390087.

87. That is not to discount opposition on the right which has also encouraged opting out, but for different reasons.

88. Jessica Bakeman, "Parents, Teachers Push 'Opt Out,' with Different Goals," April 13, 2015, http://www.capitalnewyork.com/article/albany /2015/04/8565872/parents-teachers-push-opt-out-different-goals.

89. See, for example, Chris Stewart, "Painting Education the Whitest Shade of Pale," April 2, 2015, http://citizenstewart.org/painting-education -the-whitest-shade-of-pale; Lynnell Mickelsen, "Dumping the Evidence–remind Me Again Why Anti-Testing Is 'Progressive'?" *Put Kids First*

Minneapolis, February 17, 2015, http://putkidsfirstmn.org/dumping-evidence
-remind-anti-testing-progressive.

90. The data also show that the *most* refusals came from districts with relatively more racial diversity.

91. Dave Tobin, "Cuomo: New York Teacher Evaluations System Is 'Baloney'," *Post-Standard*, January 21, 2015, http://www.syracuse.com /news/index.ssf/2015/01/cuomo_proposes_higher_standards_for_teachers _1.html.

92. Kyle Spencer, "Some Parents Oppose Standardized Testing on Principle, but Not in Practice," *The New York Times*, April 13, 2015, http:// www.nytimes.com/2015/04/14/nyregion/despite-opposing-standardized -testing-many-new-york-parents-and-students-opt-in.html.

93. Debbie Kelley, "Students Opt Out of Testing in Droves in Some Colorado Springs Schools," *Colorado Springs Gazette*, April 30, 2015, http://gazette.com/students-opt-out-of-testing-in-droves-in-some-colo rado-springs-schools/article/1550653; Jaclyn Zubrzycki, "Federal Educa-tion Department: No Reprieve for Opt-Outs," *Chalkbeat Colorado*, April 24, 2015, http://co.chalkbeat.org/2015/04/24/federal-education-department -no-reprieve-for-opt-outs.

94. Andrew Ujifusa, " 'Opt-Out' Push Gains Traction Amid Common-Core Testing—Education Week," *Education Week*, May 6, 2015, http://www .edweek.org/ew/articles/2015/05/06/opt-out-push-gains-traction-amid -common-core-testing.html.

95. Patrick Wall, "As Opt-Out Numbers Grow, Arne Duncan Says Feds May Have to Step in," *Chalkbeat New York*, April 21, 2015, http://co .chalkbeat.org/2015/04/23/as-opt-out-numbers-grow-arne-duncan-says -feds-may-have-to-step-in.

96. Todd Engdahl, "No Cow Too Sacred for Some State Board Mem-bers," *Chalkbeat Colorado*, February 15, 2015, http://co.chalkbeat.org/2015 /02/19/no-cow-too-sacred-for-some-state-board-members.

97. Zubrzycki, "Federal Education Department"; Wall, "As Opt-Out Numbers Grow, Arne Duncan Says Feds May Have to Step in."

98. Andrew Ujifusa, "Amid Cries of Overtesting, a Crazy Quilt of State Responses—Education Week," *Education Week*, July 8, 2015, http://www .edweek.org/ew/articles/2015/07/08/amid-cries-of-overtesting-a-crazy -quilt.html.

99. Michael B. Henderson, Paul E. Peterson, and Martin R. West, "The 2015 EdNext Poll on School Reform," *Education Next*, 2016, http:// educationnext.org/2015-ednext-poll-school-reform-opt-out-common-core -unions.

CHAPTER 5: THE GHOST OF EDUCATION FUTURE: TEACHERS, TESTS, AND TIME

1. Randi Weingarten, "Randi Weingarten: Why I Support the Common Core Standards," *Diane Ravitch's Blog*, May 10, 2013, http://dianeravitch.net /2013/05/10/randi-weingarten-why-i-support-the-common-core-standards.

2. Lyndsey Layton, "Turmoil Swirling Around Common Core Education Standards," *The Washington Post*, April 29, 2013, http://www .washingtonpost.com/local/education/turmoil-swirling-around-common -core-education-standards/2013/04/29/7e2b0ec4-b0fd-11e2-bbf2-a6f9e 9d79e19_story.html.

3. National Education Association, "NEA's Involvement in the Common Core State Standards," *NEA*, July 26, 2011, http://www.nea.org //home/46665.htm.

4. Jeffrey Pfeffer and Gerald R. Salancik, *The External Control of Organizations: A Resource Dependence Perspective* (Stanford University Press, 2003).

5. Terry M. Moe, *Special Interest: Teachers Unions and America's Public Schools* (Brookings Institution Press, 2011); Myron Lieberman, *The Teacher Unions: How They Sabotage Educational Reform and Why* (Encounter Books, 2000).

6. David J. Hoff, "Teachers' Unions Take Own Path on Election," *Education Week*, January 30, 2008, http://www.edweek.org/ew/articles/2008 /01/30/21electpol.h27.html; Alexander Russo, "Obama Hands NEA Endorsement to Clinton," *This Week in Education*, July 6, 2007, http://blogs .edweek.org/edweek/thisweekineducation/2007/07/obama_hands_nea _endorsement_to.html?cmp=SOC-SHR-FB.

7. National Education Association, "NEA's Involvement in the Common Core State Standards."

8. Wayne Washington, "Georgia Students Struggle on Test Tied to Common Core Math Course," *Atlanta Journal Constitution*, February 11, 2013, http://www.ajc.com/news/news/georgia-students-struggle-on-test-tied-to -common-c/nWLbm; Patricia Willens, "Panel Debates Bloomberg's School Reforms," *Schoolbook* (WNYC, November 28, 2012), http://www.wnyc.org /story/303093-panel-debates-bloombergs-school-reforms/?utm_source =sharedUrl&utm_medium=metatag&utm_campaign=sharedUrl.

9. Scott Waldman, "Test Anxiety Grips Students, Teachers," *Times Union*, April 17, 2013, http://www.timesunion.com/local/article/Test -anxiety-grips-students-teachers-4439906.php.

10. New York State United Teachers, "Common Core: Moving Too Fast on Testing," January 30, 2013, http://www.nysut.org/news/nysut

-united/issues/2013/february-2013/common-core—moving-too-fast-on
-testing.

11. New York State United Teachers, "Fact Sheet on Opting-Out of State Tests (15-01)," January 27, 2015, http://www.nysut.org/resources/all -listing/2015/january/fact-sheet-on-opting-out-of-state-tests.

12. CBS New York, "NYSUT President Reportedly Urging Parents to Boycott Common Core Exams," April 1, 2015, http://newyork.cbslocal.com /2015/04/01/nysut-president-reportedly-urging-parents-to-boycott -common-core-exams.

13. RiShawn Biddle, "Common Standards Need Common Account-ability," *Dropout Nation*, July 11, 2013, http://dropoutnation.net/2013/07 /11/common-standards-need-common-accountability.

14. Allie Bidwell, "Critics Say Growth in Common Core Delays Hurts Students, Teachers," *US News & World Report*, February 13, 2014, http:// www.usnews.com/news/special-reports/a-guide-to-common-core/articles /2014/02/13/critics-say-growth-in-common-core-delays-hurts-students -teachers.

15. Douglas O. Staiger, Robert Gordon, and Thomas J. Kane, "Identi-fying Effective Teachers Using Performance on the Job" (Washington, DC: Brookings Institution, April 2006); Stephen G. Rivkin, Eric A. Hanushek, and John F. Kain, "Teachers, Schools, and Academic Achievement," *Econo-metrica* 73, no. 2 (March 2005): 417–58.

16. Jay Price, "Common Core Education Standards Get Legislative Scrutiny," *Raleigh News-Observer*, December 17, 2013, http://www .newsobserver.com/2013/12/17/3468081/common-core-education-stan dards.html.

17. Stephanie Simon, "Teachers Union Takes on Common Core," *POLITICO*, July 11, 2014, http://www.politico.com/story/2014/07/american -federation-of-teachers-common-core-108793.html.

18. National Center for Fair & Open Testing, "Common Core Assess-ment Myths and Realities: Moratorium Needed From More Tests, Costs, Stress," September 3, 2013, http://fairtest.org/common-core-assessments -factsheet.

19. Editorial Board, "Educators Frustrated with New York's Standard-ized Tests," *Journal News*, March 24, 2015, http://www.lohud.com/story /opinion/editorials/2015/03/24/educators-frustrated-new-york-stand ardized-tests/70393712.

20. E.g., Erin Richards, "Problems Swirl Around New State Test Tied to Common Core," *Milwaukee Journal Sentinel*, February 9, 2015, http:// www.jsonline.com/news/education/problems-swirl-around-new-state-test -tied-to-common-core-standards-b99440358z1-291220931.html; Valerie

Strauss, "New Test Scoring Problems for Pearson," July 19, 2010, http://voices.washingtonpost.com/answer-sheet/standardized-tests/new-test-scoring-problems-for.html; Debbie Kelley, "Computer Attack During Standardized Testing Delays Some Exams in Colorado Springs School District," *Colorado Springs Gazette*, March 20, 2015, http://gazette.com/computer-attack-during-standardized-testing-delays-some-exams-in-colorado-springs-school-district/article/1548240; Jennifer Johnson, "North Dakota Districts Resume Common Core-Aligned Test After . . . ," *Press*, March 25, 2015, http://www.thedickinsonpress.com/news/education/3708023-north-dakota-districts-resume-common-core-aligned-test-after-delay; and Stephanie Simone, "Tenafly Officials: New Exams Facing Potential Delays," *NorthJersey.com*, July 4, 2013, http://www.northjersey.com/cm/2.1593/news/tenafly-officials-new-exams-facing-potential-delays-1.705731.

21. Valerie Strauss, "Superintendents Urge Common Core Testing Delay: 'How Can Test Data Be Valid Under Testing Conditions Like This'?" *The Washington Post*, February 6, 2015, http://www.washingtonpost.com/blogs/answer-sheet/wp/2015/02/06/superintendents-urge-common-core-testing-delay-how-can-test-data-be-valid-under-testing-conditions-like-this.

22. Quoted in Maris Vinovskis, *Overseeing the Nation's Report Card* (Washington, DC: National Assessment Governing Board, U.S. Department of Education, 1998), http://www.nagb.org/publications/95222.pdf, 5.

23. James S. Coleman et al., "Equality of Educational Opportunity" (Washington, DC: U.S. Department of Health, Education, and Welfare, Office of Education, 1966); Geoffrey D. Borman and Maritza Dowling, "Schools and Inequality: A Multilevel Analysis of Coleman's Equality of Educational Opportunity Data," *Teachers College Record* 112, no. 5 (May 2010): 1201–46.

24. Quoted in Vinovskis, Overseeing the Nation's Report Card, 6.

25. Ibid., 6.

26. Rebecca Jacobsen and Richard Rothstein, "What NAEP Once Was, And What NAEP Could Once Again Be" (25 Years of Making a Difference, Washington, DC, February 26, 2014), http://www.nagb.org/25th anniversary/assets/documents/rrothstein-paper.pdf.

27. Common Core State Standards Initiative, "English Language Arts Standards: Key Design Consideration," 2009, http://www.corestandards.org/ELA-Literacy/introduction/key-design-consideration; Victor Bandeira de Mello, "Mapping State Proficiency Standards Onto the NAEP Scales" (Washington, DC: National Center for Education Statistics, August 20, 2011), http://nces.ed.gov/nationsreportcard/pdf/studies/2011458.pdf

28. Daniel P. Resnick, "Minimum Competency Testing Historically Considered," *Review of Research in Education* 8 (1980): 3–29, http://www.jstor.org/stable/1167122.

29. National Commission on Excellence in Education, "Nation at Risk: The Imperative for Educational Reform" (Washington, DC: Author, 1983), http://www.ed.gov/pubs/NatAtRisk/risk.html.

30. National Governors Association, "Time for Results: The Governors' 1991 Report on Education" (Washington, DC: National Governors' Association, 1986).

31. Arnold F. Shober, *Splintered Accountability: State Governance and Education Reform* (Albany, NY: SUNY Press, 2010), 148, 152.

32. Office of Technology Assessment, "Testing in American Schools: Asking the Right Questions" (Washington, DC: U.S. Government Printing Office, 1992), 4.

33. *SDP Beyond the Numbers Convening: David Coleman* (Cambridge, MA, 2013), https://www.youtube.com/watch?v=IPoUmSfTTNI. at 3:47 and 13:02.

34. For a critical view of this argument, see Eric A. Hanushek and Alfred A. Lindseth, *Schoolhouses, Courthouses, and Statehouses* (Princeton, NJ: Princeton University Press, 2009).

35. Marianne Goodland, "Lobato Lawsuit Could Have Major Ramifications for K-12 School Finance," *Colorado Statesman*, March 15, 2013, http://www.coloradostatesman.com/content/994052-lobato-lawsuit-could-have-major-ramifications-k-12-school-finance.

36. Shober, *Splintered Accountability: State Governance and Education Reform,* 94.

37. Coleman et al., "Equality of Educational Opportunity," 22.

38. Dan Goldhaber, Dominic Brewer, and Deborah Anderson, "A Three-Way Error Components Analysis of Educational Productivity," *Educational Economics* 7, no. 3 (1999): 199–208.

39. National Commission for Teaching and America's Future, "What Matters Most: Teaching for America's Future" (Woodbridge, VA: Author, 1996).

40. Public Law 105–244, Section 207.

41. Jeff Archer, "Foundation Stirs Debate with Report Questioning Research on Licensure," *Education Week*, October 17, 2001.

42. Dan Goldhaber and Emily Anthony, "Can Teacher Quality Be effectively Assessed? National Board Certification as a Signal of Effective Teaching," *Review of Economics and Statistics* 89, no. 1 (2007): 134–50.

43. James Cowan and Dan Goldhaber, "National Board Certification and Teacher Effectiveness: Evidence from Washington State" (Seattle, WA: University of Washington, 2015).

44. Government Accountability Office, "Race to the Top: States Implementing Teacher and Principal Evaluation Systems Despite Challenges" (Washington, DC: Author, September 18, 2013), http://www.gao.gov/assets /660/657936.pdf, p. 19.

45. Sean C. Feeney and Carol C. Burris, "An Open Letter of Concern Regarding New York State's APPR Legislation for the Evaluation of Teachers and Principals," January 4, 2013, https://docs.google.com/viewer?a=v &pid=sites&srcid=ZGVmYXVsdGRvbWFpbnxuZXd5b3JJrcHJpbmNpc GFsc3xneDo3MjA2ODgwZmMwMjYxYWUx, 2.

46. Weingarten, "Making Common Core Standards Work Before Making Them Count," April 30, 2013, http://www.aft.org/press/speeches /making-common-core-standards-work-making-them-count.

47. Alyson Klein, "Miller on Common Core, Teacher Evaluation, and NCLB Renewal," *Education Week*, September 26, 2014, http://blogs.edweek .org/edweek/campaign-k-12/2014/09/miller_on_common_core_teacher_ .html.

48. Stephen Burd, "Liberal Democrat Is an Unlikely Foe of Teacher-Education Programs," *The Chronicle of Higher Education*, April 24, 1998, http://chronicle.com.proxy.lawrence.edu:2048/article/Liberal-Democrat -Is-an/98214.

49. Steinhauser Wendell, "Testimony Before the State Board of Education," *New Jersey Education Association*, July 9, 2014, http://www.njea .org/news/2014/07/14/agreement%20reached%20on%20parcc%20evalu ations/steinhauer-testimony-educator-effectiveness.

50. Mark Naison, "Bat History," June 17, 2013, http://www.badass teacher.org/category/history.

51. Ernest Anemone, "Badass Teachers and the Future of American Democracy," October 7, 2014, http://badassteachers.blogspot.com/2014/10 /badass-teachers-and-future-of-american.html.

52. Scholastic, Inc., and Bill & Melinda Gates Foundation, "Primary Sources: 2012 America's Teachers on the Teaching Profession," 2012, http:// mediaroom.scholastic.com/files/ps_fullreport.pdf, 124.

53. Madeloni is identified as a BAT teacher in Anemone, "Badass Teachers and the Future of American Democracy."

54. Michael Levenson, "Massachusetts Teachers Association's New President Rejects Assessments, Testing, and Other Education Policies," *Boston Globe*, June 4, 2014, https://www.bostonglobe.com/news/politics/2014 /06/05/massachusetts-teachers-association-new-president-rejects-assess ments-testing-and-other-education-policies/N4LWsYjMXyc3ON98pxnPJP /story.html.

55. Barbara Madeloni, "Common Core: A Position Statement from the Committee to Elect Barbara Madeloni," 2014, http://www.educators forademocraticunion.com/uploads/1/1/8/5/11852082/common_core.pdf.

56. Barbara Madeloni, "This Year There Is a Clear Choice: What Policies Do You Favor?" 2014, http://www.educatorsforademocraticunion.com /uploads/1/1/8/5/11852082/newflyercontrasts.pdf.

57. Massachusetts Teachers Association, "MTA President Barbara Madeloni," 2014, http://www.massteacher.org/about_mta/leadership /president.aspx; Denisha Jones, "Standing Up For Action Conference January 16th—18th," *Badass Teachers Association*, January 12, 2015, http://badassteachers.blogspot.com/2015/01/press-release-from-united -opt-out.html.

58. Linda Darling-Hammond, "A Marshall Plan for Teaching," *Education Week*, January 10, 2007.

59. Linda Darling-Hammond, "On the Common Core Standards," *Diane Ravitch's Blog*, October 24, 2013, http://dianeravitch.net/2013/10 /24/linda-darling-hammond-on-the-common-core-standards.

60. Diane Ravitch, *The Death and Life of the Great American School System* (New York, NY: Basic Books, 2010), 194.

61. Ibid., 226.

62. Joel Spring, Political Agendas for Education: From Race to the Top to Saving the Planet, 5 edition (Routledge, 2013), 40.

63. Dora Taylor, "Dump Duncan Cuz He's Flunkin': The Petition," *Seattle Education*, February 11, 2012, https://seattleeducation2010.word press.com/2012/02/11/dump-duncan-he-is-flunkin-the-petition.

64. Stephanie Simon, "Nation's Biggest Teachers Union Slams 'Botched' Common Core Implementation," *POLITICO*, February 19, 2014, http://www .politico.com/story/2014/02/national-education-association-common-core -103690.html.

65. Diane Ravitch, "BREAKING NEWS: AFT President Randi Weingarten Endorses Opt Out!" *Diane Ravitch's Blog*, March 31, 2015, http:// dianeravitch.net/2015/03/31/breaking-news-aft-president-randi-weing arten-endorses-opt-out.

66. Valerie Strauss, "Arne Duncan: 'White Suburban Moms' Upset That Common Core Shows Their Kids Aren't 'Brilliant'," *The Washington Post*, November 16, 2013, http://www.washingtonpost.com/blogs/answer-sheet /wp/2013/11/16/arne-duncan-white-surburban-moms-upset-that-common -core-shows-their-kids-arent-brilliant.

67. Carol Burris, "Who Are the 'Enemies' of Common Core?" *The Washington Post*, November 18, 2013, http://www.washingtonpost.com

/blogs/answer-sheet/wp/2013/11/18/who-are-the-enemies-of-common
-core.

68. P. L. Thomas, "Secretary Duncan and the Politics of White Outrage," *The Becoming Radical*, November 17, 2013, https://radicalscholarship
.wordpress.com/2013/11/17/secretary-duncan-and-the-politics-of-white
-outrage.

69. Laura McKenna, "Suburbia and Its Common Core Conspiracy
Theories," *The Atlantic*, February 12, 2015, http://www.theatlantic.com
/education/archive/2015/02/suburbia-and-its-common-core-conspiracy
-theories/385424.

70. Karla Reid, "Testing Skeptics Aim to Build Support for Opt-Out
Strategy," *Education Week*, March 12, 2014, http://www.edweek.org/ew
/articles/2014/03/12/24boycotts_ep.h33.html.

71. Jessica Bakeman, "Parents, Teachers Push 'Opt Out,' with Different Goals," April 13, 2015, http://www.capitalnewyork.com/article/albany
/2015/04/8565872/parents-teachers-push-opt-out-different-goals.

72. Swapna Venugopal Ramaswamy, "Common Core: Test Refusal
Pushed by Middle Class Families," *Journal News*, April 17, 2015, http://
www.lohud.com/story/news/education/2015/04/18/test-refusal-pushed
-middle-class-families/25995541.

73. National Center for Fair and Open Testing, "Common Core Assessment Myths and Realities: Moratorium Needed From More Tests, Costs,
Stress | FairTest," September 3, 2013, http://fairtest.org/common-core
-assessments-factsheet.

74. Charlie Boss, "Common Core Stirs Fear of Too Many Tests," *The
Columbus Dispatch*, November 2, 2014, http://www.dispatch.com/content
/stories/local/2014/11/02/common-core-stirs-fear-of-too-many-tests.html.

75. Valerie Strauss, "Colorado Teacher: 'I Refuse to Administer the
PARCC' Common Core Test to My Students," *The Washington Post*, September 23, 2014, http://www.washingtonpost.com/blogs/answer-sheet/wp
/2014/09/23/colorado-teacher-i-refuse-to-administer-the-parcc-common
-core-test-to-my-students/?tid=recommended_strip_1.

76. Valerie Strauss, "NY Principals: Why New Common Core Tests
Failed," *The Washington Post*, May 23, 2013, http://www.washingtonpost
.com/blogs/answer-sheet/wp/2013/05/23/ny-principals-why-new-common
-core-tests-failed.

77. New York State Education Department, "Fact Sheet: Common
Core and Assessments" (Author, 2015), http://usny.nysed.gov/docs/common
-core-assessment-faq.pdf.

78. Melissa Lazarín, "Testing Overload in America's Schools"
(Washington, DC: Center for American Progress, 2014), https://cdn

.americanprogress.org/wp-content/uploads/2014/10/LazarinOvertesting
Report.pdf, 8.

79. Ibid., 19.

80. Ibid., 20.

81. Mark Teoh et al., "The Student and the Stopwatch: How Much
Time Do American Students Spend on Testing?" (Boston, MA: TeachPlus,
2014), http://www.teachplus.org/sites/default/files/publication/pdf/the
_student_and_the_stopwatch.pdf, 8–9.

82. For their part, districts may be responding to other state laws. The
State of Ohio, for example, requires a test be given for talented-and-gifted
programs; some districts give the tests to all students in several grades. Lazarín, "Testing Overload in America's Schools," 8.

83. Trevor Thompson, Jennifer Benz, and Jennifer Agiesta, "Parents'
Attitudes on the Quality of Education in the United States" (Chicago,
IL: National Opinion Research Center, 2013), www.apnorc.org/PDFs
/Parent%20Attitudes/AP_NORC_Parents%20Attitudes%20on%20
the%20Quality%20of%20Education%20in%20the%20US_FINAL_2
.pdf, 14.

84. Michael B. Henderson, Paul E. Peterson, and Martin R. West, "The
2015 EdNext Poll on School Reform," *Education Next*, 2016, http://
educationnext.org/2015-ednext-poll-school-reform-opt-out-common-core
-unions.

85. Arne Duncan, "Beyond Bubble Tests and Bake Sales: Secretary
Arne Duncan's Remarks at the 114th Annual National PTA Convention,"
June 11, 2010, http://www.ed.gov/news/speeches/beyond-bubble-tests
-and-bake-sales-secretary-arne-duncans-remarks-114th-annual-national
-pta-convention.

86. Lynnell Mickelsen, "Dumping the Evidence–remind Me Again
Why Anti-Testing Is 'Progressive'?" *Put Kids First Minneapolis*, February 17, 2015, http://putkidsfirstmn.org/dumping-evidence-remind-anti
-testing-progressive.

87. Catherine Gewertz, "Testing Group Scales Back Performance
Items," *Education Week*, December 5, 2012, http://www.edweek.org/ew
/articles/2012/11/30/13tests.h32.html.

88. Stephen Sawchuk, "Vision, Reality Collide in Common-Core Tests,"
Education Week, April 23, 2014, http://www.edweek.org/ew/articles/2014
/04/23/29cc-promises.h33.html.

89. Debbie Kelley, "D-11 Board Votes Unanimously to Request
Change in Testing Rules," *Colorado Springs Gazette*, September 25, 2014,
http://gazette.com/d-11-board-votes-unanimously-to-request-change-in
-testing-rules/article/1538211.

90. Valerie Strauss, "Colorado School District Votes to Opt Most Students Out of Common Core Testing," *The Washington Post*, September 27, 2014, http://www.washingtonpost.com/blogs/answer-sheet/wp/2014/09/27/colorado-school-district-votes-to-opt-most-students-out-of-common-core-testing.

91. Associated Press, "Lee County Schools Rescind Vote to Opt-Out of Common Core Exams," *Florida Today*, September 2, 2014, http://www.floridatoday.com/story/news/education/2014/09/02/superintendent-lee-county-school-board-cancel-testing-opt/14954933.

92. Kelley, "D-11 Board Votes Unanimously to Request Change in Testing Rules"; Debbie Kelley, "Assessment Advocate Stands by Benefits of Common Core Testing," *Colorado Springs Gazette*, October 19, 2014, http://gazette.com/assessment-advocate-stands-by-benefits-of-common-core-testing/article/1539715.

93. Jim Siegel, "Nixing Common Core Could Let Some Ohio Schools Opt Out of State Tests," *The Columbus Dispatch*, August 21, 2014, http://www.dispatch.com/content/stories/local/2014/08/21/bill-would-let-some-schools-opt-out-of-tests.html.

94. Jim Siegel, "Common Core Repealed in Ohio? Kasich Doubts It," *The Columbus Dispatch*, September 9, 2014, http://www.dispatch.com/content/stories/local/2014/09/09/governor-no-common-core-repeal-bill-expected.html.

95. Richard A. Ross, "Testing Report and Recommendations" (Columbus, OH: Ohio Department of Education, 2015), www.dispatch.com/content/downloads/2015/01/Testing_recommendations.pdf, 1.

96. Catherine Candisky, "Board Votes to Trim Student Testing Time by 90 Minutes," *The Columbus Dispatch*, May 22, 2015, http://www.dispatch.com/content/stories/local/2015/05/21/standardized-testing-to-be-shorter.html.

97. Partnership for Assessment of Readiness for College and Careers, "PARCC States Vote to Shorten Test Time and Simplify Test Administration," May 21, 2015, http://parcconline.org/parcc-states-vote-shorten-test-time.

98. Michelle Everhart, "Ohio Politics Now: Will Changes to PARCC Testing Be Enough for Lawmakers?" *The Columbus Dispatch*, May 22, 2015, http://www.dispatch.com/content/stories/local/2015/05/22/ohio-politics-now-will-parcc-changes-be-enough.html.

99. Andrew Ujifusa, "Ohio House Passes Bill to Cut PARCC Test; Plus, Md. and Ill. Testing News," *Education Week—State EdWatch*, May 20, 2015, http://blogs.edweek.org/edweek/state_edwatch/2015/05/ohio_house_passes_bill_to_cut_parcc_test_plus_md_and_ill_testing_news.html.

100. Brian Smith, "Gov. Rick Snyder Signs $15 Billion Education Budget for 2014–15," *MLive.com*, June 24, 2014, http://www.mlive.com /lansing-news/index.ssf/2014/06/snyder_signs_education_budget.html.

101. Sean Cavanagh, "Pearson Lands Common-Core Contract in Mississippi After Testing Standoff," *Education Week—Marketplace K-12*, http:// blogs.edweek.org/edweek/marketplacek12/2014/09/pearson_lands _contract_in_mississippi_after_testing_standoff.html.

102. Emily Le Coz, "Miss. Withdraws from Common Core Testing," *The Clarion Ledger*, January 16, 2015, http://www.clarionledger.com /story/news/2015/01/16/mississippi-withdraw-parcc/21859553.

103. Erin Richards, "Latest Glitch Delays Common Core Exam in Wisconsin," *Milwaukee Journal Sentinel*, March 26, 2015, http://www.js online.com/news/education/latest-glitch-delays-common-core-exam-in -wisconsin-b99469929z1-297708641.html.

104. Molly Beck, "Cost of Common Core Tests Millions More Than Expected," *Wisconsin State Journal*, January 18, 2015, http://host.madison .com/news/local/education/local_schools/cost-of-common-core-tests -millions-more-than-expected/article_6872d4fc-10da-5b97-9ec3-95e 2d50477cb.html.

105. Patrick Marley, "Vos: Taxpayers Feel 'Ripped Off' by Badger Exam," *Milwaukee Journal Sentinel*, April 23, 2015, http://www.jsonline .com/news/statepolitics/vos-taxpayers-feel-ripped-off-by-badger-exam -b99487113z1-301067851.html.

106. Richards, "Problems Swirl Around New State Test Tied to Common Core."

107. Molly Beck, "DPI Seeking Bids for New State Test," *Wisconsin State Journal*, May 8, 2015, http://host.madison.com/news/local/education /local_schools/dpi-seeking-bids-for-new-state-test/article_ad654d06 -c041-548e-acb4-ccfcb7ae44f9.html.

108. Matt Cardoza, "Georgia Withdrawing from the Partnership for Assessment of Readiness of College and Careers (PARCC) Consortium," July 22, 2013, http://www.gadoe.org/External-Affairs-and-Policy /communications/Pages/PressReleaseDetails.aspx?PressView=default &pid=123.

109. Charlie Walton, "Script for GKAP Promotional Piece," January 10, 1990, Georgia Assisstant Superintendent's Subject Files, series 12-09-089, box 31, folder 7, Georgia State Archive, Atlanta, GA, emphasis original.

110. See Shober, *Splintered Accountability: State Governance and Education Reform*, 160.

111. Chester E. Finn, Jr., "Chicken Little Goes to School," *Flypaper*, July 24, 2013, http://edexcellence.net/commentary/education-gadfly-daily /flypaper/2013/chicken-little-goes-to-school.html.

CHAPTER 6: THE REVERIE OF THE LEFT: FOUNDATIONS, THINK TANKS, AND INTEREST GROUPS

1. Anthony Cody, "The Secret Sixty Prepare to Write Standards for 50 Million," *Education Week—Living in Dialogue*, July 6, 2009, http://blogs .edweek.org/teachers/living-in-dialogue/2009/07/national_standards _process_ign.html.

2. Anthony Cody, "National Standards a Wild Goose Chase," *Living in Dialogue*, June 8, 2009, http://blogs.edweek.org/teachers/living-in-dialogue /2009/06/national_standards_a_wild_goos.html.

3. Adam D. Sheingate, *The Rise of the Agricultural Welfare State: Institutions and Interest Group Power in the United States, France, and Japan* (Princeton, NJ: Princeton University Press, 2003); William T. Gormley, "Regulatory Issue Networks in a Federal System," *Polity* 18, no. 4 (1986): 595–620. High-wire public policy written away from the glare of the public eye had precedent, too. The watershed federal income tax overhaul in 1986 succeeded only after closing the doors. John F. Witte, *The Politics and Development of the Federal Income Tax* (Madison, WI: University of Wisconsin Press, 1986).

4. She gives an exact date: November 30, 2006. Diane Ravitch, *The Death and Life of the Great American School System* (New York, NY: Basic Books, 2010), 99.

5. Ibid., 30.

6. Ibid., 105.

7. Ibid., 102.

8. Ibid., 200–201.

9. "Why I Cannot Support the Common Core Standards," *Diane Ravitch's Blog*, February 26, 2013, http://dianeravitch.net/2013/02/26/why -i-cannot-support-the-common-core-standards.

10. Ibid.

11. Liam Julian, "Common Core's Uncommon Rise," *Philanthropy*, 2013, http://www.philanthropyroundtable.org/topic/excellence_in_philan thropy/common_cores_uncommon_rise.

12. The phrase comes from Michael Berkman and Eric Plutzer, *Ten Thousand Democracies: Politics and Public Opinion in America's School Districts* (Washington, DC: Georgetown University Press, 2005), a review of public opinion in school districts.

13. Robert Rothman, *Something in Common: The Common Core Standards and the Next Chapter in American Education* (Cambridge, MA: Harvard Education Press, 2011), 61–63.

14. Anne Bridgman, "Education Groups Agree on Plan to Improve Instructional Materials," *Education Week*, April 11, 1984, http://www.edweek.org/ew/articles/1984/04/11/05420033.h03.html.

15. Mercedes Schneider, "The Common Core License: Open for NGA and CCSSO Alteration," *Deutsch29*, April 2, 2014, https://deutsch29.wordpress.com/2014/04/02/the-common-core-license-open-for-nga-and-ccsso-alteration.

16. Ibid.

17. Jay Mathews, "Divide and Confound; Meet the New, New Math. Just Like the Old New Math—Totally Baffling," *The Washington Post*, May 23, 1993, http://www.lexisnexis.com/lnacui2api/api/version1/getDocCui?lni=3S7T-8SG0-0088-P21H&csi=270944,270077,11059,8411&hl=t&hv=t&hnsd=f&hns=t&hgn=t&oc=00240&perma=true; Debra Viadero, "8th-Grade Math Achievement Tied to Focus on Algebra, Geometry," August 4, 1993, http://www.edweek.org/ew/articles/1993/08/04/40ccsso.h12.html.

18. Emmeline Zhao, "Common Core Copyright: What Does It Really Mean? 5 Questions with Chris Minnich," *Real Clear Education*, October 8, 2014, http://www.realcleareducation.com/articles/2014/10/08/common_core_copyright_1112.html.

19. Ibid.

20. Karen Diegmueller and Millicent Lawton, "The Road Not Taken," *Education Week*, April 24, 1996, http://www.edweek.org/ew/articles/1996/04/24/31stand.h15.html.

21. Drew Lindsay, "Summit Slated for Governors, Corporations," *Education Week*, October 4, 1995, http://www.edweek.org/ew/articles/1995/10/04/05summit.h15.html.

22. Ibid.

23. Achieve, Inc., "National Education Summit Briefing, 1996" (Washington, DC: Achieve, Inc., 1996), http://www.achieve.org/files/1996NationalEducationSummit.pdf, 1.

24. Achieve, Inc., "National Education Summit Briefing Book, 2001" (Washington, DC: Achieve, Inc., 2001), http://www.achieve.org/files/2001NationalEducationSummitBriefing%20Book.pdf, 4.

25. Lori Aratani, "Project Aims to Strengthen Students' Skills," *The Washington Post*, February 16, 2006, sec. Print Edition, http://www.washingtonpost.com/wp-dyn/content/article/2006/02/08/AR2006020800112.html.

26. The 15 states *not* members of ADP were Alaska, Iowa, Kansas, Missouri, Montana, Nevada, New Hampshire, New York, North Dakota, South Carolina, South Dakota, Utah, Vermont, West Virginia, and Wyoming. Of these 15 states, all except Alaska and South Carolina adopted the Common Core.

27. Achieve, Inc., "Ready or Not: Creating a High School Diploma That Counts" (Washington, DC: Achieve, Inc., 2004), http://www.achieve.org/files/ReadyorNot.pdf, 116.

28. Julia E. Koppich, "Investing in Teaching" (New York: National Alliance of Business, 2001), http://web.archive.org/web/20040205134309/http://www.nab.com/PDF/invest_teaching_report.pdf.

29. Achieve, Inc., "Ready or Not: Creating a High School Diploma That Counts," 1.

30. State of Georgia, "Race to the Top Application for Initial Funding," January 19, 2010, http://www2.ed.gov/programs/racetothetop/phase1-applications/georgia.pdf, 45.

31. Cited in State of Minnesota, "Race to the Top Application for Initial Funding," January 2010, http://www2.ed.gov/programs/racetothetop/phase1-applications/minnesota.pdf, 51.

32. Ibid., 71.

33. Barack H. Obama, "Remarks by the President to the Business Roundtable" (Washington, DC, February 24, 2010), https://www.whitehouse.gov/node/9345.

34. Fenwick English, "The Ten Most Wanted Enemies of American Public Education's School Leadership," *University Council for Educational Administration Review* 51, no. 3 (2010): 13–18, http://www.ncpeapublications.org/attachments/article/330/November%202010%20ELR.pdf, 11.

35. Cited in ibid., 6.

36. Mercedes Schneider, *Common Core Dilemma* (New York: Teachers College Press, 2015), 21.

37. Ibid., 30.

38. Ibid., 22.

39. Ibid., 189.

40. Sean Cavanagh, "McGraw-Hill Education Shifting Away From High-Stakes Testing," *Education Week*, August 5, 2015, http://www.edweek.org/ew/articles/2015/07/31/as-mcgraw-hill-education-leaves-state-testing-market.html.

41. Thomas B. Fordham Foundation, "Thomas B. Fordham Foundation Five-Year Report, 1997–2001" (Washington, DC: Thomas B. Fordham Foundation, May 2002), http://www.edexcellencemedia.net/publications/2002/200205_tbfffiveyear/report.pdf, 5.

42. Jim Bencivenga, "Fordham at Ten" (Washington, DC: Thomas B. Fordham Foundation, 2007), http://www.edexcellencemedia.net/publications/2007/2007_fordham10yrreport/2007fordhamtenyearreport.pdf, 8.

43. Michael Petrilli and Chester E. Finn, "The State of State Standards" (Washington, DC: Thomas B. Fordham Institute, August 2006), http://edex.s3-us-west-2.amazonaws.com/publication/pdfs/State%20of%20State%20Standards2006FINAL_9.pdf, 19.

44. Education Week, "Former Federal Research Chief Backing 'National Curriculum'," *Education Week*, February 22, 1989, http://www.edweek.org/ew/articles/1989/02/22/08180020.h08.html.

45. Chester E. Finn, Jr., "On Governors and Ostriches," *Education Week*, February 14, 1996, http://www.edweek.org/ew/articles/1996/02/14/21finn.h15.html.

46. Julian, "Common Core's Uncommon Rise."

47. Michael J. Petrilli, "Petrilli Testimony on Common Core in Ohio," *Education Next*, November 20, 2013, http://educationnext.org/petrilli-testimony-on-common-core-in-ohio.

48. Michael J. Petrilli, "The RNC on the CCSSI, OMG!" April 17, 2013, http://edexcellence.net/commentary/education-gadfly-daily/flypaper/2013/the-rnc-on-the-ccssi-omg.html.

49. Conservatives for Higher Standards, "Supporters," 2013, http://highercorestandards.org/supporters.

50. Kenneth J. Saltman, *The Gift of Education: Public Education and Venture Philanthropy* (New York: Palgrave-Macmillan, 2010), 154.

51. Schneider, *Common Core Dilemma*, 57; English, "The Ten Most Wanted Enemies of American Public Education's School Leadership," 6.

52. In 2012, the NAACP's action plan did not mention Common Core, although a year later it did. See Suzanne Gamboa, "NAACP Launches Biggest Education Push Since *Brown v. Board of Ed*," *The Huffington Post*, December 6, 2012, http://www.huffingtonpost.com/2012/12/06/naacp-volunteers-education-brown-v-board-of-education_n_2253135.html.

53. NAACP, "2013 Common Core State Standards Resolution" (NAACP, 2013), http://action.naacp.org/page/-/education%20documents/2014_Common_Core_State_Standards_Resolution.pdf, 1.

54. Alyson Klein, "Miller on Common Core, Teacher Evaluation, and NCLB Renewal," *Education Week*, September 26, 2014, http://blogs.edweek.org/edweek/campaign-k-12/2014/09/miller_on_common_core_teacher_.html.

55. Carl` Chancellor, "Critical Education Standards Opposed by Conservative Group," *Center for American Progress Blog*, May 11, 2012, https://

www.americanprogress.org/issues/education/news/2012/05/11/11563
/critical-education-standards-opposed-by-conservative-group.

56. Meg Sommerfield, "Alliance for Learning: El Paso: Crossing the
Border," *Education Week*, April 13, 1994, http://www.edweek.org/ew
/articles/1994/04/13/29aaelp.h13.html.

57. Joetta L. Sack, "Group Seeks Help for Minority Achievement,"
December 15, 1999, http://www.edweek.org/ew/articles/1999/12/15/16ed
trust.h19.html.

58. Ibid.

59. Joan Richardson, "Emphasize the Ambitious: Q&A With Kati
Haycock," *Education Week*, November 1, 2011, http://www.edweek.org
/ew/articles/2011/11/01/kappan_haycock.html.

60. Kati Haycock, "Kati Haycock, President of The Education Trust,
on the Common Core Standards Initiative," *Education Trust*, September 21, 2009, http://edtrust.org/press_release/kati-haycock-president-of
-the-education-trust-on-the-common-core-standards-initiative-2.

61. Catherine Gewertz, "College and the Workforce: What 'Readiness' Means," *Education Week*, January 14, 2010, http://www.edweek
.org/ew/articles/2010/01/14/17readiness.h29.html.

62. Michele Mcneil, "NGA, CCSSO Launch Common Standards
Drive," *Education Week*, April 16, 2009, http://www.edweek.org/ew/arti
cles/2009/04/16/29standards.h28.html.

63. Kati Haycock, "Building Common College-Ready Standards,"
Change, 2010, http://www.changemag.org/Archives/Back%20Issues/July
-August%202010/building-college-readiness-full.html.

64. Lyndsey Layton, "Is It a Student's Civil Right to Take a Federally
Mandated Standardized Test?" *The Washington Post*, April 10, 2015, http://
www.washingtonpost.com/local/education/is-it-a-students-civil-right-to
-take-a-federally-mandated-standardized-test/2015/04/10/7f1b731c-d3e4
-11e4-a62f-ee745911a4ff_story.html.

65. Tim Daly, "Unmasking the 'Blame the Teacher' Crowd," *Eduwonk*,
http://www.eduwonk.com/2010/08/unmasking-the-blame-the-teacher
-crowd.html.

66. Schneider, *Common Core Dilemma*, p. 48.

67. John Thompson, "Can Education Trust Be Trusted by Teachers?"
Living in Dialogue, August 15, 2013, http://blogs.edweek.org/teachers
/living-in-dialogue/2013/08/john_thompson_can_education_tr.html.

68. John Thompson, "Can the Education Trust and Teachers Work
Together?" *The Huffington Post*, September 11, 2013, http://www.huff
ingtonpost.com/john-thompson/can-the-education-trust-a_b_3894822
.html.

69. Kati Haycock, "Calling the Nation's Civil Rights Leaders Ignorant on Testing: Really?" *Education Trust*, June 4, 2015, http://edtrust.org/the-equity-line/calling-the-nations-civil-rights-leaders-ignorant-on-testing-really.

70. Jesse Hagopian, "Resistance to High Stakes Tests Serves the Cause of Equity in Education: A Reply to 'We Oppose Anti-Testing Efforts'," *Network for Public Education*, May 5, 2015, http://www.networkforpublic education.org/2015/05/resistance-to-high-stakes-tests-serves-the-cause-of-equity-in-education.

71. American Federation of Teachers, "Where We Stand: Standards-Based Assessment and Accountability" (Washington, DC: American Federation of Teachers, June 2003), http://www.aft.org/sites/default/files/wwsstandassesaccnt0603.pdf; Lynn Olson, "An 'A' or a 'D': State Rankings Differ Widely," *Education Week*, April 15, 1998, http://www.edweek.org/ew/articles/1998/04/15/31stand.h17.html.

72. American Federation of Teachers, "Where We Stand: Standards-Based Assessment and Accountability."

73. Randi Weingarten, "Saving Public Education Not As We Know It But As It Ought to Be" (AFT National Convention, Seattle, WA, July 8, 2010), http://www.aft.org/sites/default/files/sp_weingarten070810.pdf, p. 10.

74. Sean Cavanagh, "Transparency of Common-Standards Process at Issue," *Education Week*, July 30, 2009, http://www.edweek.org/ew/articles/2009/07/30/37standardsprocess.h28.html; Sean Cavanagh, "Groups to Spread Word on Standards in States, Districts," *Curriculum Matters*, December 2, 2009, http://blogs.edweek.org/edweek/curriculum/2009/12/organizations_to_spread_word_o.html.

75. Ann Bradley, "The AFT Innovation Fund and Common Core State Standards," *The Intersection*, September 20, 2012, http://www.hunt-institute.org/resources/2012/09/the-aft-innovation-fund-and-common-core-state-standards.

76. Michele McNeil, "Race to Top Buy-In Level Examined—Education Week," *Education Week*, June 16, 2010, http://www.edweek.org/ew/articles/2010/06/16/35buyin_ep.h29.html.

77. American Federation of Teachers, "AFT Members Pass Resolution to Fulfill Promise and Potential of Common Core, Lay Out Action Plan to Fix Botched Implementation" (American Federation of Teachers, July 13, 2014), http://www.aft.org/press-release/aft-members-pass-resolution-fulfill-promise-and-potential-common-core-lay.

78. Common Core, "A Challenge to the Partnership for 21st Century Schools," September 2009, http://greatminds.net/maps/documents/reports/CConP21final-090915.pdf. Note that this "Common Core" was *not* the

same as the Common Core State Standards Initiative; instead, it was a non-profit curriculum provider of Common Core State Standards-aligned material. Its name was later changed to "Great Minds." In early 2015, after the departure of several technology companies from P21 and the retirement of some AFT staff, the union joined P21, in part because of its work on alternative school accountability systems. Stephen Sawchuk, "AFT Joins '21st Century Skills' Group," *Education Week*, January 27, 2015, http://blogs .edweek.org/edweek/teacherbeat/2015/01/aft_rejoins_p21_group.html.

79. Dennis Van Roekel, *Common Core State Standards: A Tool for Improving Education* (Washington, DC: National Education Association, 2010), http://neadental.info/assets/docs/PB30CommonCoreStateStandards 2010.pdf, 6.

80. Andrew Ujifusa and Stephen Sawchuk, "Common-Core Tensions Cause Union Heartburn," *Education Week*, February 19, 2014, http://www .edweek.org/ew/articles/2014/02/19/21commoncore.h33.html.

81. Stephanie Simon, "Nation's Biggest Teachers Union Slams 'Botched' Common Core Implementation," *POLITICO*, February 19, 2014, http:// www.politico.com/story/2014/02/national-education-association -common-core-103690.html.

82. Ann Bradley, "Teacher Training a Key Focus for Administration," *Education Week*, July 13, 1994, http://www.edweek.org/ew/articles/1994 /07/13/41prof.h13.html; "GOP Teacher Bill Attracts Some Democratic Supporters," *Education Week*, August 4, 1999, 29, 31.

83. Mary Ellen Flannery, "Bringing Common Sense to Common Core," July 1, 2013, http://www.nea.org/grants/55932.htm.

84. Richard Lee Colvin, "A New Generation of Philanthropists and Their Great Ambitions," in *With the Best of Intentions*, ed. Frederick M. Hess (Cambridge, MA: Harvard Education Press, 2005), 21–48, 25.

85. Peter Applebome, "Annenberg School Grants Raise Hopes, and Questions on Extent of Change," *The New York Times*, April 30, 1995, sec. U.S., http://www.nytimes.com/1995/04/30/us/annenberg-school-grants -raise-hopes-and-questions-on-extent-of-change.html.

86. Sarah Reckhow, *Follow the Money: How Foundation Dollars Change Public School Politics*, 1 edition (Oxford, England; New York, NY: Oxford University Press, 2012), 13.

87. Bill & Melinda Gates Foundation, "Foundation Fact Sheet," 2015, http://www.gatesfoundation.org/Who-We-Are/General-Information/Foun dation-Factsheet.

88. Bill Gates, "Annual Letter 2009," *Bill & Melinda Gates Foundation*, January 2009, http://www.gatesfoundation.org/who-we-are/resources -and-media/annual-letters-list/annual-letter-2009.

89. Bill Gates, "Speech to National Conference of State Legislatures," July 21, 2009, http://www.gatesfoundation.org/media-center/speeches/2009 /07/bill-gates-national-conference-of-state-legislatures-ncsl.

90. Bill Gates, "Speech to American Federation of Teachers" (AFT Annual Convention, Seattle, WA, July 10, 2010), http://www.aft.org/sites /default/files/sp_gates071010.pdf.

91. Bill & Melinda Gates Foundation, "Awarded Grants," *Bill & Melinda Gates Foundation*, 2015, http://www.gatesfoundation.org/How-We-Work /Quick-Links/Grants-Database#q/k=achieve%2C%20inc&sort=grantee &sortdir=asc.

92. Collaborative for Student Success, "About," 2015, http:// forstudentsuccess.org/about.

93. Alison Grizzle et al., "State Teachers of the Year Defend the Common Core," *Education Week*, May 20, 2015, http://www.edweek.org/ew /articles/2015/05/20/state-teachers-of-the-year-defend-the.html; Caralee Adams, "Higher Education Leaders Form Coalition in Support of Common Core," *College Bound—Education Week*, June 10, 2014, http://blogs.edweek .org/edweek/college_bound/2014/06/higher_education_leaders_form _coalition_in_support.html; Catherine Gewertz, "Common-Core Backers Hit States' High Proficiency Rates," *Curriculum Matters—Education Week*, May 14, 2015, http://blogs.edweek.org/edweek/curriculum/2015/05/common -core_backers_hit_states_high_proficiency_rates.html?intc=mvs.

94. Reckhow, *Follow the Money*, 150.

95. Lyndsey Layton, "How Bill Gates Pulled Off the Swift Common Core Revolution," *The Washington Post*, June 7, 2014, http://www.wash ingtonpost.com/politics/how-bill-gates-pulled-off-the-swift-common -core-revolution/2014/06/07/a830e32e-ec34-11e3-9f5c-9075d5508f0a _story.html.

96. Mercedes Schneider, "Gates Money and Common Core: Part II," *Deutsch29*, September 3, 2013, https://deutsch29.wordpress.com/2013/09 /03/gates-money-and-common-core-part-ii.

97. Valerie Strauss, "Pro-Common Core Group Takes Issue with Blog Post—and the Author Responds," *The Washington Post*, May 13, 2015, https://www.washingtonpost.com/blogs/answer-sheet/wp/2015/05/13 /pro-common-core-group-takes-issue-with-blog-post-and-the-author -responds.

98. Jack Hassard, "Why Bill Gates Defends the Common Core," *The Art of Teaching Science*, March 15, 2014, http://www.artofteachingscience .org/why-bill-gates-defends-the-common-core.

99. Diane Ravitch, "The Inside Story of How Bill Gates Bought the Common Core Standards," *Diane Ravitch's Blog*, June 8, 2014, http://

dianeravitch.net/2014/06/08/the-inside-story-of-how-bill-gates-bought
-the-common-core-standards.

100. Tony Felicio, Jr., "Open Letter," May 30, 2015, http://badassteachers
.blogspot.com/2015/05/an-open-letter-to-maryellen-elia.html.

101. English, "The Ten Most Wanted Enemies of American Public
Education's School Leadership," 6, 11.

102. Ibid., 6.

103. Ravitch, *The Death and Life of the Great American School
System*.

104. Grantmakers for Education, "Benchmarking 2012" (Portland,
OR: Grantmakers for Education, 2012), http://www.edfunders.org/sites
/default/files/Benchmarking_2012.pdf, 16.

CHAPTER 7: THROUGH A GLASS DARKLY: THE WAY FORWARD

1. Kevin Carey, "Hot Air: How States Inflate Their Educational Progress
Under NCLB," *The Education Sector*, 2006, http://www.mikemcmahon
.info/nclbstate.pdf, 10.

2. National Center for Education Statistics, "NAEP State Profiles,"
2015, http://nces.ed.gov/nationsreportcard/states.

3. John Cronin et al., "Proficiency Illusion" (Thomas B. Fordham
Institute, October 2007), http://onlinelibrary.wiley.com/doi/10.1002/jcc
.540040303/pdf, 4.

4. Michael J. Petrilli, "Nine Questions: What Does It Even Mean to
Oppose the Common Core?" *Flypaper*, January 29, 2015, http://edexcellence
.net/articles/nine-questions-what-does-it-even-mean-to-oppose-the-com
mon-core.

5. Andrew Cuomo, "New York Governor Andrew Cuomo's 2015 State
of the State Speech" (Albany, NY, January 21, 2015), http://www.governing
.com/topics/politics/gov-new-york-andrew-cuomo.html.

6. Two prominent left-wing academics even wrote a dazed essay asking
how Obama could support "right-wing" education reform. Henry A. Giroux and Kenneth J. Saltman, "Obama's Betrayal of Public Education? Arne
Duncan and the Corporate Model of Schooling," *Truthout*, December 17,
2008, http://www.truth-out.org/archive/component/k2/item/81572:obamas
-betrayal-of-public-education-arne-duncan-and-the-corporate-model-of
-schooling.

7. Michael Puma et al., "Head Start Impact Study, Final Report"
(Washington, DC: U.S. Department of Health and Human Services, January 2010), http://eric.ed.gov/?id=ED507845.

8. Ronald G. Ehrenberg et al., "Class Size and Student Achievement," *Psychological Science in the Public Interest*, 2001, 1–30, http://www.jstor .org/stable/40062283.

9. Caitlin Emma, "Fallin Signs Common Core Repeal Bill," *POLITICO*, http://www.politico.com/story/2014/06/common-core-repeal-oklahoma -mary-fallin-107499.html.

10. Associated Press, "Oklahoma Gov. Mary Fallin Issues Order Supporting Common Core," *Conservatives for Higher Standards*, December 4, 2013, http://highercorestandards.org/ap-oklahoma-gov-mary-fallin-issues -order-supporting-common-core.

11. Mary Fallin for Governor, "Mary Fallin for Governor," 2014, http://maryfallin.org/accomplishments/education.

12. Education, "The Federalist Debate: Pullman vs. Petrilli On Common Core," April 16, 2014, http://thefederalist.com/2014/04/16/the-fede ralist-debate-pullman-vs-petrilli-on-common-core.

13. Sean D. Reyes, "Common Core Standards Legal Analysis" (Utah Attorney General's Office, October 7, 2014), 6.

14. Michael Berkman and Eric Plutzer, *Ten Thousand Democracies: Politics and Public Opinion in America's School Districts* (Washington, DC: Georgetown University Press, 2005); Noel Epstein, *Who's in Charge Here? The Tangled Web of School Governance and Policy* (Washington, DC: Brookings Institution Press, 2004), http://www.brookings.edu/~/media /Files/Press/Books/2004/whosinchargehere/whosinchargehere_chapter .pdf.

15. Gallup, Inc., "Education," *Gallup.com*, http://www.gallup.com/poll /1612/Education.aspx.

16. Elizabeth A. Harris and Ford Fessenden, "'Opt Out' Becomes Anti-Test Rallying Cry in New York State," *The New York Times*, May 20, 2015, http://www.nytimes.com/2015/05/21/nyregion/opt-out-movement -against-common-core-testing-grows-in-new-york-state.html.

17. Kate Taylor, "New York Schools With Many Opting Out of Tests May Be Penalized," *The New York Times*, August 13, 2015, http://www .nytimes.com/2015/08/14/nyregion/new-york-schools-with-many-opting -out-of-tests-may-be-penalized.html.

18. Kelley Wallace, "Parents All Over U.S. Opting Out of Standardized Student Testing," *CNN*, April 24, 2015, http://www.cnn.com/2015/04 /17/living/parents-movement-opt-out-of-testing-feat/index.html.

19. "Fewer, higher, better" standards might have been beneficial given high rates of college remediation even among this population!

20. Michael J. Petrilli and Chester E. Finn, Jr., "Common Core Standards: Now What?" October 20, 2010, http://edexcellence.net/commentary

/education-gadfly-weekly/2010/october-21/common-core-standards-now
-what.html.

21. Many of the same charges were heard about NCLB as well as some suburban schools were labeled as "in need of improvement" due to a small subgroup of students not making the required increase in test scores.

22. Denise Smith Amos, "Superintendent Nikolai Vitti Promises Fewer Tests for Duval Students," *Florida Times-Union*, March 28, 2014, http://jacksonville.com/news/metro/2014-03-28/story/vitti-promises-fewer-tests -duval-students.

23. U.S. Senate, 114th Cong., 1st Sess., S. 1177 sec. 9527(a)(1)(C).

24. U.S. Senate, 114th Cong., 1st Sess., S. 1177 sec. 1111(b)(1)(A).

25. Jonathan Rothwell, "Job Vacancies and STEM Skills" (Washington, DC: Brookings Institution, July 2014), http://www.brookings.edu/~/media /research/files/reports/2014/07/stem/job-vacancies-and-stem-skills.pdf.

26. Lawrence Goodman, "Upgrading Education," *Brown Alumni Magazine*, September 2011, http://www.brownalumnimagazine.com/content /view/2982/40.

27. Elliot Eisner, "Educational Leadership: The Whole Child: Back to Whole," *Educational Leadership*, September 2005, http://www.ascd.org /publications/educational-leadership/sept05/vol63/num01/Back-to-Whole .aspx, 17.

28. Catholic Identity Curriculum Integration, "CICI Home," *Catholic Identity Curriculum Integration*, 2013, http://cici-online.org.

29. Christel Swasey, "The Story Killers," February 10, 2014, https://whatiscommoncore.wordpress.com/tag/informational-text.

30. Gracy Olmstead, "Common Core and 'Informational Texts': Fact and Fiction, Part III," *The American Conservative*, March 11, 2014, http://www.theamericanconservative.com/2014/03/11/common-core-and-info rmational-texts-fact-and-fiction-part-iii.

31. Bob Shepherd, "Commnet on How to Turn Great Literature into Informational Text," *Diane Ravitch's Blog*, December 4, 2014, http://dianeravitch.net/2014/12/04/how-to-turn-greatliterature-into-informational -text.

32. Peter Greene, "NYT CCSS ELA PR," *CURMUDGUCATION*, June 21, 2015, http://curmudgucation.blogspot.com/2015/06/nyt-ccss-ela -pr.html.

33. Kathleen Porter-Magee, "The Weak Critique of Common Core's Approach to Great Literature," *Common Core Watch*, December 17, 2012, http://edexcellence.net/commentary/education-gadfly-daily/common-core -watch/2012/the-weak-critique-of-common-cores-approach-to-great -literature.html.

34. Diane Ravitch, "MaryEllen Elia and Vicky Phillips of Gates Foundation Explain the Gates Plan for Hillsborough County," *Diane Ravitch's Blog*, May 28, 2015, http://dianeravitch.net/2015/05/28/maryellen-elia-and-vicky-phillips-of-gates-foundation-explain-the-gates-plan-for-hillsborough-county.

35. Jamie Kain, "A Confusing Job Market," *Diane Ravitch's Blog*, June 29, 2012, http://dianeravitch.net/2012/06/29/a-confusing-job-market.

36. Anthony Cody, "Common Core, China, and the Myth of Meritocracy," *Living in Dialogue*, December 30, 2013, http://blogs.edweek.org/teachers/living-in-dialogue/2013/12/common_core_and_the_myth_of_me.html.

37. Kenneth J. Saltman, *The Gift of Education: Public Education and Venture Philanthropy* (New York: Palgrave-Macmillan, 2010), 21, 31.

38. Ibid., 25. He ties these explicitly to the Common Core in Noah De Lissovoy, Alex Means, and Kenneth J. Saltman, "Creating a Pedagogy in Common: Excerpt From 'Toward a New Common School Movement'," *Truthout*, February 27, 2014, http://www.truth-out.org/opinion/item/22113-creating-a-pedagogy-in-common-excerpt-from.

39. All members are appointed by the legislature in New York and South Carolina, and four of nine are in Mississippi. In Washington, six of its board's 14 members are selected by local school boards or private schools and one is elected (the superintendent). The rest are appointed. See National Association of State Boards of Education, "State Education Governance Matrix" (National Association of State Boards of Education, January 2015), http://www.nasbe.org/wp-content/uploads/Governance-matrix-January-2015.pdf.

40. Catherine Gewertz, "State Lawmakers Assert Influence Over Standards," *Education Week*, July 9, 2014, http://www.edweek.org/ew/articles/2014/06/23/36stateboards.h33.html.

Index

About the Author

Arnold F. Shober, PhD, is an associate professor of government at Lawrence University, Appleton, WI. He is the author of *Splintered Accountability: State Governance and Education Reform* (2010), *The Democratic Dilemma of American Education* (2012), and shorter works on school boards, teacher quality, school choice, and American federalism. He received the Faculty Award for Excellence in Scholarship from his institution in 2015.